17 Pastern
18 Toes
19 Nails
20 Forefoot
21 Sternum (Breastbone)
22 Chest
23 Flank
24 Thigh (Upper thigh)
25 Stifle (Knee)
26 Second thigh (Lower thigh)
27 Hock (Heel)
28 Rear pastern
29 Hind foot
30 Pads
31 Tail (Brush, flag, rudder, stern)
32 Croup
33 Loin
34 Back
35 Withers (Top of the shoulders)
36 Crest of neck

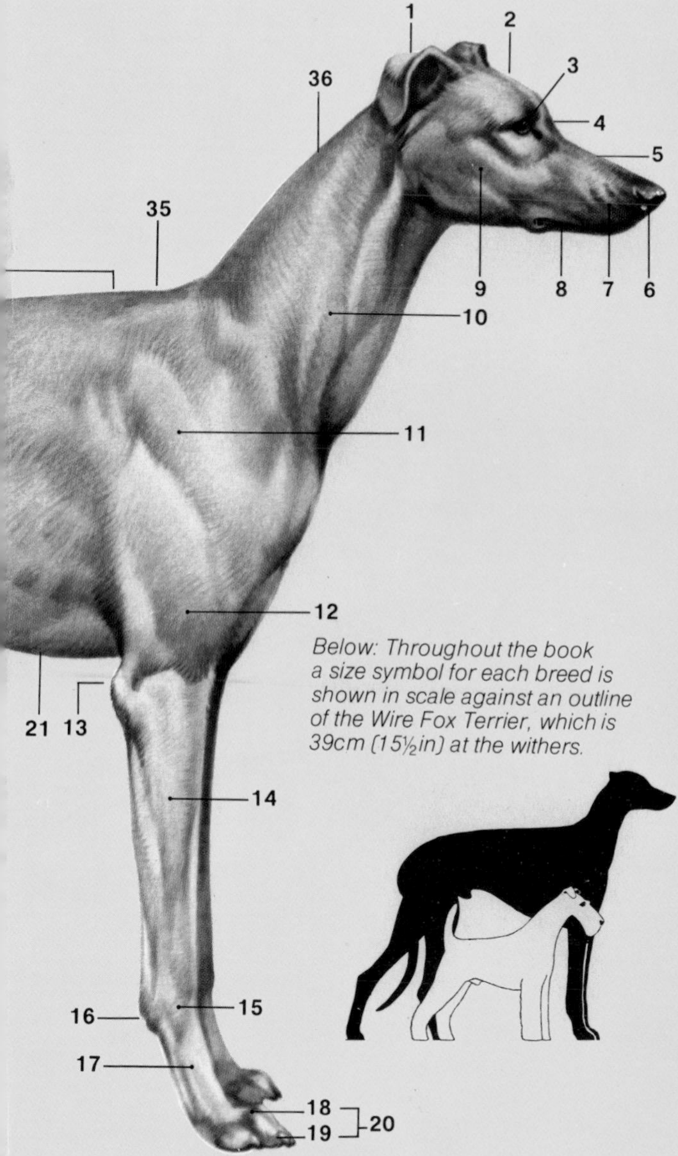

Below: Throughout the book a size symbol for each breed is shown in scale against an outline of the Wire Fox Terrier, which is 39cm (15½in) at the withers.

Dandie Dinmont Terrier

Labrador Retrievers

AN ILLUSTRATED GUIDE TO

DOGS

A practical guide designed to help you choose the most suitable dog for you and your home

Joan Palmer

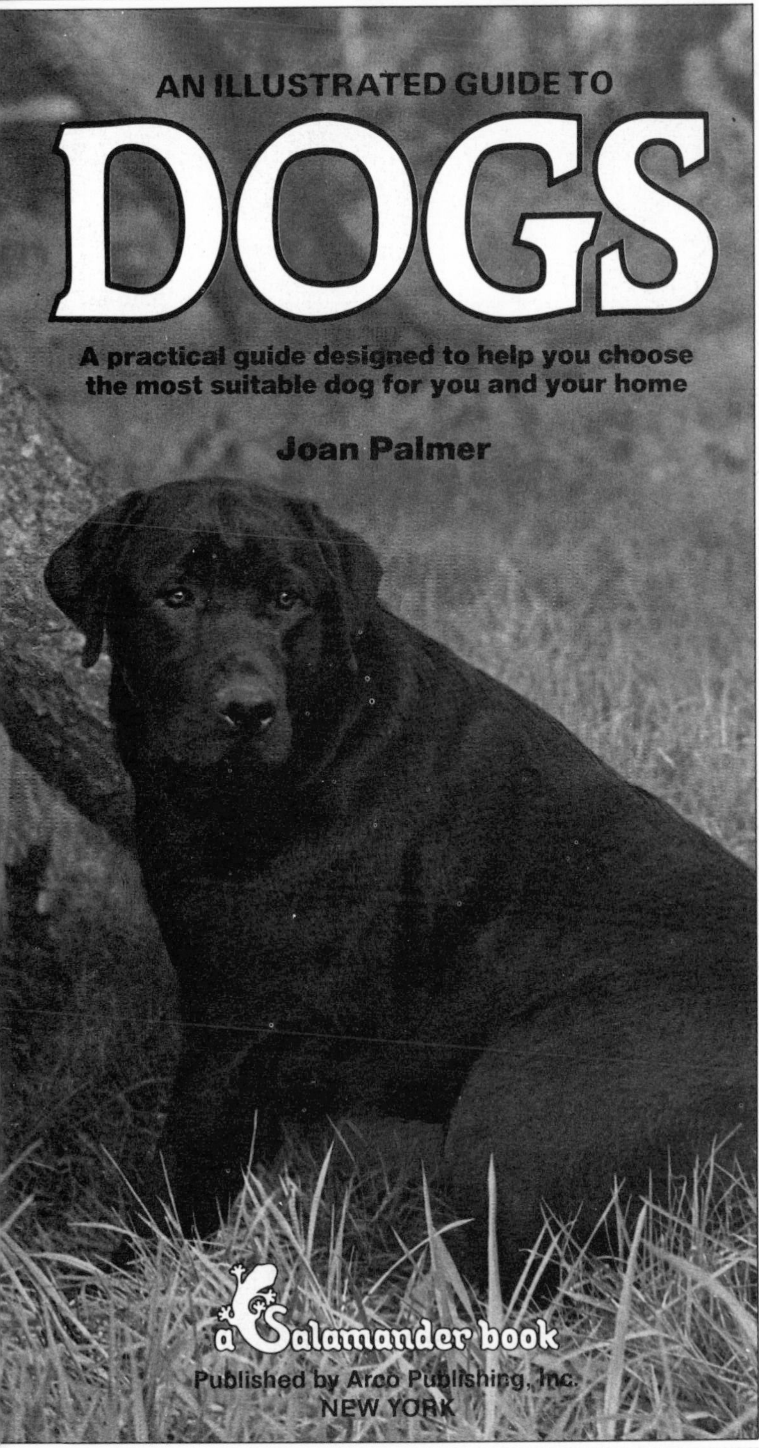

a Salamander book

Published by Arco Publishing, Inc.
NEW YORK

A Salamander Book

Published by
Arco Publishing, Inc.,
219 Park Avenue South,
New York,
N.Y. 10003,
United States of America.

Library of Congress catalog card number **81-68053**

ISBN 0-668-05362-3

All correspondence concerning the contents of this volume should be addressed to Salamander Books Ltd.

This book may not be sold outside the USA and Canada.

Publisher's note: Some material in this book has previously appeared in *A Dog of Your Own*.

Contents

Text and colour illustrations are cross-referenced throughout as follows: 64▸

The breeds are arranged in order of increasing weight. Page numbers in Roman type refer to text entries; those in **bold** to colour illustrations.

Author: Joan Palmer has been a committee member of The National Dog Owners' Association of Great Britain for the past 16 years. A busy freelance journalist, Joan contributes to various journals and newspapers and has a number of books to her credit.

Consultant: Bruce Sessions, formerly Senior Editor and Consultant to *International Dog Fancy Magazine*, is a widely respected American expert.

Editor: Geoff Rogers
Designer: Roger Hyde

Colour artwork: John Francis (Linden Artists), John Green (John Martin & Artists) © Salamander Books Ltd.
Line drawings: Glenn Steward (John Martin & Artists) © Salamander Books Ltd.
Photographs: See page 240 for credits.
Colour and monochrome reproductions: Bantam Litho Ltd., Essex, England.
Filmset: Modern Text Typesetting Ltd., Essex, England.

Printed in Belgium by
Henri Proost & Cie, Turnhout.

CHIHUAHUA

Good points
- *Ideal for town dwellers*
- *Intensely loyal and affectionate*
- *Keenly intelligent*
- *Guard dog in miniature*
- *Inexpensive to keep*

Take heed
- *May snap at teasing children*
- *Strong willed*
- *Hates the cold*

The Chihuahua is keenly intelligent, fiercely protective and cheap to keep. Also, being the world's tiniest dog, it is the least likely to fall foul of the landlord.

The adult Chihuahua usually takes a few weeks to reveal its true personality, keeping its new owner under careful surveillance, perhaps giving the impression that it is shy. Actually, it is weighing up which of them is to be master in the home!

Size
Weight between 0.9-2.7kg/2-6lb (under 1.8kg/4lb preferred for show). There is no desired height in this breed's standard.

Exercise
Contrary to belief, the Chihuahua is ready, and able, to walk as far as most owners would wish, although it doesn't object to an occasional ride in a shopping basket. The fact that its exercise requirements are moderate makes this breed an ideal choice of pet for the elderly.

Grooming
The Chihuahua should be groomed with a soft brush. A rub down with the proverbial velvet glove, or pad, will make the coat gleam. Nails must be regularly clipped and the ears kept clean.

Feeding
The requirement of a very small Chihuahua should be 57-85g (2-3oz) of cooked minced beef or branded dog food, with a handful of puppy biscuits. These dogs fare best on two or three small meals rather than one large daily feed. Bigger specimens can manage up to ½ can (376g, 13.3oz size) of branded dog food, or the equivalent, and a handful of dog biscuits.

Health care
Not as delicate as one might imagine, but they dislike the cold and appreciate a coat to keep them warm when out of doors in winter. These dogs are definitely not designed for kennel living.

Watch out for the molera, a small opening on top of the skull. The Chihuahua's molera, unlike that of a human baby, may never fill in, so a blow on the head could prove fatal. This breed is prone to hiccups; a spasm can often be cured by lifting the pet purposefully up and down. They also have a tendency to shiver, a habit that evokes sympathy from onlookers and generally makes the owner seem the villain of the piece, folk wrongly imagining that the Chihuahua is terrifed or frozen.

Origin and history
Named after the state of Chihuahua in Mexico, the Chihuahua is believed to have been the sacred dog of the Incas. Nevertheless, it seems likely that a few may have been used by the American Indians in their cooking pots. There is also a theory that Chihuahuas were once fierce little dogs living in holes in the ground, which could well account for their inclination to huddle together in every warm nook and cranny. 17▸

PAPILLON (And Phalène)

Good points
- *Affectionate*
- *Dainty size*
- *Good house dog*
- *Trainable for competitive obedience*
- *Usually strong and healthy*

Take heed
- *Not keen on visitors*
- *Possessive towards owners*

The Papillon is a toy spaniel that takes its name from the French word for 'butterfly'. The breed is often referred to as the 'Butterfly Dog' because of the manner in which its ears are set on the head, fringed like a butterfly's wings. The Phalène is identical except that the ears are dropped, and this variety is known as the 'moth'.

The Papillon is an affectionate, lively little dog. It is resilient, whelps easily, is a good walker, and can adapt to extremes of climate. Its attractive appearance and friendly nature make it the ideal family pet. But, like many toy breeds, it has a tendency to be possessive towards its owners and often resents visitors to the home.

Size
The ideal height at the withers is 20-28cm (8-11in). The dog will appear to be slightly longer than high when properly furnished with ruff and hind fringes.

Exercise
Like quite a number of toy breeds, the Papillon will happily walk its owner off his feet, or be content with a walk around the park. One thing is sure: you won't tire it!

Grooming
Daily grooming is required to keep this breed in good condition.

Feeding
Recommended would be ⅓-½ can (376g, 13.3oz size) of a branded meaty product, with biscuit added in equal part by volume; or 1-1½ cups of a dry food, complete diet, mixed in the proportion of 1 cup to ½ cup of hot or cold water.

Above: The dainty and affectionate Papillon – ideal for limited space.

Origin and history
Believed to be a descendant of the Dwarf Spaniel of the 16th century and to have originated in Spain, the dainty little Papillon has been included in many paintings, including some by Rubens and Van Dyke. The Phalène, or Continental Toy Spaniel, is identical except for its drop ears. In the United States and the United Kingdom they are judged as one breed with almost identical standards except for colour variations, but specimens over 30cm (12in) cannot be shown in America.

The French Fédération Cynologique Internationale (FCI) separates the breeds by both type and weight variations, those over 2.5kg (5½lb) in weight entering a separate class. Papillons have done well in obedience classes. 17▶

POMERANIAN

Good points
- *Adaptable*
- *Devoted to owner*
- *Handy size*
- *Happy nature*
- *Ideal for apartment living*

Take heed
- *Will yap if unchecked*
- *Thinks it is a 'big' dog, so bigger dogs may be provoked!*

The Pomeranian is a happy, active little dog that will adapt cheerfully to life in a one-roomed apartment or a spacious dwelling, revelling in the role of lap dog or enjoying walks with its owner. Alternatively, it will amuse itself adequately in a garden. It makes a faithful and devoted companion.

Size
Dog 1.8-2kg (4-4½lb); bitch 2-2.5kg (4½-5½lb).

Exercise
It is wrong to think that toy breeds are of use for little else except sitting decoratively on their owner's knees, and the Pomeranian is no exception. True, they adore being pampered and petted, but they are also lively little dogs, quite able to walk as far as their owner would wish—often further. Alternatively, they will exercise themselves quite happily in a garden.

Grooming
This is not the breed for those who cannot spare the time for daily grooming. Indeed, the Pomeranian has two coats to care for: a short fluffy under-coat, and a long straight top-coat covering the whole of the body. Daily brushing with a stiff brush is a must. The coat should be damped with cold water, and the moisture rubbed in with the fingertips; finally the dog is rubbed down with a towel.

Working from the head, part the coat and brush it forward from roots to tips. Make a further parting and repeat this procedure until the whole dog has been covered.

The Pomeranian requires regular trimming; obtain advice from a breeder or breed club as to how this should be carried out.

Feeding
Recommended would be ⅓-½ can (376g, 13.3oz size) of a branded meaty product, with biscuit added in equal part by volume; or 1-1½ cups of dry food, complete diet, mixed in the proportion of 1 cup to ½ cup of hot or cold water.

Origin and history
The Pomeranian takes its name from Pomerania, in Germany, and is generally thought to be of mid-European origin. However, it is a member of the Spitz family, which could mean that its history began in the Arctic Circle.

The known history of the breed dates from the mid-18th century when it was introduced to several European countries. It became very popular until, following the raiding of the Summer Palace in Peking in 1860 and the appearance of the Imperial Pekingese, some of its popularity was usurped by that breed.

The Pomeranian, in those early days, was a very much larger dog, up to 13.6kg (30lb) in weight, and it was bred down until, by 1896, show classes for Pomeranians were divided into those for exhibits over and under 3.6k (8lb). The British Kennel Club withdrew challenge certificates for the over 3.6kg (8lb) variety in 1915. The American Pomeranian club was formed in New York in 1900. 17▸

JAPANESE CHIN (Japanese Spaniel)

Good points
- *Affectionate*
- *Loyal family dog*
- *Hardy*
- *Good with children*

Take heed
- *That silky coat tends to shed!*
- *Guard against exertion and overheating in warm weather due to breathing difficulties*

The Japanese Chin (sometimes called Japanese Spaniel), might, at first glance, be mistaken for the Pekingese, and it is possible that the two breeds may have evolved from a common stock. It is, however, a high-stepping, graceful dog that is taller in the leg and has a much lighter body than the Pekingese.

The Japanese Chin, it must be remembered, *is* a 'spaniel' and there are some similarities with the King Charles Spaniel, whose origin can also be traced to Japan. However, it has much more of the perky confidence of the tinier breeds than the slower-moving spaniel, and is a lively but dignified little oriental that likes nothing better than to be the centre of attention and is miserable if its advances are thwarted.

Size
1.8-3.2kg (4-7lb).

Exercise
This is a happy little dog that will delight in going for walks and playing games with all the family. It will walk as far as its owners wish, or be happy with a run in the park. The Japanese Chin is quite tough, despite its delicate structure, and will enjoy careful handling by youngsters. But it does like to climb, so be careful it does not fall.

Grooming
Daily grooming with a pure bristle brush will maintain the Chin's luxurious silky coat in good condition. Always give this breed a bath before a show!

Feeding
170-227g (6-8oz) of cooked minced beef, or ½ can (376g, 13.3oz size) of branded dog food, with a handful of dog biscuits, will keep the Chin in excellent health. Lean meat scraps and the occasional non-splintery bone will be enjoyed and, like most small breeds, the Japanese Chin will find lots of pleasure in doggie chews. Remember that dogs should not be given cakes or sweets.

Origin and history
This breed was, for over 1000 years, a favourite of the Japanese emperors, one of whom decreed that all Japanese Chin should be worshipped; some tiny specimens were even kept in hanging cages in the manner of small oriental birds.

The breed is reputed to have found its way to Europe with returning seamen in medieval times. However, the Japanese Chin did not make its appearance in the British show ring until 1862, and is not recorded as being shown in the United States until 20 years later.

Two Japanese Chin were presented to Queen Victoria by Commodore Perry on his return from the Far East in 1853, and this did much to promote the breed. Although they never gained the popularity of the Pekingese, they had a fairly staunch following up until the First World War, when their numbers diminished. Registrations have been on the increase in recent years, and it has become a dependable show dog. 21▸

SMALL GERMAN SPITZ (Kleinspitz)

Good points
- *Adaptable to town or country*
- *Beautiful*
- *Excellent guard*
- *Loyal companion*
- *Intelligent*
- *Ideal for apartments*

Take heed
- *Likes to bark*
- *Suspicious of strangers*

The Small German Spitz is the small variety of the Great German Spitz (Gross-spitz). The only difference between the types is in size; characteristics and conformation are the same.

This is a happy, extremely intelligent little dog. It makes an excellent companion, does not need a great deal of exercise, and adapts well to life in town or country. It usually loves its owners deeply, but does not care much for strangers. Perhaps its only drawback is that it rather likes the sound of its own voice! It is unlikely to chase sheep: guard duty and the protection of its beloved home are far more important.

Size
Height: 28cm (11in) maximum at withers, weight not more than 3.4kg (7½lb). (The Gross-spitz stands about 40cm [15¾in] high).

Exercise
Despite its ability to cover immense areas at speed, the Spitz does not require a great deal of exercise; members of this variety can live quite happily in a small town house.

Grooming
Vigorous daily brushing is necessary if you don't wish to be always vacuuming your carpet!

Feeding
Recommended would be ⅓-½ can (376g, 13.3oz size) of a branded meaty product, with biscuit added in equal part by volume; or 1-1½ cups of a dry food, complete diet, mixed in the proportion of 1 cup of feed to ½ cup of hot or cold water.

Origin and history
It is difficult to pinpoint the origin of this variety of Spitz, for the prehistoric remains of such types have been found throughout Asia and the Pacific, and drawings of similar dogs were found among the remains of the ancient Pharaohs. There are a number of Spitz varieties, all of which are very similar in character and type. Indeed, in the late Sir Richard Glyn's 'Champion Dogs of the World' (Harrap), reference is made to a white variety of Spitz established in German Pomerania some 160 years ago and bred in different sizes. Some of the smallest size, and of various colours, were introduced into the UK under the name of Pomeranian and became well established.

The larger varieties attracted little attention in Germany or elsewhere until the end of the last century, when a breed club was formed in Germany. The club divided the breed into varieties by colour and size.

About the same time the Russians began to develop the Spitz varieties which were distributed throughout Russia under the name of Laika. A Laika was the first dog sent into Earth orbit.

The Russians divided their standard Laikas into the four subvarieties, the East Siberian, West Siberian, Russian and Russian-Finnish, the latter being the smallest. They are still used as gundogs and hunt elk and bear.

YORKSHIRE TERRIER

Good points
- *Affectionate*
- *Healthy and fearless*
- *Good watchdog*
- *Suits apartment living*

Take heed
- *Lengthy show preparation*
- *Needs weekly bath*
- *Difficult to determine pup's size and colouring*

The Yorkshire Terrier is one of the most popular dogs of the day. It rivals the Chihuahua for the title of the world's smallest dog. It is unlikely to be over-awed by larger animals, however, and is not the ideal choice for the stand-offish, because it wants to make friends with everybody. It has been described as a big dog inhabiting a small dog's body; in fact it thinks it is enormous!

Size
Weight up to 3.2kg (7lb).

Exercise
The Yorkie is well suited to town and apartment living, but will prove tireless on a country walk.

Grooming
Many Yorkie owners are content for their pet to have a somewhat scruffy 'shaggy dog' look as long as they know that it is clean and healthy. The show aspirant, however, has a busy time ahead, for the Yorkshire Terrier is exhibited on a show box, which displays its immaculate coat to advantage, a condition that can be achieved only through endless grooming, shampooing and oiling. The show Yorkie spends much of its life, away from the ring, in curlers!

Feeding
Similar to that of other toy breeds, with four meals given in puppyhood, reducing to one meal at a year old, comprising ½ can of branded dog food, or the bought meat equivalent (approximately 199-227g, 7-8oz), lightly cooked and supplemented by biscuits. Lean meat scraps can be given, and bones are appreciated, but never chicken bones.

Above: The Yorkshire Terrier looks its best when groomed for a show.

Health care
The Yorkie has strong, terrier-type teeth, but it is as well to have them scaled by a veterinarian at regular intervals. Toy breeds tend to lose their teeth at an early age (sometimes as early as three), but the avoidance of titbits will preserve them for as long as is possible.

Origin and history
Unlike the Chihuahua, the Yorkie cannot trace its ancestry back to antiquity, for it has been with us for little more than 100 years. It is believed that the breed evolved through the crossing of the Skye Terrier with the old Black and Tan Terrier, although it is rumoured that the Maltese Terrier and the Dandie Dinmont Terrier may also have contributed to producing this game little breed, which is renowned as a ratter. 17▸

MALTESE TERRIER (Maltese)

Good points
- *Adaptable about exercise*
- *Extremely good with children*
- *Healthy*
- *Long-lived*
- *Sensitive*
- *Sweet-natured*

Take heed
- *Needs fastidious daily grooming*

The Maltese Terrier is a good-tempered dog that makes the ideal family pet. It is reliable with children, adaptable about exercise, and usually healthy, and it generally remains playful throughout its long life.

Size
Not over 25cm (10in) from ground to top of shoulder.

Exercise
Can manage a long walk or be content with a stroll in the park.

Grooming
Most important. Use a bristle brush every day from puppyhood and use baby powder on legs and underside to keep the animal clean between baths. Obtain advice from the breeder about show preparation; this breed may not be the ideal choice for new show aspirants.

Feeding
Recommended would be ⅓ can (376g, 13.3oz size) of a branded meaty product, with biscuit added in equal part by volume; or 1-1½ cups of a dry food, complete diet, mixed in the proportion of 1 cup of feed to ½ cup of hot or cold water. Such a diet is, of course, offered purely as a guide. The owner may occasionally substitute lightly cooked minced beef, mixed with biscuit. Water must be available to all breeds at all times.

Origin and history
The Maltese Terrier is described as the oldest of European toy breeds. However, there is some controversy as to whether it originated in Malta, although the breed has certainly existed there for centuries. The Maltese Terrier also found its way to China and the Philippines, probably due to enterprising Maltese traders.

Like the Papillon, the Maltese has been depicted by many famous artists, including Goya, Rubens, and the famous animal painter Sir Edwin Landseer, who in 1930 produced a portrait entitled *The Lion Dog from Malta – the last of his race,* which shows their rarity on the island at that time. The breed first became established in the United Kingdom during the reign of Henry VIII and was a popular pet among elegant ladies. It had a class of its own for the first time in Birmingham, England, in 1864, since when it has gained popularity in both the United Kingdom and the United States. 18▶

Above: Maltese puppies will make reliable companions for children.

ITALIAN GREYHOUND

Good points

- *Affectionate*
- *Easy to train*
- *Graceful appearance*
- *Intelligent and obedient*
- *Odourless*
- *Rarely moults*

Take heed

- *Wounded by harsh words*
- *Should not be kept in a kennel*

The Italian Greyhound is the perfect Greyhound in miniature, a graceful dainty animal that makes an ideal house pet. It does, however, need plenty of exercise and will enjoy a day's rabbiting, should the opportunity arise.

Size

The most desirable weight is. 2.7-3.6kg (6-8lb), and not exceeding 4.5kg (10lb).

Exercise

Certainly not the dog to keep shut up indoors all day. It thrives on plenty of exercise, but adapts well to town living with adequate walks and off-the-lead runs.

Grooming

The Greyhound needs little more than a rub down with a silk handkerchief. But remember that this breed feels the cold, hates the wind and rain, and needs a coat. Care must be taken of the teeth.

Below: The Italian Greyhound is a sensitive and lively companion.

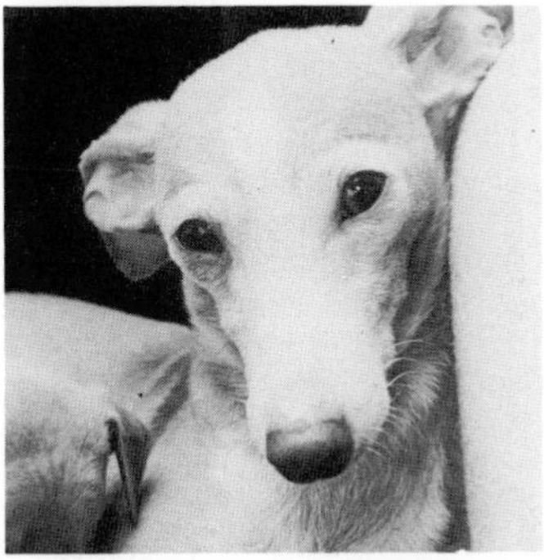

Regular scaling by a veterinarian is recommended (this applies to all toy breeds), but cream of tartar – mixed into a paste on a saucer with a little water, and applied with cotton wool – will often remove unsightly stains.

Feeding

About ½ can of a branded meaty product (376g, 13.3oz size), with biscuit added in equal part by volume; or 1-1½ cupfuls of a dry food, complete diet, mixed in the proportion of 1 cup of feed to ½ cup of hot or cold water.

Origin and history

This obedient and easy-to-train little dog is thought to originate from the Greyhounds depicted on the tombs of the Pharaohs. But it has existed in its present form for centuries and takes its name from its great popularity in 16th century Italy. It was favoured by Queen Victoria, who did much to popularize so many toy breeds during her long reign. Unfortunately for the breed, some English Toy Terrier blood was introduced in an effort to reduce the size further. This spoiled the breed character, and in an effort to restore it several dogs were imported from America. Alas, this did little to help matters and by the early 1950s only five registrations with the British Kennel Club remained. However, fresh stock was imported from Italy and, thanks to the determined efforts and dedication of breeders, the Italian Greyhound was once more firmly established as a stable breed by the early 1970s. 18▸

ENGLISH TOY TERRIER (Toy Manchester Terrier)

Good points
- *Affectionate*
- *Easy to care for*
- *Good with children*
- *Intelligent*
- *Lively*
- *Good at expelling vermin*

Take heed
- *Tends to be a one-person dog that resents outsiders*

The English Toy Terrier, which in the USA is called the Toy Manchester Terrier, is a most attractive, affectionate and game little dog, marvellously intuitive and loyal, but tending to attach itself to one person to the exclusion of others. It is usually healthy, easy to keep clean, odourless and an easy whelper if you wish to breed.

Size
The ideal weight is 2.7-3.6kg (6-8lb), and a height of 25-30cm (10-12in) at the shoulders is most desirable.

Exercise
Adapts well to town living provided adequate walks and off-the-lead runs are possible.

Grooming
A daily brushing will suffice. One of the advantages of this short-coated breed is that it does not shed. The coat can be massaged to effect a sheen; or equally beneficial is a weekly teaspoonful of cod liver oil in the food. Dry the coat with a towel after excursions on rainy days. Although the breed is robust it will, in common with most toy breeds, appreciate a warm coat in bitter weather.

Feeding
Recommended would be ⅓-½ can (376g, 13.3oz size) of a branded meaty product, with biscuit added in equal part by volume; or 1-1½ cups of a dry food, complete diet, mixed in the proportion of 1 cup of feed to ½ cup of hot or cold water. The owner may occasionally substitute lightly cooked minced beef, mixed with biscuit. Lean meat scraps are appreciated. Water must be available to all breeds at all times.

Origin and history
(See also Manchester Terrier)
The English Toy is a smaller version of the Manchester Terrier, once a prodigious ratter and descended from the old Black and Tan Rough-haired Terrier. Their fitness owes something to the Italian Greyhound and the Whippet. The breed began in England under the name Toy Manchester Terrier, and was later known variously as Toy Black and Tan, and Miniature Black and Tan. They were recognized as English Toy Terriers (Black and Tan) by the British Kennel Club in 1962. 18▸

Below: The elegant, compact and lively English Toy Terrier.

MINIATURE PINSCHER

Good points

- *Delightful hackney gait*
- *Easy to look after*
- *Fearless*
- *Good house dog*
- *Intelligent*
- *Rarely moults*
- *Suitable for town or country life*

Take heed

- *Do not overfeed*

The Miniature Pinscher (or Min Pin), sometimes called the 'King of the Toys', makes an ideal pet for the town dweller who, nonetheless, wants a lively sporting companion, not averse to an occasional day's rabbiting. It will follow a scent and give a good account of itself in obedience competitions. The breed's hackney gait is a delight to watch, as it trots along like a dainty little horse. It has the added advantages of rarely moulting and of requiring the minimum of attention to its coat.

Size

The height is 25-30cm (10-12in) at the withers. (There are some slight differences in the US standard as regards acceptable colour and size.)

Exercise

The Min Pin will exercise itself in a reasonable-sized garden or accompany its owner on a day-long trek. This adaptable dog will be happy living in a flat and being taken for walks around the park, or living a free country life.

Grooming

A daily brush and rub down with a chamois leather will keep the Min Pin gleaming.

Feeding

About ½ can of a branded meaty product (376g, 13.3oz size), with biscuit added in equal part by volume; or 1-1½ cupfuls of a dry food, complete diet, mixed in the proportion of 1 cup of feed to ½ cup of hot or cold water.

Above: The Miniature Pinscher is a neat, proud and alert toy dog.

Origin and history

The Miniature Pinscher is not a smaller version of the Dobermann Pinscher, but a much older breed descended from the German Smooth-haired Pinscher. It is suggested that the Italian Greyhound and the Dachshund contributed to its make-up. It achieved pedigree status by the Pinscher-Schnauzer Klub in 1895.

The Min Pin's tail is docked, and its cropped ears can be pricked or dropped. Indeed, were it not for these characteristics and colour variations, one might be forgiven for mistaking it at first glance for an English Toy Terrier. The broad skull and bulging eyes, once prevalent in the breed, have been replaced by the wedge-shaped head preferred in the Dobermann. 18▸

GRIFFON (Griffon Bruxellois, Griffon Brabançon. The Griffon Bruxellois is known in the USA as the Brussels Griffon).

Good points
- *Happy temperament*
- *Hardy*
- *Intelligent*
- *Long-lived*
- *Obedient*
- *Suitable for town or country living*

Take heed
- *No drawbacks known*

The Griffon is an attractive, happy little dog that makes a first-class family pet. It has an almost monkey-like face, with a knowing expression, and is hardy, intelligent and terrier-like in temperament. The breed, which is essentially Belgian, was originally used as a guard and catcher of vermin, particularly in stable yards. However, it took the fancy of royalty, thereby becoming a fashionable house pet.

There are two varieties, the Griffon Bruxellois and the Griffon Brabançon. The only difference is in the coat: the Bruxellois is a rough-coat, and the Brabançon a smooth-coat. Rough-coats and smooth-coats can appear in a single litter. The only variation in the breed standard is in the coat: roughs are harsh, wiry and free from curl, preferably with an under-coat; smooths are short and tight.

Size
Weight: 2.3-5kg (5-11lb), most desirable 2.7-4.5kg (6-10lb).

Exercise
Like most toy breeds it adapts well to town life and does not need a great deal of exercise, but a romp in the countryside will be greatly appreciated.

Grooming
The rough-coat needs twice yearly stripping: best to seek advice, or have this done professionally. The smooth-coat should be brushed, towelled, and gently rubbed down with the proverbial velvet glove or a piece of chamois leather. Watch with this and other small breeds that the nails do not grow too long. Purchase the proper nail clippers for the job from a pet store or pharmacy, and be particularly careful to cut down only to the 'quick'.

Feeding
About ½ can of a branded meaty product (376g, 13.3oz size), with biscuit added in equal part by volume; or 1-1½ cupfuls of a dry food, complete diet, mixed in the proportion of 1 cup of feed to ½ cup of hot or cold water.

Origin and history
The Griffon was first exhibited at the Brussels Exhibition in 1880 and is a truly Belgian breed. It seems likely that it derives from the Affenpinscher, to which it certainly bears a facial resemblance; the introduction of the Pug may be responsible for the Brabançon, or smooth-coat, which in the early days was not recognized.

An enthusiastic Griffon owner was the late Queen Astrid of the Belgians. Before World War I, the popularity of Griffons in their country of origin was immense, but the breeding programme was severely affected by the war.

Griffons have fortunately now found their way to most countries of the world, but showing differences exist. In its native land the Griffon is shown with cropped ears, a practice that is illegal in the United Kingdom, Scandinavia and Australia, and dependent on individual state law in the USA. 18▸

Pomeranian 8▸
Papillon 7▸
Phalène 7▸
Smooth-coated Chihuahua 6▸
Long-coated Chihuahua 6▸
Yorkshire Terrier 11▸

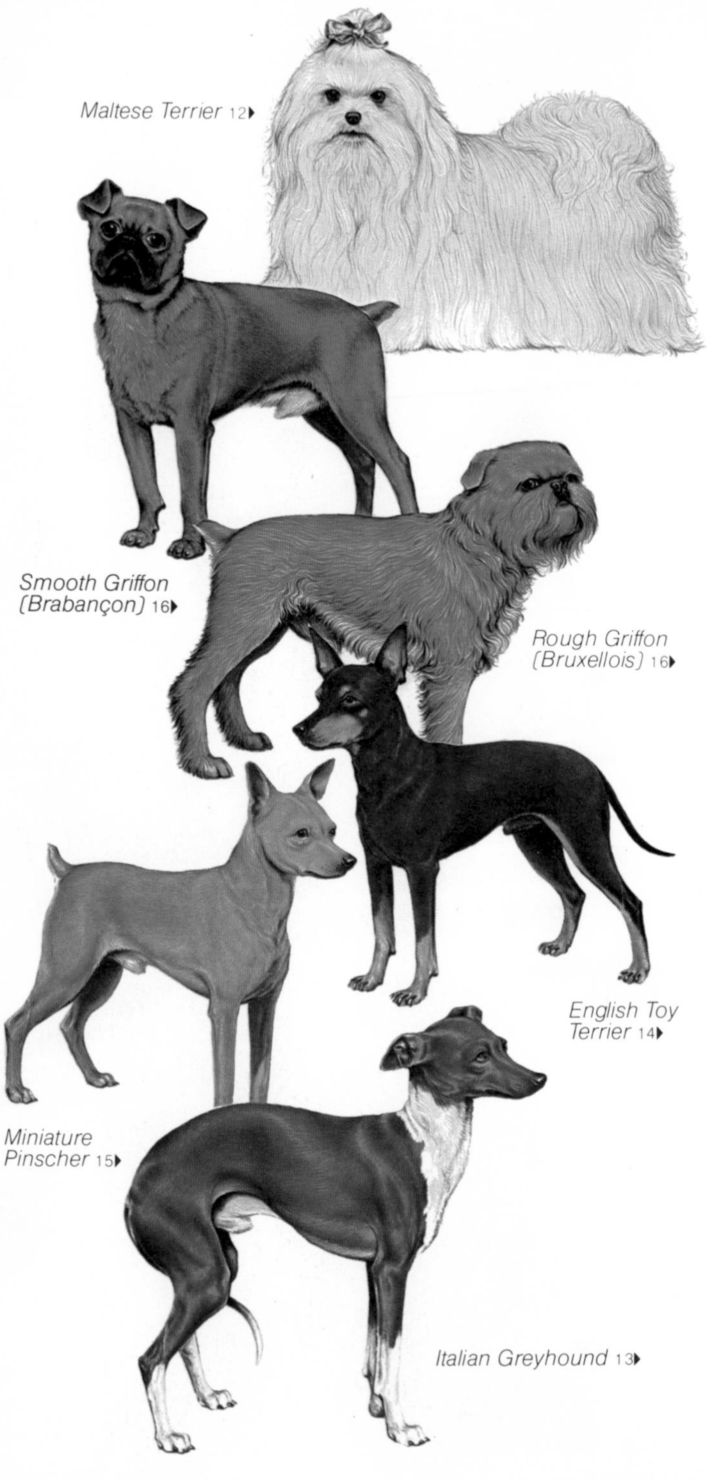

Maltese Terrier 12▸
Smooth Griffon (Brabançon) 16▸
Rough Griffon (Bruxellois) 16▸
English Toy Terrier 14▸
Miniature Pinscher 15▸
Italian Greyhound 13▸

Lowchen 33▸

Affenpinscher 34▸

Bichon Frise 35▸

Toy Poodle (English saddle, or lion, clip) 36▸

Australian Silky Terrier 38▸
Tibetan Spaniel 39▸
Mexican Hairless 85▸
Chinese Crested 42▸

Japanese Chin 9▸
Miniature Smooth-haired Dachshund 40▸
Miniature Long-haired Dachshund 40▸
Miniature Wire-haired Dachshund 40▸
Pekingese 37▸

King Charles Spaniel (Ruby) 45▸

King Charles Spaniel (Tricolour) 45▸

Cavalier King Charles Spaniel (Blenheim) 46▸

Norfolk Terrier 44▸

Norwich Terrier 43▸

Border Terrier 47▸
Australian
Terrier 48▸
Cairn Terrier 49▸
Shih Tzu 53▸
Lhasa Apso 52▸

Bedlington Terrier 68▸
Miniature Poodle
(Lamb clip) 69▸
Pug 54▸
Irish Terrier 81▸
Shetland
Sheepdog 70▸

Miniature Schnauzer 65▸
Schipperke 50▸
West Highland
White Terrier 55▸
Scottish Terrier 64▸
Sealyham Terrier 62▸

German Hunt Terrier 71▸
Lakeland Terrier 60▸
Welsh Terrier 61▸
Standard Smooth-haired Dachshund 66▸
Standard Wire-haired Dachshund 66▸
Standard Long-haired Dachshund 66▸

Wire Fox Terrier 58▸
Smooth Fox Terrier 57▸
Jack Russell Terrier 59▸
Dandie Dinmont Terrier 63▸
Glen of Imaal Terrier 86▸
Skye Terrier 79▸

French Bulldog 82
Miniature
Bull Terrier 95
Boston Terrier 80
Tibetan
Terrier 72
Manchester
Terrier 56
Basenji 76

Beagle 73▶
Drever 74▶
Dachsbracke 74▶
Swedish
Vallhund 75▶
Pembroke
Welsh Corgi 77▶
Cardigan
Welsh Corgi 78▶

Bull terrier 95▸

Staffordshire Bull Terrier 93▸

American Staffordshire Terrier 94▸

American Cocker Spaniel 83▸

English Cocker Spaniel 84▸

Finnish Spitz 91▸

Norrbotten Spitz 90▸

Japanese Spitz 89▸

Pumi 88▸

Hungarian Puli 92▸

Whippet 113▸
Medium Pinscher 96▸
Australian Kelpie 114▸
Standard Schnauzer 96▸
Kerry Blue Terrier 115▸
Kromfohrländer 87▸

LOWCHEN

Good points
- *Affectionate*
- *Happy nature*
- *Intelligent*
- *Healthy*
- *Good show dog*

Take heed
- *No drawbacks known, except perhaps the need for skilful clipping*

The Lowchen is a member of the Bichon family, sharing with the imperial Pekingese the title of little lion dog , because of the practice of clipping it in the traditional poodle exhibition cut, the lion clip, which, complete with mane and tufted tail, gives it the appearance of a lion in miniature. It is an affectionate, happy, healthy little dog, known in Europe for several centuries.

Size
Height: 25-33cm (10-13in) at the withers. Weight: 1.8-4.1kg (4-9lb).

Exercise
This breed adapts well to town or country; although usually presented more suitably for decoration than for sporting activity, it will enjoy regular walks in the park, or a run in the countryside. But many of the exotic breeds are kept in breeding and exhibition kennels where, although extremely well looked after, they never have the chance of a muddy scamper.

Below: Seemingly fragile, the Lowchen is robust and full of energy.

Grooming
Clipping is best left to the expert, at any rate until a pattern has been studied and absorbed. Meanwhile, a daily brushing will keep the Lowchen looking handsome.

Feeding
Recommended would be ⅓-½ can of a branded meaty product (376g, 13.3oz size), with biscuit added in equal part by volume; or 1-1½ cupfuls of a dry food, complete diet, mixed in the proportion of 1 cup of feed to ½ cup of hot or cold water. Always ensure that the dog has an ample supply of water.

Origin and history
The Lowchen is thought to be a French dog. It is registered with the FCI as of native origin, under the title 'petit chien lion'. Certainly it was known in both France and Spain from the late 1500s, and is thought to have been favoured by the beautiful Duchess of Alba, for a dog bearing a strong similarity to the Lowchen appears in a portrait of that lady painted by the Spanish artist Francisco Goya (1746-1828). Probably the breed evolved in the Mediterranean area about the same time as the Maltese, the Bichon Frise and the Bichon Bolognese.

The Lowchen is now a frequent contender in the show ring in many countries, but it has yet to become popular as a pet. 19▸

AFFENPINSCHER

Good points
- *Affectionate*
- *Intelligent*
- *Cute monkey-like appearance*
- *Excellent ratter despite small frame*
- *Good watchdog*

Take heed
- *No drawbacks known*

The Affenpinscher is an enchanting little breed, with an almost monkey-like appearance, whence the prefix 'Affen', which is the German word for monkey. In its country of origin it is often called the 'Zwergaffenpinscher' ('Zwerg' means dwarf). The French have dubbed it the 'moustached devil'. In any event it is an appealing, comical little dog, the smallest of the Schnauzers and Pinschers alert, gentle and affectionate, but always ready to defend.

Size
Height: 24-28cm (9½-11in).
Weight: 3-4.1kg (6½-9lb).

Exercise
Like most toy dogs it will be content with a walk around the park, but it will gladly walk you off your feet if that is your pleasure.

Grooming
Regular brushing will keep the Affenpinscher in good condition.

Feeding
Recommended would be ⅓-½ can of a branded meaty product (376g, 13.3oz size), with biscuit added in equal part by volume; or 1-1½ cupfuls of a dry food, complete diet, mixed in the proportion of 1 cup of feed to ½ cup of hot or cold water. When giving a dry feed, ensure that the dog has—as always—an ample supply of water.

Origin and history
Miniature Pinschers and Affenpinschers were, until 1896, classified as one breed. In that year, at the Berlin show, it was decided that the long-coated variety should be known as the Affenpinscher.

The Affenpinscher is an ancient German breed that was depicted by Jan van Eyck (1395-1441) and Albrecht Dürer (1471-1528). There is, however, some controversy as to its origin, though its nationality has never been in doubt. Some believe it to be related to the Brussels Griffon; others attribute the Brussels Griffon to the Affenpinscher; a third school of thought is that the Affenpinscher is a toy version of the German coarse-haired terrier, the Zwergschnauzer. In any event, this delightful breed was recognized by the American Kennel Club in 1936, and has now achieved recognition in the United Kingdom, being represented in the 1980 Crufts Dog Show. 19▶

Above: The Affenpinscher's comical looks hide a sturdy watchdog.

BICHON FRISE (Bichon Bolognese)

Good points
- *Good pet*
- *Happy temperament*
- *Adaptable*
- *Intelligent*
- *Loves human company*
- *Attractive, lamb-like appearance*

Take heed
- *Requires meticulous grooming*

The Bichon Frise has been recognized by the British and American Kennel Clubs only over the past 10 years. It is a most appealing and happy little dog, which will surely become more popular when the public become acquainted with the breed.

Size
Height: less than 30cm (12in), smallness being highly desirable.

Exercise
Will enjoy a romp if you can bear to clean up that muddy coat afterwards! It will fit well into town living and regular walks, but will enjoy the occasional off-the-lead country run and a game in the garden.

Grooming
This is not the breed for novice exhibitors, or for those who are not prepared to spend time in meticulous grooming, bathing, trimming and scissoring. The effect, when complete, should be of an elegant white 'powder puff', the head and body trimmed to give a rounded effect, but showing the eyes. Hair around the feet should also be trimmed. Ask the breeder for a showing and grooming chart, and for a demonstration.

Feeding
Recommended would be ⅓-½ can of a branded meaty product (376g, 13.3oz size), with biscuit added in equal part by volume; or 1-1½ cupfuls of a dry food, complete diet, mixed in the proportion of 1 cup of feed to ½ cup of hot or cold water. Always ensure that the dog has ample water.

Origin and history
The Bichon, like the Caniche, is a descendant of the Barbet (water spaniel), from which the name Barbichon originates; later it was abbreviated to Bichon.

The little dogs are said to have originated in the Mediterranean area and were certainly introduced by sailors to the Canary Islands prior to the 14th century. There were then four varieties: the Bichon Ténériffe, the Bichon Maltaise, the Bichon Bolognese and the Bichon Havanais. The breed later found favour with the French and Spanish nobility and was included in paintings by Francisco Goya (1746-1828).

A period of obscurity followed until, after World War I, soldiers took a few when they left France. A breed standard was written up in France in 1933, when the name 'Bichon à poil frise' (curly-coated Bichon) was adopted, and the word Ténériffe omitted from its title. Crufts Dog Show in London included a class for the Bichon Frise for the first time in 1980.

The Bichon Frise was first introduced into America in 1956, and from further imports a few years later breeding began in earnest. The breed was registered with the American Kennel Club in October 1972 and classified in the Non-Sporting Group of the AKC in April 1973.

The Bolognese is very similar to the Bichon Frise and is registered with the Fédération Cynologique Internationale) as an Italian breed. 19▸

TOY POODLE

Good points
- *Affectionate*
- *Intelligent and long-lived*
- *Good sense of fun*

Take heed
- *Noisy if unchecked*
- *Not ideal as a child's pet*
- *Sensitive*
- *Suggest veterinary examination prior to purchase*

The Poodle has a character full of fun. It is intelligent and obedient. In the United Kingdom, it has proved a useful competitor in obedience competitions. It has a fondness for water, if the owner permits, but is much favoured for the show ring where, exhibited in the traditional lion clip, it is a beauty to behold. It is also, debatably, the most difficult breed to prepare for the ring, involving the handler in a day's canine beauty treatment.

Size
Height at shoulder should be under 28cm (11in).

Exercise
The Poodle will enjoy a ball game in the garden, practising obedience exercises or trotting beside you in the park.

Grooming
Use a wire-pin pneumatic brush and a wire-toothed metal comb for daily grooming. The lion clip is an essential for the show ring, but pet owners generally resort to the more natural lamb clip, with the hair a short uniform length. It is possible to clip your own dog with a pair of hairdressers' scissors. However, if, despite the help which is usually available from the breeder, you find the task tedious, there are numerous poodle parlours to which you should take your dog every six weeks. Regular bathing is essential.

Feeding
One third to ½ can (376g, 13.3oz size) of a branded, meaty product, with biscuit added in equal part by volume; or 1-1½ cupfuls of a dry complete food, mixed in the proportion of 1 cup of feed to ½ cup of hot or cold water.

Health care
Fanciers will confirm that the Standard Poodle is the soundest of the varieties. It is possible to acquire healthy Toy and Miniature stock, but care should be taken to purchase from a breeder who puts quality ahead of daintiness. Watch out for signs of ear trouble, nervousness or joint malformations. Teeth need regular scaling.

Origin and history
The Poodle was originally a shaggy guard, a retriever and protector of sheep, with origins similar to the Irish Water Spaniel and, no doubt, a common ancestor in the French Barbet and Hungarian Water Hound.

The Poodle may not be, as many suppose, solely of French origin. It originated in Germany as a water retriever; even the word poodle comes from the German 'pudelnass' or puddle, and from this fairly large sturdy dog, the Standard Poodle, the Miniature and the Toy have evolved.

The breed has been known in England since Prince Rupert of the Rhine, in company with his Poodle, came to the aid of Charles I in battle. The breed was favoured also by Marie Antoinette who, rumour has it, invented the lion clip to match the uniform of her courtiers. It is also a popular breed in the United States. 19▸

PEKINGESE

Good points
- *Loyal and affectionate*
- *Brave guard dog*
- *Healthy and intelligent*

Take heed
- *Aloof, independent nature*
- *Subject to eye trouble*
- *Needs daily grooming*
- *Guard against exertion and overheating in warm weather*

'You have to say please to a Peke.' So said a well-known Pekingese breeder. Tell one off and it will sulk until you feel *you're* in the wrong!

The Pekingese likes to remind its owners of its regal background, and expects to be petted and pampered. It is not, however, a delicate creature; in fact, it is fearless and fun, and loves having toys to play with.

It is good with children, but comes into its own as an adult's sole companion, being the centre of attention and, preferably, having the run of the house. The restricted and neglected Peke is apt to become destructive through boredom. The Peke has a mind of its own and is condescending by nature. But when it decides to offer you its affection, you could not wish for a more loyal and loving companion.

Size
Dogs: 3.2-5kg (7-11lb). Bitches: 3.6-5.4kg (8-12lb).
There is not, as is often supposed, a miniature Pekingese, but within a litter may be found 'sleeve' specimens weighing no more than 2.7kg (6lb). Sleeve Pekes are so called because they could be concealed in the flowing sleeves of the Chinese mandarins.

Exercise
The Peke will happily trudge across fields with its owner, or be content with a sedate walk.

Grooming
The Pekingese needs daily brushing with a brush of soft bristles. The grooming of the underside is usually carried out with the Peke lying on its back, the rest of the job being tackled with the pet standing on a table, or on one's lap. Grooming a dog on a table is good preparation for a possible show career! It isn't necessary to bath a Peke frequently; as an alternative, talcum powder can be applied and brushed through the coat.

Feeding
The adult Pekingese thrives on about 170-227g (6-8oz) of meat supplemented by biscuits and the occasional non-splintery bone. Like most breeds, they appreciate vitamin tablets, which they will learn to beg for like sweets. An accessible water bowl is, of course, a 'must' for this and all breeds.

Origin and history
This regal little lion dog came to Europe following the Boxer Rebellion when, in 1860, the British invaded the Summer Palace in Peking and five Imperial Pekingese were looted from the women's apartments. Previous to this, it had been forbidden for anyone other than the Chinese royal family to own a Peke, and their theft was punishable by death.

One of the Pekes taken by the British was presented to Queen Victoria; it was appropriately named 'Looty', lived until 1872, and was the subject of a painting by Landseer. 21▸

AUSTRALIAN SILKY TERRIER

Good points
- *Alert*
- *Affectionate*
- *Dainty nature*
- *Excellent rat catcher*
- *Hardy*
- *Makes a good pet*

Take heed
- *No drawbacks known*

The Australian Silky Terrier is a dainty little dog, similar to the Yorkshire Terrier in appearance. It is alert and hardy, and has a merry and affectionate nature.

The Official Standard states: 'The dog is compact, moderately low set, of medium length, with a refined structure, but of sufficient substance to suggest the ability to hunt and kill domestic rodents. It should display terrier characteristics, embodying keen alertness, activity and soundness.'

Size
The most desirable weights are 3.6-4.5kg (8-10lb). Height approximately 23cm (9in) at the withers.

Exercise
Despite its small stature the Silky has well-developed terrier instincts and is a first-class ratter. It will adapt well to apartment living and town walks, but is in its element chasing across the fields, getting that straight, silky coat into magnificent disarray.

Below: The hardy Australian Silky Terrier—an excellent pet.

Grooming
Ideally the Silky should have a well-groomed appearance, which calls for a coat length of 12.5-15cm (5-6in) from behind the ears to the set-on of the tail. Legs from knees and hocks to feet should be free from long hair.

Feeding
Recommended: ⅓-½ can of a branded, meaty product (376g, 13.3oz size), with biscuit added in equal part by volume; or 1-1½ cupfuls of a dry food, complete diet, mixed in the proportion of 1 cup of feed to ½ cup of hot or cold water.

Origin and history
The Australian (or Sydney) Silky Terrier was derived from crossing Yorkshire Terriers with Skye Terriers, some say by cross-breeding with the Australian Terrier, which has Norwich and Cairn Terrier and probably also Dandie Dinmont in its make-up.

The breed, which in America is shown in toy classes under the name of Silky Terrier, has been recognized in the United States since 1959, but is a relative newcomer to the United Kingdom, where separate standards now exist for the Australian Terrier and the Australian Silky Terrier. 20▸

TIBETAN SPANIEL

Good points
- *Confident*
- *Easy to train*
- *Happy nature*
- *Intelligent*
- *Good household pet*
- *Suitable for town or country*

Take heed
- *No drawbacks known*

The Tibetan Spaniel is an attractive small dog, with a happy, if independent, nature. It is easily trained and makes an ideal family pet, being reliable with children. In appearance it resembles a rather large Pekingese. It is also an enjoyable dog to show.

Size
Weight: 4-6.8kg (9-15lb) is ideal. Height about 25cm (10in).

Exercise
This dog requires average walks and off-the-lead runs.

Grooming
Needs daily brushing.

Feeding
Half to 1 can (376g, 13.3oz size) of a branded, meaty product, with biscuit added in equal part by volume; or 1½ cupfuls of a dry complete food, mixed in the proportion of 1 cup of feed to ½ cup of hot or cold water.

Origin and history
The Tibetan Spaniel was first discovered in the Tibetan monasteries where, to quote a reference in *Champion Dogs of the World* (G. Harrap, 1967), 'Reports indicate that it still turns the prayer-wheel of Tibetans who seek to reap the rewards of a devout life without the inconvenience of physical exertion'. However, this charming practice may have ceased since the Chinese takeover and outlawing of dogs. It is a close relative of the Tibetan Terrier and Lhasa Apso, both of which also originate from Tibet. The Tibetan Spaniel was first seen in England in 1905. 20▸

Below: Three beautiful Tibetan Spaniels – ideal show dogs.

MINIATURE DACHSHUND

Good points

- *Courageous*
- *Loyal family pet*
- *Great sense of fun*
- *Good watchdog*

Take heed

- *Prone to disc trouble – don't let it jump, or get overweight*
- *Self-willed*
- *Slightly aggressive to strangers*

Smooth-haired

The Dachshund (or Teckel) was bred as a badger hound in its native Germany. Badger hunting required a short-legged hound, with a keen sense of smell, coupled with courage and gameness; a dog that could burrow – an ability, which, if unchecked, today's pet Dachshund will demonstrate in your garden. The Dachsie just loves to dig!

Some Dachsunds are still bred as hunting dogs and will bravely tackle an opponent larger than themselves, such as the badger. They would also defend their owner until death. However, their role nowadays is mainly as a companion. They like children, but can be a little aggressive with strangers if unchecked. They are affectionate, full of fun and, despite their short legs, can cope with as much exercise as you can give them. They have a large bark for their size and are good watchdogs.

Size

Long-haired, Smooth-haired and Wire-haired: Ideal weight 4.5kg (10lb). It is most important that judges should not award a prize to any dog exceeding 5kg (11lb).

Exercise

Regular exercise is important as the tendency to put on weight must be discouraged. This doesn't mean you should take your Dachsie on 10-mile treks every day, but short, frequent walks are a must, with plenty of runs in a well-fenced garden.

Grooming

The Dachshund's coat is easy to keep in condition. The Smooth-haired needs only a few minutes' attention every day with a hound glove and soft cloth. A stiff-bristled

Below: The Smooth-haired Miniature Dachshund – an easy-care family pet.

Long-haired

Wire-haired

brush and comb should be used on the Long-haired and Wire-haired varieties.

Feeding

About ½ can (376g, 13.3oz size) of a branded, meaty product, with biscuit added in equal part by volume; or 1-1½ cupfuls of a dry complete food, mixed in the proportion of 1 cup of feed to ½ cup of hot or cold water.

Origin and history

The Dachshund was bred as a badger hound, or hunting dog, and is known to have existed prior to the 16th century and to have been derived from the oldest breeds of German hunting dog, such as the Bibarhund.

When the German Dachshund Club was formed in 1888, there was only one variety—the Smooth-haired Dachshund, whose wrinkled paws, then a characteristic, have been almost bred out. Today there are three varieties, with miniatures of each type: the Smooth-haired, Wire-haired and Long-haired. The Wire-haired Dachshund arose through crossing with the Scottish, Dandie Dinmont and other terriers, the Long-haired by crossing the Smooth-haired with the spaniel and an old German gundog, the Stöberhund.

Both bandiness, due to a weakness in the tendons, and exaggerated length have now been eradicated from the breed.

In his book *The Dachshund* (Popular Dogs), the late Eric Fitch Daglish refers to the severe blow dealt on dog breeding in the United Kingdom and elsewhere, during the 1914-18 war. 'All breeds were affected,' he writes, 'but none, perhaps, so tragically as the Dachshund. Ever since its appearance among us the little Teckel had been recognized as the national dog of the Teutonic Empire, and with the outbreak of hostilities he came in for a share of the scorn heaped on everything made in Germany.' This sad state of affairs continued in the United Kingdom and other parts of Europe during the Second World War, when Dachshunds were unfairly discarded, shouted at and even stoned in the streets because of their German ancestry. Happily this is now long past and the sporty, lovable Dachshund has come again to the fore in popularity polls.

The miniatures, like the standards, were also introduced for a purpose. Towards the end of the 19th century, German sportsmen required a hound to go to ground after rabbits. Some were produced by chance, the smaller, weaker members of a litter, but there also appears to have been a miniature type, known as the Kaninchenteckel, which was intentionally produced by mating lightweight Dachshunds to toy terriers or Pinschers. The early miniatures apparently had little of the quality of the show Dachshund about them, but selective breeding produced a far better type—for many years known as the dwarf Teckel—but with the shallow chest, short head and full eye of its predecessor. 21▸

CHINESE CRESTED

Good points
- *No hairs on the carpet!*
- *Intelligent and devoted*
- *Good with children*

Take heed
- *Apt to be greedy*
- *Some folk find the reptilian skin unpleasant*
- *Can die of a broken heart if parted from its beloved owner*

The Chinese Crested has much to recommend it, as both pet and show dog. It is a handy size, clean, and odourless, and does not shed. It is dainty, alert, intelligent, courageous and gentle. It seldom requires veterinary aid and is a free whelper. It adjusts to cold or warm climates as its body temperature is 4°F (2.2°C) higher than that of humans; in fact, it has its own central heating system, the body feeling hotter to the touch after the animal has eaten. It has the ability to grip with its paws in a charming, almost human fashion.

A strange fact about the breed is that in almost every litter there are one or two haired pups, known as 'powder puffs'. Although these haired specimens have been excluded from selective breeding over a period of years, they are still apparent. Many people believe that the power puffs are nature's way of keeping the hairless pups warm. And some think that breeding a hairless dog with a powder puff results in healthier stock, the powder puff being allegedly the stronger. The powder puff dog will command only a very moderate price as a household pet.

Size
Varies considerably, maximum weight 5.4kg (12lb).

Exercise
The Chinese Created is a lively little dog and enjoys a brisk walk. However, it happily works off a lot of surplus energy running after, and playing with, the chews and other toys that it so likes.

Grooming
The Chinese Crested needs frequent bathing, and the skin should be regularly rubbed with baby oil to prevent cracking and to keep it smooth to the touch. Care must be taken to prevent sunburn and to maintain the skin free of blackheads—to which they are prone in adolescence—and other blemishes. Facial hair and whiskers are usually removed.

Feeding
Usually a rather greedy dog, this breed should nonetheless be content with ½-¾ can of branded dog food (376g, 13.3oz size) or the fresh meat equivalent, and a cupful of small dog biscuits. It is a good ideal to keep a bowl of biscuits accessible, so that the animal may help itself when peckish, but remove them if your pet becomes overweight.

Health care
These dogs lack premolar teeth, and thus it is inadvisable to give them bones. They are also allergic to wool.

Origin and history
Up until 1966, an elderly lady in the United States owned the only examples of the Chinese Crested in the world. Mrs Ruth Harris introduced four of these to the United Kingdom. Today the Chinese Crested is thriving, and classes for the breed are being included in an increasing number of dog shows. It is recognized by the British Kennel Club, but has yet to achieve Championship Show status. 20▸

NORWICH TERRIER

Good points
- *Adaptable to most life-styles*
- *Equable temperament*
- *Fearless*
- *Good with children*
- *Hardy*
- *Lovable*

Take heed
- *No drawbacks known*

Prior to 1964 the Norwich Terrier and the Norfolk Terrier were recognized as one breed by the British Kennel Club. In 1964 the Norwich gained independent status as the prick-eared variety of the two. Its appearance and characteristics are otherwise identical with its Norfolk kin. In the USA both prick-eared and drop-eared varieties were known as the Norwich Terrier until 1 January 1979, when separate breeds were recognized.

The Official Standard states: 'A small, low, keen dog, compact and strong, with good substance and bone. Excessive trimming is not desirable. Honourable scars from fair wear and tear should not be penalized unduly.'

Size
Ideal height 25cm (10in) at the withers; this must not be attained by excessive length of leg.

Exercise
The Norwich Terrier will settle for regular walks if living in a town, but is happiest when allowed off-the-lead runs in the countryside. It is adept at ratting and rabbiting.

Grooming
Little grooming or trimming is required.

Feeding
Recommended would be ½-1 can of a branded meaty product (376g, 13.3oz size), with biscuit added in equal part by volume; or 1½ cups of a dry, complete food, mixed in the proportion of 1 cup of feed to ½ cup of hot or cold water. Increase rations if the terrier is in hard exercise.

Origin and history
There is some controversy as to whether Colonel Vaughan of Ballybrick, Southern Ireland, or Mr Jodrell Hopkins, a horse dealer from Trumpington, England, deserves credit for founding the Norwich Terrier breed.

Colonel Vaughan hunted in the 1860s with a pack of small red terriers that had evolved from the Irish terrier. As there were many outcrosses, terriers with drop and prick ears came about, and breeders tended to crop the ears of the drop-eared animals until the practice became illegal. When it did, the Norwich Terrier Club protested loudly about the admittance of the drop-eared variety; when the breed was recognized by the Kennel Club, the Norwich Terrier Club requested that the standard should call for only those with prick ears.

Mr Jodrell Hopkins owned a bitch, a number of whose pups came into the hands of his employee, Frank Jones. Mr Jones crossed them with other terriers, including the Irish and the Glen of Imaal Terrier, using only small examples of these breeds; the progeny were known as 'Jones' or 'Trumpington' Terriers. There is a breeder who claims a direct line from Mr Jones' dogs to the Norwich of today.

The Norwich is a breed that has not been spoilt; for, perhaps surprisingly, it has—like the Norfolk—never gained great popularity. 22▸

NORFOLK TERRIER

Good points
- *Adaptable to most life-styles*
- *Equable temperament*
- *Fearless*
- *Good with children*
- *Hardy*
- *Lovable*

Take heed
- *No drawbacks known*

The Norfolk Terrier co-existed with the Norwich Terrier for more than a century until, in 1932, it gained recognition by the British Kennel Club. There were two types, those with drop ears and those with erect ears. However, in 1964 the British Kennel Club agreed to separate the types, the breed with drop ears becoming the Norfolk Terrier, the prick-eared variety henceforth being known as the Norwich Terrier. The appearance and size of the breed is otherwise the same. They are gay, hardy little dogs with an equable temperament, adapt well to almost any life-style, and are fearless and sporty. (In the United States the Norfolk Terrier was known as the Norwich Terrier (Drop ear) until 1 January 1979, when it was officially recognized as a separate breed.)

Below: The Norfolk Terrier is full of terrier liveliness and energy. Although it will adapt to town living, it likes nothing better than a good scamper in the fields in search of adventure.

Size
Ideal height 25cm (10in) at the withers.

Exercise
The Norfolk Terrier will settle for regular walks in a town, but is in its element enjoying off-the-lead runs in the countryside, and is adept at ratting and rabbiting.

Grooming
Little grooming or trimming is required.

Feeding
Recommended would be ½-1 can of a branded meaty product (376g, 13.3oz size), with biscuit added in equal part by volume; or 1½ cups of a dry, complete food, mixed in the proportion of 1 cup of feed to ½ cup of hot or cold water. Increase rations if the terrier is in hard exercise.

Origin and history
These sporty little terriers from the eastern counties of England were once popular with Cambridge students; the dogs were red in colour, rarely weighed more than 4.5kg (10lb), and included both prick-eared and drop-eared varieties. They were shown at dog shows from 1870. 22▸

KING CHARLES SPANIEL

Good points
- *Hardy, despite small stature*
- *Clean*
- *Loves children*
- *Usually gets on with other pets*

Take heed
- *Needs monthly bath*
- *Watch out for canker in ears*
- *Needs daily grooming*
- *Not suited to outdoor kennels*

The King Charles Spaniel (Black and Tan variety) is known in the USA as the English Toy Spaniel, the varieties of which are Prince Charles (tricolour), Ruby (red) and Blenheim (chestnut and white).

In 1903 an attempt was made in the United Kingdom to change the breed name to Toy Spaniel. However, the change was opposed by King Edward VII, a devotee of the breed, and it has retained the name, probably attributed to it because of Van Dyck's 17th-century paintings, which showed King Charles with these pets.

The King Charles is an ideal choice. It is a good mixer, marvellous with children and – despite its small stature – very hardy. It does, however, require daily grooming, regular bathing and, like the Pekingese, to have its eyes wiped every day; care must also be taken lest canker should develop in those well-concealed ears.

Size
The most desirable weight is 3.6-6.4kg (8-14lb).

Exercise
The King Charles will look forward to its daily outings, whether accompanying its owner on a shopping trip or going for a scamper in the park. It will be quick to learn how to carry its lead or a newspaper. Don't forget to rub it down with a towel after it has been out in the rain.

Grooming
Regular brushing with a bristle brush is essential. Examine paws for any trace of interdigital cysts, and ears for canker, often detectable by an unpleasant smell. Wipe eyes with cotton wool dipped in a weak saline solution to keep them clear of unsightly 'tear streaks'.

Feeding
About ½-1 can (376g, 13.3oz size) of a branded, meaty diet, with biscuit added in equal parts by volume; or, if a dry food, complete diet is used, 1½ cupfuls of feed mixed in the proportion of 1 cup of dry feed to ½ cupful of hot or cold water; or minced beef, lightly cooked, with biscuit added. Meat scraps are acceptable, as are canine chocolate drops as a reward or treat, but don't spoil those teeth by giving your dog cakes or sweet biscuits.

Origin and history
The King Charles is generally thought of as a British breed, but it can be traced back to Japan in 2000BC. The original breed was much in evidence at the English 16th-century court, when it closely resembled the present-day, longer-nosed Cavalier King Charles. As short-nosed dogs became fashionable, the King Charles Spaniel evolved.

The breed has many royal associations; one was found hidden in the folded gown of Mary, Queen of Scots, after her execution, and Macaulay, in his *History of England,* recalls how King Charles II endeared himself to his people by playing with these spaniels in St James's Park, 'before the dew was off the grass'. 22▸

CAVALIER KING CHARLES SPANIEL

Good points
- *Hardy, despite small stature*
- *Clean*
- *Loves children*
- *Usually gets on with other pets*

Take heed
- *Needs monthly bath*
- *Watch out for canker in ears*
- *Needs daily grooming*
- *Not suited to outdoor kennels*

Many people find it hard to distinguish between the King Charles and the Cavalier King Charles Spaniel; the Cavalier is larger, and there are marked differences in the head formation – the skull is almost flat between the ears and its stop is much shallower than that of the King Charles. However, it has the same characteristics of courage, hardiness and good nature, which makes it a suitable pet for any age group.

Size
Weight: 5.4-8.2kg (12-18lb). A small, well-balanced dog within these weights is desirable.

Exercise
Normal exercise requirements. Will adapt easily to town or country living. It should not, however, be kennelled out of doors.

Grooming
Regular brushing with a bristle brush is essential. Examine paws for any trace of interdigital cysts, and ears for canker, often detectable by an unpleasant smell. Wipe eyes with cotton wool dipped in a weak saline solution to keep them clear of unsightly 'tear streaks'.

Feeding
About ½-1 can (376g, 13.3oz size) of a branded, meaty diet, with biscuit added in equal parts by volume; or, if a dry food, complete diet is used, 1½ cupfuls of feed mixed in the proportion of 1 cup of dry feed to ½ cupful of hot or cold water; or minced beef, lightly cooked, with biscuit added.

Above: The attractive Cavalier King Charles makes a fine pet.

Meat scraps are acceptable, as are canine chocolate drops as a reward or treat, but don't spoil those teeth by giving your dog cakes or sweet biscuits.

Origin and history
Reports by Pepys and other British diarists tell us that King Charles II spent more time playing with his 'toy spaniels' during Council meetings that he did dealing with matters of state. He even took his dogs into his bedchamber.

The Cavalier and the King Charles originate from common stock. When it became fashionable to produce a King Charles Spaniel with a short nose, the original type almost disappeared; but in the late 1920s, a group of breeders combined to bring back the old type of King Charles, prefixing its name with the word 'cavalier' to distinguish it from the newer, quite separate variety. 22▸

BORDER TERRIER

Good points

- *Good-natured*
- *Handy size*
- *Hardy*
- *Reliable*
- *Sporty working dog*
- *Unspoilt breed*
- *Fine guard dog*

Take heed

- *Needs space for exercise*

The Border Terrier is the smallest of the working terriers. It is a natural breed that evolved in the Border counties of England and Scotland, where its task was to worry foxes from their lair.
It is a hardy, unspoilt dog with an equable temperament, and usually gets on well with other animals.

Size
Weight: dog, 5.9-7kg (13-15½lb); bitch, 5.2-6.4kg (11½-14lb).

Exercise
The Border Terrier has immense vitality and is able to keep pace with a horse. It is unfair to keep one unless you can give it adequate exercise.

Grooming
The coat needs a little trimming to tidy up for the show ring, but otherwise requires the minimum of grooming.

Feeding
Recommended would be ½-1 can of a branded meaty product (376g, 13.3oz size), with biscuit added in equal part by volume; or 1½ cups of a dry, complete food diet, mixed in the proportion of 1 cup of feed to ½ cup of hot or cold water. Increase rations if the terrier is in hard exercise.

Origin and history
The Border Terrier was derived in the Border counties of England and Scotland in the middle of the 19th century, when it was the practice to produce a terrier tailor-made for the task it would perform. Sportsmen wanted a hardy dog able to run with hounds and bolt the fox from its lair.

The Border Terrier, with its otter-like head, still works with hounds, and has been less changed to meet the dictates of the show ring than almost any other breed. It was recognized by the British Kennel Club in 1920. 23▸

Below: The unspoilt Border Terrier has boundless energy for work.

AUSTRALIAN TERRIER

Good points

- *Courageous*
- *Devoted to children*
- *No human enemies*
- *Hardy*
- *Keen, alert watchdog*

Take heed

- *Has aggression of a natural ratter—watch out for the neighbour's cat!*

The Australian Terrier is a loyal and devoted dog, game, hardy, and utterly reliable with toddlers. It has no human enemies, but will give a good account of itself when called to do battle with other dogs. It is an exceptionally alert watchdog but, having given the alarm, is more likely to kill intruders with kindness. It makes an excellent companion, and its alertness and speed combine to make it an excellent ratter. The Aussie's coat is weather-resistant, so it can be kept either in the home or in an outdoor kennel.

Size

Average weight about 4.5-5kg (10-11lb)—in Australia, approximately 6.4kg (14lb). In both the United Kingdom and Australia, the desired height is approximately 25cm (10in) at the withers. (The desired UK weight seems to be changing in line with that recommended by the Australian Kennel Club.)

Exercise

This is an active and keen scenting dog with the skill and courage to hunt and attack food for itself. Nowadays it is rarely asked to use these abilities, but it should have the opportunity to unleash its energy with regular walks and off-the-lead scampers. Nonetheless, it will adapt to apartment living.

Grooming

Regular grooming with a bristle brush will stimulate the skin and encourage a good coat growth. If you are planning to show your Aussie, bath it at least a fortnight before the show; but during spring and summer, when show dates may be close together, don't bath on each occasion, as frequent washing will soften the coat.

Feeding

About ½-¾ can of a branded meaty product (376g, 13.3oz size), with biscuit added in equal part by volume; or 1½ cupfuls of a complete, dry food, mixed in the proportion of 1 cup of feed to ½ cup of hot or cold water.

Fat is an essential ingredient if you want the animal to have a healthy coat; so if the meat given in the daily ration is low in fat content, a teaspoonful of corn oil should be added to the daily feed.

Origin and history

The Australian Terrier was known by various names until 1889, the year in which a club was formed in Melbourne to foster the breed, which had been evolved from several varieties of British terriers brought to Australia by settlers.

The dogs of the settlers were all derived from British stock. Sporting types, capable of hunting and killing vermin, were highly prized. There was, however, the need for a small, game watchdog to guard the lonely homestead in isolated areas.

It is believed that the development of the purebred Australian Terrier derived from the progeny of a Yorkshire Terrier bitch smuggled in aboard a sailing ship in a lady's muff and mated to a dog resembling a Cairn Terrier. 23▸

CAIRN TERRIER

Good points
- *Intelligent*
- *Adaptable*
- *Hardy*
- *Gay disposition*
- *Can live indoors or out*
- *Family companion*

Take heed
- *A bundle of energy; needs the opportunity to release it*

The game little Cairn Terrier comes from Inverness in Scotland and, although a popular show dog elsewhere, and drawing large entries in terrier classes, it is still in Scotland that the Cairn really comes into its own as a family pet. Indeed, when I lived in a Scottish village during World War II, it seemed as if every villager was the proud possessor of a perky Cairn.

The Gaelic word 'cairn' means a heap of stones, and is therefore a most suitable name for a terrier that goes to ground. It is an affectionate, sporty little dog with an almost rain-resistant coat, very active, and rarely stubborn, and it makes an ideal family companion.

Size

Weight 6.4kg (14lb).

Exercise

The Cairn is an energetic dog and also an expert killer of rodents. It is in its element trotting with its owner across the fields, or playing a lively ball game with children. It will adapt to controlled walks on the lead and sedate town living, as long as it has a good-sized garden to romp in.

Grooming

The Cairn is an easy dog to groom or, indeed, to prepare for the show ring, as it is presented in a 'natural' condition. It should be brushed and combed, and have any excess feathering removed from behind the front legs and the tail. Any long hairs about the ears and on the underside should also be removed for tidiness.

Feeding

Small terriers do well on ¾ can of branded dog food (376g, 13.3oz size) or the fresh meat equivalent, supplemented with biscuits.

The Cairn is not a greedy dog and may prefer to have two small meals each day, rather than receiving its rations all in one go. It also enjoys the occasional large dog biscuit to chew.

A daily teaspoon of cod liver oil will keep the Cairn in good health.

Origin and history

It is on record that James VI of Scotland (James I of England) ordered from Edinburgh half a dozen 'earth dogs or terrieres' to be sent as a present to France and these, it is believed, were forerunners of the present-day Cairn, suggesting that more than 300 years ago a working terrier of this type was used for killing vermin in Scotland. Indeed, Mr J.W.H. Beynon in his work, *The Popular Cairn Terrier,* says that every Highland chieftain, in ancient days, had his pack of hounds and terriers, the latter being used to bolt the foxes, badgers and smaller fur-bearing vermin. He also writes that, as far as he could learn, the oldest known strain of Cairns is that founded by the late Captain MacLeod of Drynoch, Isle of Skye, which goes back over 150 years.

Mr John MacDonald, who for over 40 years was gamekeeper to the Macleod of Macleod, Denvegan Castle, kept this strain alive for many years, the Cairn then being known as a Short-haired Skye Terrier. 23▸

SCHIPPERKE

Good points
- *Affectionate*
- *Excellent guard*
- *Good with children*
- *Handy size*
- *Hardy*

Take heed
- *Not suitable for kennel life*
- *Needs affection and individual attention to thrive*

The Schipperke is a delightful breed that originated in Belgium, where its job was to guard canal barges when they had been tied up for the night. The name Schipperke is, in fact, Flemish for 'little captain'.

Apart from being an excellent guard dog, the Schipperke is a most affectionate animal, and particularly good with children. It is also hardy and long lived. However, it needs individual attention and likes to be treated as a member of the family; it also takes a while to accept strangers.

Size
The weight should be about 5.4-7.3kg (12-16lb).

Exercise
A Schipperke can walk up to 6 miles or more without any sign of fatigue; but it can manage with a great deal less exercise if its owner lives in a town.

Grooming
The Schipperke has a dense hard coat that needs very little regular grooming.

Feeding
Feeding is no problem: a Schipperke will eat anything that is offered to it, and one good meal a day, perhaps with biscuit at night, will suffice. Recommended for its size would be ½-1 can of a branded meaty product (376g, 13.3oz size), with biscuit added in equal part by volume; or 1½ cupfuls of a dry, complete food mixed in the proportion of 1 cup of feed to ½ cup of hot or cold water.

Origin and history
The Schipperke originated in Belgium, but is often thought to be a Dutch dog, probably because Belgium and the Netherlands have been one country in the past. The breed is well over 100 years old; some claim it to be nearer 200 years old, but there are no records to support this theory.

How the breed evolved is subject to conjecture. Some classify it as a member of the Spitz family, others as the result of a terrier/Pomeranian cross. However, it seems likely that the Schipperke and the Groenendael have a common ancestor, the Schipperke closely resembling a smaller example of that other fine Belgian breed. 25▸

Below: The compact Schipperke has a sharp and lively expression.

LUNDEHUND (Puffin Dog; Puffin Hound)

Good points
- *Alert*
- *Active*
- *Robust*
- *Intelligent*
- *Able to climb well*
- *Excellent hunter*
- *Faithful companion*

Take heed
- *No drawbacks known*

The Lundehund has existed for centuries on two islands off the coast of northern Norway, but is little known outside Scandinavia. For many years it was impossible to export a breed member and this may still be the case. The breed is derived from the Miniature Elkhound.

Size
Weight approximately 5.9-6.4kg (13-14lb). Height: dog 31.5-35.5cm (12½-14in); bitch 30-34cm (12-13½in).

Exercise
This little dog is a hunter skilful at scaling rocks and precipices. Kept as a pet it is happiest if exercised freely.

Grooming
Daily brushing with a stiff-bristled brush should be sufficient.

Feeding
Half to 1 can (376g, 13.3oz size) of a branded, meaty product, with biscuit added in equal part by volume; or 1½ cupfuls of a dry, complete food, mixed in the proportion of 1 cup of feed to ½ cup of hot or cold water.

Origin and history
The Lundehund, or Puffin Dog, is a Spitz variety that received recognition in Scandinavia in 1943. Its job in life is to locate puffins' nests in rocks and crevices, and to retrieve the eggs and birds, the puffin being a welcome addition to the islanders' meal table. Puffin-hunting is an art that has existed in Scandinavia for at least 400 years.

This dog has five functional toes on each foot (normally there are four); and in the upper part of the ears, the cartilage ends meet and can shut when the ears are partly raised. It is thought that this may prevent water penetrating.

Below: The lively Lundehund, a skilled hunter from Scandinavia.

LHASA APSO

Good points
- *Affectionate*
- *Confident*
- *Good with children*
- *Hardy*
- *Excellent show dog*
- *Suitable for town or country*

Take heed
- *Needs lots of grooming*
- *Not keen on strangers*

The Lhasa Apso, like the Tibetan Terrier and Tibetan Spaniel, comes from the mountains of Tibet. It is a shaggy little dog, rather like an Old English Sheepdog in miniature, and makes an excellent pet, the only possible drawback being its natural suspicion of strangers.

Size
Ideal height: 25cm (10in) for dogs; bitches slightly smaller.

Exercise
This lively breed needs plenty of walks and off-the-lead runs.

Grooming
Brushing and combing daily—and not for a few minutes only.

Below: The Lhasa Apso from Tibet is a solid, gay and assertive dog.

Feeding
Half to 1 can (376g, 13.3oz size) of a branded, meaty product, with biscuit added in equal part by volume; or 1½ cupfuls of a dry, complete food, mixed in the proportion of 1 cup of feed to ½ cup of hot or cold water.

Origin and history
This is the dog that the Dalai Lama of Tibet offered to the Chinese emperors. It existed for centuries in the Tibetan mountains until brought to Europe, and elsewhere, by early explorers and missionaries. The words lhasa apso mean 'goat-like' and it was perhaps as guard and protector of the wild goats of Tibet that this glamorous breed of today first found favour. It was first seen at a European show in 1929. 23▸

SHIH TZU (Chrysanthemum Dog)

Good points
- *Affectionate*
- *Hardy*
- *Intelligent*
- *Loves children and animals*
- *Suitable for town or country*

Take heed
- *Best to tie back the topknot with a bow, or your pet could develop eye trouble*

Above: The affectionate Shih Tzu needs daily grooming for good looks.

The Shih Tzu is a happy and attractive little house-pet which adores human company and hates to be neglected. It is extremely intelligent, arrogant, and looks forward to the long, daily grooming sessions for which time must be allocated if you decide to buy this delightful breed.

Size
Weight 4.5-8.2kg (10-18lb); ideally 4.5-7.3kg (10-16lb). Height at the withers not more than 26.5cm (10½in).

Exercise
Short, regular walks, and off-the-lead runs.

Grooming
Daily brushing with a pure bristle brush. Do not neglect this task or combing out tangles will be painful. Keep the topknot from getting into the eyes and take care that the ears are free of matted hair.

Feeding
Half to 1 can (376g, 13.3oz size) of a branded, meaty product, with biscuit added in equal part by volume; or 1½ cupfuls of a dry, complete food mixed in the proportion of 1 cup of feed to ½ cup of hot or cold water.

Origin and history
The Lhasa Apso was highly prized by the Dalai Lama of Tibet who would habitually give prized specimens to emperors of China. It is likely that the Chinese may have crossed the Apso with the Pekingese to develop the Shih Tzu. As with the Imperial Pekingese, export of the Shih Tzu from China was forbidden, and it was not until the death of Empress Tzu-hsi in 1908 that the little shaggy dogs were smuggled out to Europe. 23▸

PUG

Good points

- *Happy disposition*
- *Good with children*
- *Intelligent*

Take heed

- *Over-feeding will result in a gross, short-lived dog*
- *Guard against vigorous exertion, bad ventilation and over-heating in warm weather*

The Pug is a gay little dog, which looks extremely elegant if not allowed to indulge its inherent greed. It makes a charming family pet, provided care is taken that it does not develop respiratory trouble through over-heating or vigorous exercise, for with its flat, squashed-looking face it can encounter similar breathing difficulties to the Bulldog.

Like the Bulldog, the Pug also has a tendency to snore. But it shares the foolhardiness of the Chihuahua and certain other toy breeds, in believing that attack is the best form of defence. A classic example is the death of the Empress Josephine's 'Fortune', the pampered beast that bit Napoleon on his mistress's wedding night, and met with an untimely end after an encounter with the cook's Bordelaise Bulldog.

Size

The weight should be 6.4-8.2kg (14-18lb).

Exercise

An energetic dog, the Pug will relish more exercise than many breeds of similar size. But remember that gluttony and a tendency to over-weight go hand in hand, as will fatness and lethergy if the animal's greed is undulged. The Pug will do best walking on the lead, and should not indulge in vigorous exercise for fear of respiratory trouble.

Grooming

A good daily brushing should be sufficient for good looks.

Feeding

About ½-¾ can of branded dog food (376g, 13.3oz size) or approximately 227g (8oz) of fresh meat daily, supplemented by dog biscuits. Some fanciers prefer to feed meat raw and this must be a matter of choice and, indeed, of the dog's preference. But remember that cooked meat is generally free of bacteria, and that guard dogs are often fed on raw meat to keep them on their mettle!

Origin and history

The Pug found its way to France with the Turkish Fleet in 1553. The little dogs were brought by the sailors as gifts for their ladies, and were subsequently known as 'Little Turks'. They also found favour in Holland, where the tinge of their coat was likened to the colour of the House of Orange. When William and Mary of Orange journeyed to Britain to ascend the throne in 1689, a number of Pugs accompanied them. For a period of almost 300 years the breed enjoyed a popularity similar to that of the Poodle today.

Alas, most Pugs were permitted to eat sweetmeats and other delicacies, and became so fat that they were regarded by many as an abomination. They gradually declined in numbers until in 1864 even Queen Victoria had difficulty in locating one to add to her kennels. However, some 20 years later the Pug Dog Club was formed and efforts were made to improve and standardize the breed, resulting in the elegant and solid little Pug we know today. 24▸

WEST HIGHLAND WHITE TERRIER

Good points
- *Attractive appearance*
- *Easy to train*
- *Gets on well with other dogs*
- *Good with children*
- *Handy size*
- *Suitable for town or country*

Take heed
- *No drawbacks known*

The West Highland White Terrier is a game, hardy little dog that originated in Argyle, Scotland. In recent years it has gained tremendous popularity because of its attractive appearance, sporting instincts and handy size. It gets on well with children and other dogs and makes the ideal family dog.

The West Highland White's coat is one of the breed's most striking features. It consists of a hard outer coat and soft under-coat.

Size
About 28cm (11in) at the withers. There is no weight standard for this dog in the United Kingdom or the United States.

Exercise
The Westie will adapt to town or country, and will live either indoors or in a kennel. However, it will be happiest as a family pet allowed to share the comfort of the fireside, but given adequate free runs in the countryside. Remember that it was originally used as a working terrier, and its job was to hunt fox and badger. It is also, of course, a good ratter. This breed will enjoy an energetic ball game.

Grooming
Although the Westie may be the ideal choice for someone who wants a healthy and active dog, it is perhaps not so ideal for the show aspirant who does not want to spend much time on grooming. The Westie's coat must be brushed and combed every day, and have surplus stripped twice a year. The neckline is particularly important, and straggly hairs should be removed from ears and tail. Ideally, the Westie's coat should be approximately 5cm (2in) in length, with the neck and throat hair shorter. It is probably wise to ask the breeder to demonstrate what is required before you make your purchase, and to let you have a grooming chart with full instructions. If you feel you cannot handle the task yourself, you can entrust it to a dog grooming parlour.

Feeding
One to 1½ cans (376g, 13.3oz size) of a branded meaty product with biscuit added in equal part by volume; or 3 cupfuls of a dry, complete food mixed in the proportion of 1 cup of feed to ½ cup of hot or cold water. The Westie loves burrowing in the earth, often retrieving a long-discarded, much-loved bone; so do let it have the occasional marrow or chop bone to get its teeth into—but no splintery bones, please.

Origin and history
The first West Highland White Terrier clubs were formed in 1905, when breeds such as the Cairn Terrier and Skye Terrier, which in the past had all been classified as Small Highland Working Terriers, attained individual status.

It does appear that in the late 1800s there existed a white Scottish Terrier, or Scottie, a strain of which was bred by Colonel Malcolm of Poltalloch, from which the name Poltalloch Terrier was derived; they were also known as Roseneath Terriers. 25▸

MANCHESTER TERRIER

Good points
- *Alert and intelligent*
- *Clean*
- *Good family dog*
- *Great sporting companion*
- *Long-lived*
- *Suitable for town or country*

Take heed
- *Tends to be a one-person dog*

The Manchester Terrier is an ideal choice for those seeking a small, hardy dog that causes no trouble and makes a great sporting companion. It will fit well into family life, but does tend to attach itself to one person.

It is long lived and seldom ill. It can live indoors or outside in a heated kennel, but will be happiest if given a place by the fireside.

Size
Desired height: dog 40.5cm (16in); bitch 38cm (15in). In America the Manchester Terrier is shown in two varieties: the Toy and the Standard. The Toy Variety (known elsewhere as the English Toy Terrier) has an upper weight limit of 5.4kg (12lb). The Standard Variety should be over 5.4kg (12lb) and under 10kg (22lb) in weight.

Exercise
The Manchester is in its element running free in the countryside. Town dwellers need not rule out this breed, however, if they can offer regular walks, off-the-lead runs and a garden.

Grooming
Manchesters do not like rain, despite its proverbial frequency in their place of origin, and should be rubbed with a towel if they get wet. Otherwise, a daily brushing will keep this essentially clean animal looking smart. Its coat condition is always an indication of health.

Feeding
Half to 1 can (376g, 13.3oz size) of a branded meaty product, with biscuit added in equal part by volume; or 1½ cupfuls of a complete, dry food, mixed in the proportion of 1 cup of feed to ½ cup of hot or cold water.

Origin and history
The Manchester Terrier can trace its lineage back to the old hunting 'Black and Tan' Terrier, which, in the north of England, had the reputation of rat killer supreme.

The Manchester Terrier—once closely related to a white English terrier that seems to have disappeared, probably because of its tendency to deafness—has evolved as a reliable household pet, retaining its sporting instincts while fitting happily into a home that requires an alert, lively pet. It is usually good with children.

At one time the Manchester Terrier and the English Toy Terrier were shown as Black and Tan Terriers with a weight division. The English Toy Terrier is now separately classified in England, but in the USA, where the Manchester Terrier is popular, breeding of toys and standards is permitted.

A number of Manchesters were exported from the United Kingdom to the United States, Canada and (later) Germany in the 1800s, and it is thought (see Dobermann Pinscher) that the Manchester aided the make-up of the Dobermann, certainly as far as its short, shiny black and tan coat was concerned. Earlier Manchesters had cropped ears, a practice that became illegal in the United Kingdom in 1895. 28▶

SMOOTH FOX TERRIER

Good points
- *Alert*
- *Intelligent*
- *Good family pet*
- *Second to none as a rat-catcher*
- *Smart appearance*
- *Useful medium size*

Take heed
- *Needs plenty of exercise*

The word terrier comes from the Latin word 'terra' meaning 'earth', the job of the terrier being to kill vermin and to worry or 'boot' the fox from its lair.

The Smooth Fox Terrier is arguably the smartest terrier bred for this purpose. It enjoyed almost unrivalled popularity just before and after the Second World War, and is always a popular contender in the show ring, though it has been said that the elegance of this terrier has been attained at the expense of its former hunting ability. It makes an ideal family pet.

Size
About 7.3-8.2kg (16-18lb) for a dog and 6.8-7.7kg (15-17lb) for a bitch in show condition are appropriate weights.

Exercise
The terrier once called 'the little athlete of the dog world' deserves a chance to live up to that title. It will adjust to a regular trot around the park—on a lead, of course—but deserves the opportunity for frequent off-the-lead runs, preferably in the country.

Grooming
Daily brushing with a stiff brush. Trimming is required a few weeks before a show, paying particular attention to the inside and outside of ears, jaw, and muzzle. Usually a chalk block is used to ensure that the coat is snowy white.

Feeding
Recommended would be ½ to 1 can of a branded, meaty product (376g, 13.3oz size), with biscuit added in equal part by volume; or 1½ cupfuls of a dry, complete food, mixed in the proportion of 1 cup of feed to ½ cup of cold or hot water.

Above: The Smooth Fox Terrier is a supreme working dog and makes an intelligent family pet.

Origin and history
The Smooth-coated Fox Terrier has been around in its present form for at least 100 years. Before then, almost all terriers that went to earth were known simply as fox terriers.

It was in 1862 at the Birmingham, England, National Dog Show that the breed first made its debut in the show ring. Its ancestry probably came about through the terriers in the English counties of Cheshire and Shropshire, and also a hound variety, the Beagle. 27▸

WIRE FOX TERRIER

Good points
- *First-rate companion*
- *Good with children*
- *Intelligent*
- *Smart appearance*
- *Splendid ratter*
- *Trainable*

Take heed
- *Needs plenty of exercise*
- *Defends itself if provoked*

The Wire-haired Fox Terrier is, when well turned out, a delightful sight to see. It is intelligent, cheerful, and easily trained; a first-rate children's companion, with the typical terrier's 'get up and go'. Nowadays it is seen more frequently than the Smooth-coated variety.

Size
A full-size well-balanced dog should not exceed 39cm (15½in) at the withers—the bitch being slightly lower—nor should the length of back from withers to root of tail exceed 30cm (12in). Weight 8.2kg (18lb) in show condition, a bitch about 0.9kg (2lb) less, with a margin of 0.45g (1lb) either way.

Exercise
The Wire-haired Fox Terrier will enjoy nothing more than going rabbiting with its master. It adores sniffing out vermin and is not afraid of a fight, despite its usual good nature. It adapts well to life as a household pet, but really deserves a country home rather than apartment life.

Grooming
Hand stripping is required in spring, summer and autumn—more frequently if it is the intention to show. Normally a daily brushing will suffice, but watch the coat carefully as terriers are susceptible to eczema. Chalking is usual for a show.

Feeding
Recommended would be ½ to 1 can of a branded, meaty product (376g, 13.3oz size), with biscuit added in equal part by volume; or 1½ cupfuls of a dry, complete food, mixed in the proportion of 1 cup of feed to ½ cup of cold or hot water.

Above: The Wire Fox Terrier is a popular show, working and pet dog.

Origin and history
The Wire-haired Fox Terrier is a separate breed from the Smooth-coat, although in conformation the breeds are the same. It undoubtedly derived from the wire-haired terriers around the British coalmining areas of Durham, Wales and Derbyshire, where it had existed for some time before gaining the attention of fanciers. It did not appear in the ring until 1872. For a number of years its popularity lagged far behind the Smooth-coat, but now the position has been reversed. 27▸

JACK RUSSELL TERRIER

Good points
- *Affectionate*
- *Handy size*
- *Sporty companion*
- *Full of character*
- *Adapts well to home life*

Take heed
- *Excitable in a pack*
- *Not yet a pedigreed breed*

The Jack Russell Terrier has become immensely popular in recent years. New owners often become incensed on finding that the breed they have sought and acquired cannot be registered with the British Kennel Club, for it is not as yet a pedigreed dog. The British Kennel Club is aware of efforts to standardize the breed, but unable to accept it while there is so much variation in colour, size and form.

Size
The Jack Russell Terrier Club of the United Kingdom has drawn up a provisional breed standard aiming to produce a uniform type of Jack Russell Terrier allowing for two different heights: 28-38cm (11-15in) at the shoulder, and under 28cm (11in) at the shoulder.

Exercise
The Jack Russell Terrier will adapt well to life as a household pet provided regular walks are given. However, it is really in its element in the countryside, ferreting, facing badgers or after foxes, for they are game little working dogs that like to be active. Packs of Jack Russells are kept at most hunt kennels.

Grooming
A daily brushing with a stiff brush.

Feeding
Recommended would be ½ to 1 can of a branded, meaty product (376g, 13.3oz size), with biscuit added in equal part by volume; or 1½ cupfuls of a dry, complete food, mixed in the proportion of 1 cup of feed to ½ cup of cold or hot water. Increase the amont if the terrier is working.

Origin and history
Reverend Jack Russell, a sporting parson in Devonshire, England, who died almost 100 years ago, built up a strain of wire-haired fox terriers that would hunt with his hounds, go to ground and bolt the fox. The dogs were, in fact, hunt terriers. Jack Russell not only bred his unique hunt terriers but also judged terriers at West Country shows and was one of the earliest members of the Kennel Club. It could be that when the breed is established and proper records of pedigree are kept, we may yet see the Jack Russell listed with pedigreed dogs. Certainly the Jack Russell Terrier Club is working very hard towards achieving this aim. 27▸

Below: The Jack Russell Terrier, a sporty companion full of character.

LAKELAND TERRIER

Good points
- *Excellent with children*
- *Fine guard with strong warning bark*
- *Good family dog*
- *Handy medium size*
- *Sporty, but adapts well to home life*

Take heed
- *Might be too lively for the elderly*

The Lakeland Terrier is similar in appearance to the Welsh and Airedale Terriers. It makes a first-class family pet, being of sound temperament and convenient size, and is also a fine guard. It has been used in the past for both fox and badger hunting, but nowadays is kept mainly as a pet and has, in recent years, been a very successful contender in the show ring.

Size
The average weight of a dog is 7.7kg (17lb), bitch 6.8kg (15lb). The height should not exceed 37cm (14½in) at the shoulder.

Exercise
Unless they choose a toy breed, like the Yorkshire Terrier, nobody should choose a terrier unless they want a pet with plenty of zip. The Lakeland Terrier, true to its breed, is gay and fearless, always ready for a walk or a game. It is suitable for apartment living as long as its owner can provide regular exercise and, hopefully, those much loved days out in the country for off-the-lead runs.

Grooming
Trimming the Lakeland for the show ring requires some skill. Daily brushing will help keep the coat tidy but, even for a pet, professional stripping in spring, summer and autumn is recommended.

Feeding
Recommended would be ½-1 can of a branded, meaty product (376g, 13.3oz size), with biscuit added in equal part by volume; or 1½ cupfuls of a dry, complete food, mixed in the proportion of 1 cup of feed to ½ cup of cold or hot water.

Origin and history
The Lakeland Terrier originated in the Lake District of England, hence its name, but was originally known as the Patterdale Terrier after the place it was first worked with the local hunts. Although known as a working dog long before, the Lakeland did not make an appearance in the show ring until a Breed Club was formed in 1912. The breed was recognized in 1921 and well established by 1931. 26▸

Below: A Lakeland Terrier trimmed for competition in the show ring.

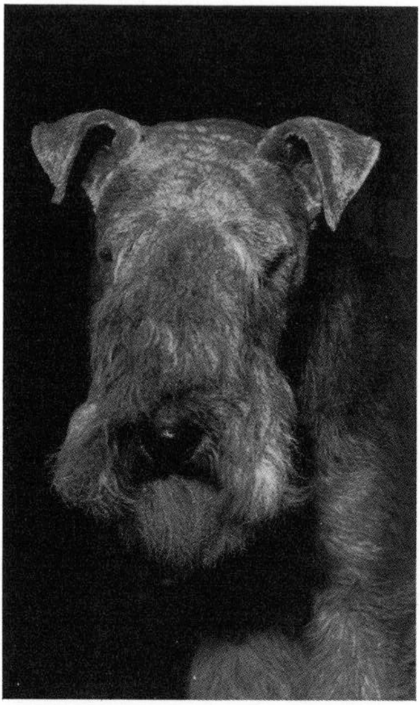

WELSH TERRIER

Good points
- *Affectionate*
- *Bold*
- *Good temperament*
- *Great fun*
- *Handy size*
- *Obedient*
- *Good with children*

Take heed
- *No drawbacks known*

The Welsh Terrier has much in common with the Airedale, Irish and Lakeland Terriers and resembles a small Airedale in appearance. It makes a good household pet, generally has a good temperament, and is affectionate, obedient and great fun.

Size
The height at shoulder should not exceed 39.5cm (15½in). In working condition, 9-9.5kg (20-21lb) is a fair average weight.

Exercise
Regular daily walks and a romp in the garden will suffice, but like most terriers it will appreciate a run in wide open spaces. They were, after all, originally bred to run with a pack of hounds.

Grooming
The Welsh Terrier's coat needs stripping twice yearly and regular brushing to maintain it in show condition, but many pet owners resort to clipping their terriers. The coat is usually left on in winter to provide extra warmth.

Feeding
One to 1½ cans (376g, 13.3oz size) of a branded meaty product, with biscuit added in equal part by volume; or 3 cupfuls of a dry food, complete diet, mixed in the proportion of 1 cup of feed to ½ cup of hot or cold water.

Origin and history
The Welsh Terrier—like its close relation, the Irish Terrier—is of Celtic origin. In fact, two strains

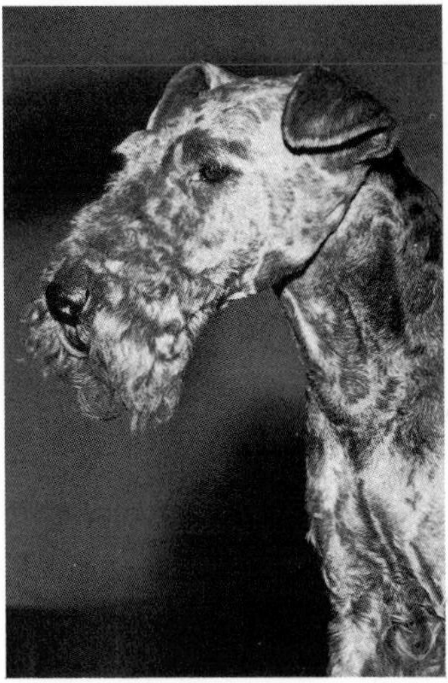

Above: The compact Welsh Terrier adapts well to family life.

once existed side by side: that evolved by the Welsh from a purpose-bred Coarse-haired Black and Tan Terrier, and an English variety achieved through crossing the Airedale and the Fox Terrier. These two types caused much argument while recognition for the breed was being sought. However, the English variety appears to have died out, and the true Celtic strain was presented in 1885, the Welsh Terrier Club being founded a year later. The following year the Welsh Terrier was awarded championship status by the British Kennel Club. The first Welsh Terriers were taken to America in 1888, but not in any numbers until after 1901. 26▸

SEALYHAM TERRIER

Good points
- *Beautiful appearance*
- *Devoted*
- *Good with children*
- *Sporting*
- *Excellent show dog*

Take heed
- *Enjoys a scrap*
- *Needs lots of grooming*
- *Obstinate*

The Sealyham was bred as a rat and badger hunter but has evolved into an elegant pet and show dog for those with time to devote to its coiffure.

The popularity of the breed diminished after the Second World War, being overtaken by the West Highland White Terrier, for which it is occasionally mistaken although resemblance is slight, except in colour. Perhaps its depleted numbers were not a bad thing, as first class stock is now being produced.

The Sealyham is a game, lovable little terrier that becomes devoted to its owners and is reliable with children. However, it can be obstinate and snappy if not firmly, but kindly, disciplined when young.

Size
Weight: dog should not exceed 9kg (20lb); bitch should not exceed 8.2kg (18lb). Height should not exceed 30cm (12in) at the shoulder.

Exercise
This dog will adapt happily to regular walks around the park and off-the-lead runs. But give a Sealyham the chance and it will enjoy getting gloriously dirty scampering in the wet, muddy countryside.

Grooming
The Sealyham needs hand stripping at least twice a year, and daily combing with a wire comb to remove surplus hair. As mentioned elsewhere, stripping by the inexperienced can prove a disastrous experience for both owner and dog, so do have the job done professionally, or ask an expert to show you how. Clipping is excusable for the older dog, but will ruin the coat for showing.

Feeding
One can (376g, 13.3oz size) of a branded meaty product, with biscuit added in equal part by volume; or 1½ cupfuls of a dry food, complete diet, mixed in the proportion of 1 cup of feed to ½ cup of hot or cold water. And it will just love bones!

Origin and history
The Sealyham takes its name from Sealyham in Haverfordwest, Wales, UK, where the breed was created in the mid-1800s, using other terriers with proven ability as hunters of fox, badger and vermin. (Some say that the Sealyham owes its existence to a terrier imported into Wales from Belgium in the 15th century.) Haverfordwest formed the first Sealyham Terrier Club in 1908, and Fred Lewis, founder of the Sealyham Terrier Club, is said to have done much to improve the strain. The breed was recognized by the British Kennel Club three years later. The American Kennel Club also recognized the breed in 1911.

The Sealyham has been very successful around the world as a show dog, particularly in America, where the breed made its show debut in California in September 1911. The American Sealyham Terrier Club was formed in 1913 to promote the breed both as a show dog and as a working terrier. 25▸

DANDIE DINMONT TERRIER

Good points
- *Courageous*
- *Intelligent*
- *Devoted to owner*
- *Keen sense of humour*
- *Excellent watchdog*

Take heed
- *Tends to be a one-person dog, whose friendship and respect must be earned*

Although once popular as a badger and fox hunter, the Dandie Dinmont is now kept mainly as a household pet: indeed, they fare better indoors as a single pet than living with their fellows in kennels. They do, however, tend to be a little suspicious of strangers, giving all their devotion to their owner. They are excellent guard dogs with a bark that should deter any burglar.

Size
The height should be 20-28cm (8-11in) at the top of the shoulder. Length from top of shoulder to root of tail should be not more than twice the dog's height, but preferably 2.5-5cm (1-2in) less. The ideal weight for a dog in good working condition is 8.2kg (18lb).

Below: The Dandie Dinmont will make a devoted pet and watchdog.

Exercise
The Dandie Dinmont is an adaptable dog and will be happy whether put to work killing foxes or enjoying the role of an old lady's pet. It would, however, be unfair to keep this active, inquisitive breed in a home without a garden.

Grooming
Grooming is not a difficult task, the only equipment needed being a stiff brush and comb. Old hairs should be removed with finger and thumb, allowing the undercoat to come through. Incidentally, don't use a trimming knife, because this will ruin the coat. Brush daily for good looks.

Feeding
Recommended would be ½-1 can of a branded meaty product (376g, 13.3oz size), with biscuit added in equal part by volume; or 1½ cupfuls of a dry, complete food mixed in the proportion of 1 cup of feed to ½ cup of water.

Origin and history
Most Dandies can be traced back to the late 1700s, to an individual named Piper Allan, something of a character of his day, who had two Dandie Dinmonts, called Charlie and Peachem. Also well known is James Davidson, who was renowned for his 'pepper and mustard' terriers, so called because of their colour: it was from Davidson that Sir Walter Scott acquired his dogs, and indeed it was from a character in his novel 'Guy Mannering' that the breed received its name. 27▸

SCOTTISH TERRIER

Good points

- *Straightforward and honest*
- *Reliable temperament*
- *Fine guard*
- *Utterly loyal*
- *Home-loving*

Take heed

- *Has little time for strangers; best for a childless couple or unattached owner*

The Scottish Terrier or Scottie has been aptly described as a gentleman. It is an honest dog, that will not look for trouble but on finding it will always fight fairly. It is a devoted companion to its owner, but has little time for strangers and is not the most suitable of dogs for a family with children or a couple intending to add to their family. It will fight fox or badger, but enjoys itself just as much in an energetic ball game, and likes nothing better than carrying a stick or a ball in its mouth. Altogether an attractive and sporty little animal.

Size

Weight: 8.6-10.4kg (19-23lb).
Height: 25-28cm (10-11in).

Exercise

The Scottie loves nothing more than being out of doors and it would be wrong to deprive it of romps in the garden or regular walks several times a day. It can live happily either indoors or in an outside kennel, heated in winter.

Grooming

The Scottie needs daily brushing and combing, particularly its fine beard, and should be trimmed in spring and autumn.

Feeding

Recommended would be 1-1½ cans of a branded meaty product (376g, 13.3oz size), with biscuit added in equal part by volume; or 3 cupfuls of a dry, complete food, mixed in the proportion of 1 cup to ½ cup of hot or cold water.

Origin and history

The Scottish Terrier, once known as the Aberdeen Terrier, and generally known as the Scottie, has existed in various forms for many centuries, but it was not until after 1800 that line breeding began. The first Scottish Terrier Club was formed in Scotland in 1892, when a standard was laid down for the breed. 25▸

Below: The devoted Scottish Terrier makes a strong, sporty companion.

MINIATURE SCHNAUZER

Good points
- *Attractive appearance*
- *Intelligent*
- *Obedient*
- *Long-lived*
- *Good with children*
- *Suitable for town or country*

Take heed
- *Happiest living indoors rather than in outside kennels*

The Miniature Schnauzer is the perfect Schnauzer in miniature, an attractive little dog, with appealing bushy eyebrows. It is good-natured, adores children, and is happiest living with the family indoors, rather than being relegated to an outside kennel. It is long-lived and easy to train, and often does well in obedience competitions.

Size
The ideal height for bitches should be 33cm (13in) and for dogs 35.5cm (14in).

Exercise
The Miniature Schnauzer can be kept in town or country, and does not require a great deal of space, although it does enjoy a garden to romp in and looks forward to good walks and off-the-lead runs.

Grooming
This breed needs to be hand stripped in spring and summer—more often if a show career is envisaged. Have this professionally done, or get instructions from the breeder—the breed club is sure to have an instruction leaflet—as clumsy, inexperienced hands can ruin a good temperament. A good weekly brushing is essential, and the removal of any dead hair in the under-coat.

Feeding
Recommended would be ½-1 can (376g, 13.3oz size) of a branded meaty product, with biscuit added in equal part by volume; or 1½ cupfuls of a dry food, complete diet, mixed in the proportion of 1 cup to ½ cup of hot or cold water.

Above: The Miniature Schnauzer will make friends with everyone it meets.

Origin and history
The Miniature Schnauzer is a replica in miniature of its bigger brother, the Standard Schnauzer, there being some 10cm (4in) difference in height between them. There is strong support for the suggestion that the Miniature Schnauzer evolved through crossing the Standard Schnauzer with the little Affenpinscher, although a Pomeranian or even a Fox Terrier may have been used.

This miniature variety was bred in Germany for at least a century before finding its way to the United Kingdom in 1928, when a black bitch was imported, followed in 1930 by two pepper-and-salt champions. About this time it also began to gain popularity in the United States, where the breed is extremely popular nowadays. Its spread among British fanciers has been somewhat slower, but the breed has been awarded Challenge Certificates since 1935. 25▸

STANDARD DACHSHUND (Teckel, Dachel, Dacksel, Badger Hound)

Good points

- *Affectionate*
- *Loyal family pet*
- *Sense of fun*
- *Watchdog with loud bark*

Take heed

- *Prone to disc trouble*
- *Self-willed*
- *Slightly aggressive with strangers, if unchecked*

Smooth-haired

The Dachshund (or Teckel) was bred as a badger hound in its native Germany. What was needed was a short-legged hound, with a keen sense of smell, coupled with courage and gameness; and a dog that could burrow – an ability that, if unchecked, today's Dachshund will demonstrate in your garden.

Some Dachshunds are still bred as hunting dogs and will bravely tackle an opponent larger than themselves, such as the badger. They would also defend their master until death. However, their role nowadays is mainly as a companion. They may be a little aggressive with strangers, if unchecked, but are affectionate and full of fun. Despite their short legs they can cope with as much exercise as you can give them. They have a loud bark for their size, and are first-class watchdogs.

Size

Long-haired: middle weight up to 8.2kg (18lb) for dogs and 7.7kg (17lb) for bitches.
Smooth-haired: dogs should not exceed 11.3kg (25lb); bitches should not exceed 10.4kg (23lb).
Wire-haired: dogs should weigh 9-10kg (20-22lb) and bitches 8.2-9kg (18-20lb).

Below: The Long-haired Dachshund's thick soft hair protects it against thorns, heat, cold and rain.

Long-haired

Wire-haired

Exercise
Regular exercise is important, as the tendency to put on weight must be discouraged. This does not mean you must take your pet on 10-mile treks, but short, frequent walks are advisable, with plenty of runs in a well-fenced garden.

Grooming
The Dachshund's coat is easy to keep in condition. The Smooth-coat needs only a few minutes' attention every day with a hound glove and soft cloth. A stiff-bristled brush and comb should be used on the Long-hair and the Wire-hair.

Health care
Disc trouble can befall the Dachshund because of its long back and stubby little legs. Anyone who has seen a young dog paralysed, while otherwise in good health, will recognize the need to keep their pet's weight within the breed standard and to prevent it from leaping on and off furniture. Treatment varies from injections of cortisone to an operation; some owners swear by an osteopath!

The Dachshund's teeth are prone to tartar. Regular scaling is recommended, but stains can be removed with a paste of water and cream of tartar, applied with a bit of cotton wool.

Feeding
Suggested would be ¾ can (376g, 13.3oz size) of a branded meaty product, with biscuit added in equal part by volume; or 1½ cupfuls of a dry food, complete diet, mixed in the proportion of 1 cup of feed to ½ cup of hot or cold water. A satisfactory menu for an adult may be based on 21g (¾oz) of food for each 454g (16oz) the dog weighs, from half to three quarters of this amount being given as meat.

Origin and history
The Dachshund was bred as a badger hound, or hunting dog, and is known to have existed before the 16th century and to have been derived from the oldest breeds of German hunting dog, such as the Bibarhund.

When the German Dachshund Club was formed in 1888, there was only one variety, the Smooth-haired Dachshund, whose wrinkled paws, then a characteristic, have now been almost bred out. Today there are three varieties, with miniatures of each type: the Smooth-hair, Wire-hair and Long-hair. The Wire-hair was introduced through crossing with the Scottish, Dandie Dinmont and other terriers, the Long-hair by crossing the Smooth-hair with the spaniel and an old German gundog, the Stöberhund. The bandiness in the breed, due to a weakness in the tendons, has now been eradicated, as has exaggerated length.

In Europe during both World Wars, the Dachshund, recognized as the national dog of the Teutonic Empire, was often discarded, shouted at, or even stoned in the streets because of its German ancestry. Happily this sorry state of affairs has long since passed and the sporty, lovable Dachshund is again popular. 26▸

BEDLINGTON TERRIER

Good points

- *Adores children*
- *Always keeps its figure*
- *Good family pet*
- *Well behaved*
- *Good watchdog*
- *Easy to train*

Take heed

- *Could be dangerous in a pack*
- *Formidable fighter if provoked*

The Bedlington Terrier is an attractive, hardy little dog that resembles a shorn lamb in appearance.

It is a dog whose dainty appearance and love of children belies its first-rate watchdog qualities. It is also a breed that trains easily, and a number have been used successfully in obedience competitions.

The Breed Standard states: 'A graceful, lithe, muscular dog, with no sign of either weakness or coarseness. The expression in repose should be mild and gentle, though not shy or nervous. When roused, the eyes should sparkle and the dog look full of temper and courage.'

Size

Height should be about 40.5cm (16in) at the shoulder, allowing slight variation below in the case of a bitch and above in the case of a dog. Weight should be 8.2-10.4kg (18-23lb).

Exercise

The Bedlington, like most terriers, is a lively, inquisitive breed and will enjoy an off-the-lead run or energetic ball game. It will, however, adapt very happily to apartment life as long as it is given regular adequate walks.

Grooming

This breed's coat does not shed, which makes it a boon for the house-proud, the dead hairs staying in the coat until they are combed out.

The breed should be trimmed regularly (otherwise the coat will become tangly) and given a good brushing every day with a fairly stiff brush. Do not bath the animal too often or this may weaken its coat. Hair should be removed from inside the dog's ears fairly regularly, which can be done quite simply by pulling the hair with finger and thumb or tweezers.

Feeding

Recommended would be ¾-1 can of a branded meaty product (376g, 13.3oz size), with biscuit added in equal part by volume; or 1½ cupfuls of a dry food, complete diet, mixed in the proportion of 1 cup of feed to ½ cup of hot or cold water.

Origin and history

It is possible that the Greyhound or Whippet played some part in the origin of the Bedlington Terrier, and the soft topknot gives strength to the suggestion that it may share common ancestry with the Dandie Dinmont Terrier. Certainly a strain of similar terriers existed with tinkers in Rothbury Forest, Northumberland, in the 18th century, and in 1820 a Mr J. Howe came to Bedlington, Northumberland, with a bitch named Phoebe. This bitch was given to a man called Joseph Ainsley, who mated Phoebe to a dog named Old Piper, producing Young Piper, the first dog with the new name 'Bedlington' Terrier. From that time, 1825, systematic breeding of the Bedlington began. The breed was shown in the ring during the 1860s and the first Bedlington Terrier Club was formed in 1875. 24▸

MINIATURE POODLE

Good points
- *Affectionate*
- *Good sense of fun*
- *Intelligent and long-lived*

Take heed
- *Noisy if unchecked*
- *Not ideal as a child's pet*
- *Sensitive*
- *Best to have veterinary examination prior to purchase*

The Poodle has a character full of fun. It is intelligent, obedient and, in the United Kingdom, has proved a useful competitor in obedience competitions. It has a fondness for water, if the owner permits, but is much favoured for the show ring where, exhibited in the lion clip, it is a beauty to behold.

Size
Height at shoulder should be under 38cm (15in) but not under 28cm (11in).

Exercise
The Poodle will enjoy a ball game in the garden, practising obedience exercises or trotting beside you in the park. The miniature variety is a good choice for the apartment dweller.

Grooming
Use a wire-pin pneumatic brush and a wire-toothed metal comb for daily grooming. The lion clip is an essential for the show ring, but pet owners generally resort to the more natural lamb clip, with the hair a short uniform length. It is possible to clip your own dog with a pair of hairdressers' scissors. However, if, despite the help which usually is available from the breeder, you find the task tedious, there are numerous pet and poodle parlours to which you should take your dog every six weeks. Bath regularly.

Feeding
Recommended would be ¾-1 can of a branded meaty product (376g, 13.3oz size), with biscuit added in equal part by volume; or 1½ cupfuls of a dry food, complete diet, mixed in the proportion of 1 cup of feed to ½ cup of hot or cold water.

Health care
Fanciers will confirm that the Standard Poodle is the soundest of the varieties. It is possible to acquire healthy Toy and Miniature stock, but care should be taken to purchase from a breeder who puts quality ahead of daintiness. Watch out for signs of ear trouble, nervousness or joint malformations. Teeth need regular scaling.

Origin and history
The Poodle was originally a shaggy guard, a retriever and protector of sheep, with origins similar to the Irish Water Spaniel and, no doubt, a common ancestor in the French Barbet and Hungarian Water Hound.

The Poodle may not be, as many suppose, solely of French origin. It originated in Germany as a water retriever; even the word poodle comes from the German 'pudelnass' or puddle, and from this fairly large sturdy dog, the Standard Poodle, the Miniature, and the Toy have evolved.

The breed has been known in England since Prince Rupert of the Rhine, in company with his poodle, came to the aid of Charles I in battle. The breed was favoured also by Marie Antoinette who, rumour has it, invented the lion clip by devising a style to match her courtiers' uniform. 24▸

SHETLAND SHEEPDOG

Good points
- *Beautiful*
- *Intelligent*
- *Faithful*
- *Ideal for competitive obedience*
- *Intuitive*

Take heed
- *Best kept in the home (not in a kennel)*
- *May be wary of strangers*

The Shetland Sheepdog is the perfect Rough Collie in miniature, a handy size for the owner who feels, perhaps, that the Rough Collie is too large for his home.

The Sheltie is a good family dog, but a little wary of strangers. It does not take kindly to being petted by those it does not know. It is faithful, supremely intelligent, and generally gives a good account of itself at training classes and in obedience competitions. It is good with horses, and a few are still used as sheepdogs.

Size
Ideal height measured at the withers 35.5cm (14in) for a bitch, 37cm (14½in) for a dog.

Exercise
Provided the Sheltie has a largish garden in which to expend its energy, and receives regular daily walks, it will be happy.

Grooming
Not so difficult to keep spick and span as might be believed. Brush regularly with a stiff-bristled brush and use a comb to avoid tangles, particularly behind the ears. Frequent bathing is unnecessary, but is advisable when the bitch loses her winter coat. The Sheltie is meticulous about its appearance and will often clean itself.

Feeding
One to 1½ cans (376g, 13.3oz size) of a branded meaty product, with biscuit added in equal part by volume; or 3 cupfuls of a dry food, complete diet, mixed in the proportion of 1 cup of feed to ½ cup of hot or cold water.

Above: The Shetland Sheepdog, an obedient and faithful companion.

Origin and history
The Sheltie originated in the Shetland Islands off the north coast of Scotland, an area also famous for its tiny Shetland ponies, which, like the Shetland Sheepdog, have been bred with thick coats to protect them against the harsh climate.

The breed has bred true for some 125 years, but controversy at one time existed as to aims and requirements, the ideals of the club formed at Lerwick in 1908 conflicting with the desires of the Shetland Collie Club, whose desire was simply to produce a Collie in miniature. Both groups were similarly named. Luckily, agreement was reached in 1914 when the English Shetland Sheepdog Club was formed, and the Sheltie received separate classification by the Kennel Club. Today the breed's popularity is universal. 24▸

GERMAN HUNT TERRIER (Deutscher Jagdterrier)

Good points

- *First-class hunter, retriever and gundog*
- *Good traveller*
- *Robust*

Take heed

- *Needs a lot of exercise*
- *Somewhat aggressive*

The German Hunt Terrier is a popular breed in its country of origin. It is also well established in Austria and other German-speaking regions. It has yet, however, to be recognized by the English or American Kennel Clubs. It can be kept as a household pet, but is essentially a worker, needing plenty of exercise, and has a somewhat aggressive temperament.

Size

Weight: dog 8.8-10kg (19½-22lb); bitch 7.3-8.2kg (16-18lb). Height at the withers not more than 40.5cm (16in).

Exercise

Needs plenty of exercise. The German Hunt Terrier is a good car traveller and rarely suffers from sickness.

Grooming

Daily brushing is required.

Feeding

Half to 1 can (376g, 13.3oz size) of a branded, meaty product, with biscuit added in equal part by volume; or 1½ cupfuls of a dry, complete food, mixed in the proportion of 1 cup of feed to ½ cup of hot or cold water.

Origin and history

This is an essentially German breed derived from crossing the English Fox Terrier with the Lakeland and others, with a view to creating a hardy, dark-coated terrier. The first results were not encouraging although good working terriers were produced. However, by 1925, a satisfactory German Hunt Terrier had evolved that was able to go to earth and retrieve small game from land or water. It is a courageous dog willing to take on fox and boar as well as rats and small rodents, but has a somewhat aggressive terrier temperament.

The Association of the German Hunt Terrier has a list of work tests designed specifically for the breed. It accepts for breeding only Hunt Terriers that have achieved high pass marks. 26▸

Left: Bred in Germany as a working dog, the German Hunt Terrier can be kept as a pet but may be fierce.

TIBETAN TERRIER

Good points
- *Charming 'shaggy' appearance*
- *Happy disposition*
- *Good house pet*
- *Weatherproof coat*
- *Popular show dog*
- *Effective watchdog*
- *Adaptable*

Take heed
- *No drawbacks known*

The Tibetan Terrier is one of three small Tibetan breeds, the others being the Tibetan Spaniel and the Lhasa Apso, both of which are dealt with elsewhere. There is also a Tibetan Mastiff, which is a much larger breed.

The Tibetan Terrier, which in appearance resembles a small Old English Sheepdog, is in truth not a terrier at all, having no history of going to earth.

Size
Height at shoulders: dog should be 35.5-40.5cm (14-16in); bitches should be slightly smaller.

Exercise
The Tibetan Terrier enjoys an off-the-lead scamper and the freedom of a garden; otherwise normal, regular walks will suffice.

Grooming
Needs a thorough brushing every day to maintain smartness.

Feeding
Half to 1 can (376g, 13.3oz size) of a branded meaty product, with biscuit added in equal part by volume; or 1½ cupfuls of a complete, dry food, mixed in the proportion of 1 cup of feed to ½ cup of hot or cold water.

Origin and history
Bred in the monasteries of Tibet, with a history of all-purpose farm work, the Tibetan breeds first reached Europe at the beginning of this century, when both the Lhasa Apso and the Tibetan Terrier were referred to as Lhasa Terriers. The situation became somewhat confused, and in 1934 the British Kennel Club formed the Tibetan Breeds Association.

The Tibetan Terrier standard is included in the British Kennel Club's Utility group, and over the past 10 years the breed has attracted quite a number of enthusiasts. At the time of writing, however, the Tibetan Terrier has still to be recognized by the American Kennel Club. 28▸

Below: Not a true terrier, the Tibetan Terrier was bred for farm work in its native land. It is now increasing in popularity.

BEAGLE

Good points

- *Healthy*
- *Adores children*
- *Good with other pets*
- *Intelligent*
- *Merry and affectionate*
- *Good show dog*

Take heed

- *Will wander if gate is left ajar*
- *Will soon grow fat if given titbits*

The Beagle is a merry, affectionate little fellow, loving humans and other pets alike. The Beagle adores children and is a wonderful companion, equally ready for a romp or to lie by your feet on the hearthrug. This breed is equally at home in a small house or a mansion, and will guard its home and owner faithfully. It is not a barker, being mostly heard at the chase, in full cry. But, like most other hounds, it has the wanderlust, so care must be taken never to leave the garden gate ajar.

The Breed Standard states: 'A merry hound whose essential function is to hunt, primarily hare, by following a scent. Bold with great activity, stamina and determination. Alert, intelligent and of even temperament. A sturdy and compactly-built hound, conveying the impression of quality without coarseness.'

Size

It is desirable that height from ground to withers should neither exceed 40.5cm (16in) nor fall below 33cm (13in). In the United States there are two size varieties for showing purposes: below 33cm (13in), and over 33cm (13in) but not exceeding 38cm (15in).

Exercise

Exercise is no problem, because Beagles keep themselves fit as easily in a small garden as on a farm. But, like most dogs, they should be taken for a walk every day. They are notoriously healthy and robust, so you rarely need the services of a veterinarian.

Grooming

The short coat of the Beagle is tough and weatherproof, and needs no grooming. It is recommended that after a muddy walk the Beagle is left in its box for an hour to clean itself up.

Feeding

One meal a day is sufficient for a full-grown Beagle, with no titbits afterwards, as this is a breed that is inclined to put on weight. One to 1½ cans (376g, 13.3oz size) of a complete meaty diet, to which biscuit should be added in equal part by volume, is adequate; or 3 cupfuls of a dry food, complete diet, mixed in the proportion of 1 cup of feed to ½ cup of water.

Origin and history

The Beagle is one of the smallest of the hounds, embodying all their virtues in the least compass. An ancient breed, it has proved a joy to sportsmen for hundreds of years; Beagles were first mentioned by name in writings published in 1475. Followed on foot and on horseback, they have been hunted in packs after hare from time immemorial, and were first imported into the United States for this purpose.

Beagles are esteemed all over the world and have hunted many different quarries in varying climates, including jackal in the Sudan and Palestine, wild pig in Ceylon and deer in Scandinavia. In the USA and Canada they are used as gundogs to seek out and retrieve game, and to hunt by scent in competitive Field Trials. 29▶

DREVER

Good points
- *Equable temperament*
- *Excellent nose*
- *Steady but slow worker*
- *Popular show dog in its native Sweden*
- *Good house pet*

Take heed
- *No drawbacks known*

The Drever is little known outside Scandinavia. It is, however, one of Sweden's most popular dogs.

It is a steady, though slow worker, and has a good nose for trekking fox, wild boar and roe deer, and will also drive them towards the gun. It has found favour in Scandinavia as a house pet. A similar dog, the Strellufs-stövare, is bred in Denmark.

Size
Height: dog 31.5-38cm (12½-15in); bitch 29-35.5cm (11½-14in).

Exercise
Needs plenty of exercise. Happiest when hunting.

Grooming
Normal daily brushing.

Feeding
One to 1½ cans (376g, 13.3oz size) of a branded, meaty product, with biscuit added in equal part by volume; or 3 cupfuls of a dry, complete food, mixed in the proportion of 1 cup of feed to ½ cup of hot or cold water.

Origin and history
The Drever is one of the most popular dogs in Sweden, a national breed said to have been derived from the mating of other Swedish hunting dogs with Dachshunds – there is something of the Dachshund and the Beagle in their appearance. At the beginning of the century, the breed was known by the German name of Dachsbracke. However, as it began to alter to meet Swedish requirements, the name was changed and recognition sought with the Swedish Kennel Club under the new name of Drever. This was achieved in 1949 and recognition by the FCI followed in 1953. This breed is not recognized by the British or American Kennel Clubs. It is a strong, muscular dog, bearing some resemblance to the Dachshund. Colours are red and white, yellow and white, or tricolour. White must not predominate but must be apparent from all angles. These white patches on the Drever's coat help to make the dog more visible when it is being used to track down deer in the thick forests of its Swedish homeland. 29▸

DACHSBRACKE

The Dachsbracke is little known outside Germany. The breed is a close relative of the Swedish Drever and many authorities refer to the Dachsbracke and Drever as one. There are three varieties, the Westphalian, the Erz mountains and the Alpine; the former, the smallest of the three, is almost extinct.

The breed stands between 34 and 42cm (13½-16½in), has a short, dense coat and bears a passing resemblance to the Dachshund. A litter was bred in Britain in 1949. However, the Dachsbracke is not recognized by the British or American Kennel Clubs. It gained recognition in Germany in 1896. 29▸

SWEDISH VALLHUND (Västgötaspets)

Good points

- *Active*
- *Excellent drover/cattle dog*
- *Loyal*
- *Affectionate*
- *Intelligent*
- *Effective guard dog*

Take heed

- *No drawbacks known*

The Vallhund or Västgötaspets is a Swedish breed, similar in appearance to the Welsh Corgi. It is an active, intelligent worker and is rapidly gaining popularity in many parts of the world.

Size

Height: dog 33cm (13in), bitch 31.2cm (12.3in).

Exercise

Fares best if given plenty of exercise.

Grooming

Normal daily brushing.

Feeding

One to 1½ cans (376g, 13.3oz size) of a branded meaty product, with biscuit added in equal part by volume; or 3 cupfuls of a dry food, complete diet, mixed in the proportion of 1 cup of feed to ½ cup of hot or cold water.

Origin and history

The Västgötaspets, to give it its Swedish name, looks something like a Cardigan/Pembroke Corgi cross. There is certainly a connection between the Corgi and this attractive breed, but it is impossible to determine whether it evolved as the result of Vikings taking Corgis to Sweden, or if Swedish dogs brought to Britain developed the Corgi. The Swedes certainly claim credit for this fine little cattle dog, which owes its present development to a Swedish breeder, Björn von Rosen. 29▸

Below: The Vallhund was developed in Sweden as a fine cattle dog.

BASENJI (Zande Dog, Belgian Congo Dog, Congo Bush Dog, Bongo Terrier, Congo Terrier, Nyam-Nyam Terrier)

Good points
- *Adaptable to most climates*
- *Has no bark*
- *Gentle with children*
- *No 'doggie' smell*

Take heed
- *Does not like rain*
- *Bitches may come into season only once a year*
- *Mischievous*

The Basenji (the name is the translation of a native word meaning 'bush thing') is an interesting and attractive breed, its main claim to fame being that it has no bark. But only the bark is absent; the Basenji will growl and whine like other breeds, and can express itself feelingly with a distinctive chortle or yodel. The breed's vocal cords are present and it is believed that training, over thousands of years, to hunt game silently may account for their characteristic quietness.

The breed is well known for its gentle disposition and love of children, though it can be aloof with strangers. It has great curiosity and mischievousness.

Appealing features are its curling tail, high set and lying over to one side of the back, its habit of washing with its paw like a cat, and its forehead full of 'worried' wrinkles.

Size
Ideal height: dog 43cm (17in) at the shoulder; bitch 40.5cm (16in); but an inch either way should not penalize an otherwise well-balanced specimen. Ideal weight: dog 10.9kg (24lb); bitch 9.5kg (21lb).

Exercise
The Basenji is a great hunter and if not exercised has a tendency to put on weight. It is fleet-footed, tireless, and enjoys a daily walk and off-the-lead run. It is, incidentally, a breed that is particularly good with horses.

This is a breed that should not be kept in an outside kennel. It is essentially a house dog, which loves to stretch out in front of the fire, or to indulge in its strange habit of reclining in places off the ground. It is suitable for apartment living as long as it is given sufficient exercise.

Grooming
Regular use of a hound glove is recommended to keep the coat in good condition.

Feeding
About 1½-2 cans of branded dog food (376g, 13.3oz size), with an equal volume of biscuit, or 3 cupfuls of dry food, complete diet, mixed in the proportion of 1 cup of feed to ½ cup of hot or cold water; or ¼kg (½lb) of fresh meat, with biscuit. Green vegetables should be added to Basenji fare. They are also inveterate grass eaters and should have ample access to fresh grass.

Origin and history
Dogs of the Basenji type are depicted in many of the carvings in the tombs of the Pharaohs, and it is believed that these dogs were brought as precious gifts by travellers from the lower reaches of the Nile.

The Basenji almost disappeared from public view from Ancient Egyptian times until the mid-19th century, when it was discovered by explorers in the Congo and Southern Sudan.

The foundation stock recognized today derived from the Belgian Congo, with further imports from Sudan and Liberia. 28▸

PEMBROKE WELSH CORGI

Good points

- *Devoted companion*
- *Excellent guard*
- *Fond of children*
- *Hardy*
- *Tireless*

Take heed

- *Needs training when young – the inherent tendency to nip must be discouraged*

The Welsh Corgi (Pembroke) has, like the Cardigan, been worked in South Wales for many centuries, but has evolved as a popular and affectionate pet, particularly because it is a breed much favoured by the British royal family, whose pets have been known to take the occasional, much publicized nip!

Size

Weight: dog 9-10.9kg (20-24lb); bitch 8.2-10kg (18-22lb). Height: 25-30cm (10-12in) at the shoulder.

Exercise

Although traditionally a worker, the Pembroke adapts well to life as a domestic pet, with daily walks of average length. But beware: if you do not give sufficient exercise this breed will soon lose its figure!

Below: Daily exercise will keep the Pembroke Welsh Corgi looking trim.

Grooming

Daily brushing needed. The breed has a water-resistant coat.

Feeding

Give ½-1 can (376g, 13.3oz size) of a branded meaty product, with biscuit added in equal part by volume; or 1½ cupfuls of a dry food, complete diet, mixed in the proportion of 1 cup of feed to ½ cup of hot or cold water.

Origin and history

The Welsh Corgi (Pembroke) has worked in South Wales since the Domesday Book survey was instigated by William the Conqueror in the 11th century. Its traditional task was to control the movement of cattle by nipping at their ankles, and then getting quickly out of range. It has, however, a bolder temperament than the Cardigan.

Some say that the Pembroke derives from stock brought to Wales by Flemish weavers who settled in the locality and crossed their dogs with Welsh native stock; others point out the similarity that exists between the Welsh Corgi (Pembroke) and the Swedish Västgötaspets, suggesting that trading between the Welsh and the Swedes introduced the breed to Wales.

In any event, the Welsh Corgi (Pembroke) has been exhibited in Britain since 1925, receiving separate classification from the Welsh Corgi (Cardigan) in 1934. It is, perhaps, one of the best-known breeds in Britain, because of its association with Her Majesty Queen Elizabeth II. 29▸

CARDIGAN WELSH CORGI

Good points

- *Devoted companion*
- *Excellent guard*
- *Fond of children*
- *Quieter temperament than the Pembroke*

Take heed

- *This breed had eye defects in the past, so seek a veterinarian's advice if necessary.*

The Welsh Corgi (Cardigan) has been known and worked in South Wales for centuries. It is hardy, fond of children, and tireless, and, despite its original task of nipping the heels of cattle to bring them into line, has a more equable temperament than the Pembroke, and is less likely to nip the heels of unsuspecting visitors.

Size

Height as near as possible to 30cm (12in) at the shoulder. Weight: dog 10-11.8 kg (22-26lb); bitch 9-10.9kg (20-24lb).

Exercise

Although traditionally a worker, the Cardigan adapts well to life as a domestic pet, with daily walks of average length. But beware: if you do not give sufficient exercise this breed will soon lose its figure!

Grooming

Daily brushing needed. The breed has a water-resistant coat.

Feeding

Give ½-1 can (376g, 13.3oz size) of a branded meaty product, with biscuit added in equal part by volume; or 1½ cupfuls of a dry food, complete diet, mixed in the proportion of 1 cup of food to ½ cup of hot or cold water.

Health care

Avoid letting your pet jump from heights, especially if overweight; this could lead to painful spine trouble. The Cardigan is also prone to eye defects (progressive retinal atrophy); fortunately, these have now been almost eradicated from the breed.

Origin and history

The Welsh Corgi (Cardigan) has worked in South Wales since the Domesday Book survey was instigated by William the Conqueror in the 11th century. Its traditional task was to control the movement of cattle by nipping at their ankles, and then getting out of range.

The breed first made its appearance in the British show ring in 1925, classified as one breed with the Welsh Corgi (Pembroke); it received separate classification in 1934. Welsh folklore contains many references to this dependable, ancient breed, which has perhaps missed out on popularity due to the British royal family's particular fondness for its Pembrokeshire cousin. 29▸

Below: The beautiful markings of a blue merle Cardigan Welsh Corgi.

SKYE TERRIER

Good points
- *Beautiful in appearance*
- *Pleasant disposition*
- *Patient*
- *Devoted to its owner*

Take heed
- *Needs plenty of grooming*
- *Does not take kindly to strangers*

The Skye Terrier originated on the Isle of Skye in the Hebrides and is, despite its beautiful appearance, a relentless fighter if aroused. It is not a vicious dog, but tends to give total trust and devotion to its owner and has little time for strangers. Considerable care has to be given to the grooming of this breed. If given the chance they are valiant hunters, having been bred to hunt fox, otter and badger.

Size
Height 25cm (10in), total length 105cm (41½in), weight 11.3kg (25lb); bitch slightly smaller.

Exercise
It would be unfair to buy this gay little breed purely as a fashionable accessory, for they are tireless and enjoy nothing better than a long country walk and romp in fresh air.

Grooming
The Skye should be brushed daily and combed once a week with a wide-toothed comb. Incidentally, the coat does not reach its full beauty until the third year.

Feeding
Recommended would be 1-1½ cans of a branded meaty product (376g, 13.3oz size), with biscuit added in equal part by volume; or 3 cupfuls of a dry, complete food, mixed in the proportion of 1 cup of feed to ½ cup of hot or cold water.

Origin and history
The Skye Terrier is a legend – not only in Scotland, but throughout the world – because of the tale of Greyfriars Bobby, whose statue stands near Greyfriars churchyard, Edinburgh. Following his master's death, Bobby would each day, for the next 14 years, visit the café that he had frequented with his master, where he would be given a bun, before retracing his steps to his master's grave, where he spent his days until his own death from old age, when the statue was erected in his memory.

The Skye evolved from the small earth dogs kept in Scotland to hunt foxes, badgers and other vermin. Although the Cairn and other breeds existed in the Highlands it would seem that the Skye owes its appearance to no-one, although the Highland terriers in early days were not separate breeds. 27▸

Above: Full of energy, the handsome Skye Terrier makes a devoted pet.

BOSTON TERRIER (Formerly American Bull Terrier)

Good points
- *Affectionate*
- *Excellent guard*
- *Good with children*
- *Rarely sheds coat*

Take heed
- *Not for outside kennelling*
- *Not the easiest type to breed and/or produce for showing*
- *Watch out for eye trouble*

The Boston Terrier is a lively and attractive American breed. It is intelligent and trainable, and makes a delightful companion, always ready for a walk or a game. However, achieving the desired markings can be a show aspirant's nightmare, and bitches frequently require caesarean section in whelping.

Size
Weight: not more than 11.3kg (25lb).

Exercise
This breed will happily settle for an on-the-lead walk, if you do not have a garden to offer it more freedom of movement. It is essentially a pet dog and should not be confined in an outside kennel.

Grooming
Daily brushing is needed. In the United States ears are cropped in some states according to state law. This practice is illegal in the United Kingdom. The coat rarely sheds.

Feeding
Half to 1 can (376g, 13.3oz size) of a branded, meaty product, with biscuit added in equal part by volume; or 1½ cupfuls of a dry, complete food mixed in the proportion of 1 cup of feed to ½ cup of hot or cold water.

Health care
The Boston is robust but, as in the case of the Pekingese and other round-eyed breeds, watch that dust and foreign bodies do not penetrate the eyes.

Origin and history
The Boston Terrier, sometimes called the 'American gentleman', can trace its ancestry from the mating of a crossbred Bulldog/terrier called Judge, imported to the United States from the United Kingdom in 1865. To later progeny were added a dash of English and Staffordshire Bull Terrier, until the dog we know today evolved. At first it was known as the American Bull Terrier, but as a result of objections from other Bull Terrier clubs it was renamed the Boston Terrier after the city responsible for its development. 28▸

Below: The Boston Terrier combines determination, strength and grace.

IRISH TERRIER

Good points
- *Alert*
- *Loyal protector*
- *Courageous*
- *Excellent ratter*
- *Good with children*
- *Trains easily*
- *Not as snappy as most terriers*

Take heed
- *Can be a prodigious fighter*

To describe the Irish Terrier as a dog that looks like a small Airedale with a self-coloured yellow coat would far from satisfy the many lovers of this ancient and most attractive breed. We have today in the Irish a fine watchdog, a loyal protector and a most excellent family pet, the only drawback being its somewhat exaggerated reputation for fighting other dogs. True to its terrier blood it is tremendously courageous, and stories of faithfulness to its master are legion.

Size
The most desirable weight in show condition is: dog 12.3kg (27lb); bitch 11.3kg (25lb). Height at the shoulders should be approximately 46cm (18in).

Exercise
The Irish Terrier is a sporty little dog, which has been trained successfully to the gun and is first-class at destroying vermin. It has also been a creditable performer in obedience competitions. It will, however, adapt happily to life as a household pet provided it has a garden to romp in and is taken for walks and off-the-lead runs.

Grooming
Like the Airedale, the Irish Terrier will need hand stripping several times a year and it is best to have this done professionally—at least until you have learned the knack.

Feeding
Recommended would be 1-1½ cans of a branded meaty product (376g, 13.3oz size), with biscuit added in equal part by volume; or 3 cupfuls of a dry, complete food mixed in the proportion of 1 cup of feed to ½ cup of hot or cold water.

Origin and history
Irish sources say that the Irish Terrier was established in the country even before the arrival of their patron saint, St Patrick, some going so far as to say that the Irish Terrier is a smaller version of another of their national dogs, the Irish Wolfhound; but the relationship seems somewhat remote. It is more likely that the Irish Terrier is a descendant of the Black and Tan Wire-haired Terriers whose purpose was to hunt fox and destroy vermin in Britain some 200 years ago. Study of the Welsh and Lakeland Terriers will show the similarity between the breeds and it would certainly seem that all have the old Black and Tan Terrier as a common ancestor. It is said that in the area around County Cork in Ireland a large Wheaten Terrier existed that could have been the forerunner of the Irish Terrier.

The standard breeding of the Irish Terrier did not take place until 1879 before which there was considerable variation of type, size and colour; it is said that the Irish Terrier in Antrim was black, brown and white, whereas those in Whitley were of a reddish colour and those in Kerry were black or black/brown. In 1879 a specialist Breed Club was formed, and in the following years the Irish Terrier in its present form and colour became tremendously popular. 24▸

FRENCH BULLDOG

Good points
- *Affectionate and devoted pet*
- *Loves human company*
- *Easy to train*
- *Adaptable*
- *Intelligent and alert*

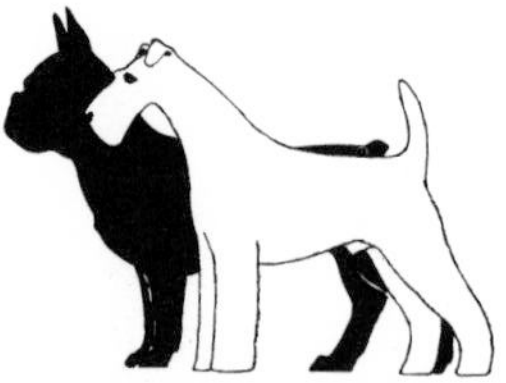

Take heed
- *Lubricate facial creases with petroleum jelly to prevent soreness.*

The French Bulldog is a devoted animal and makes the ideal family pet. It has a keen, clownish sense of humour, is intelligent, and adapts well to town or country living. It is perhaps the healthiest of the Bulldogs and does not suffer from the over-developments or nasal difficulties of the Boston Terrier and the English Bulldog.

Size
The ideal weight is 12.7kg (28lb) for dogs and 10.9kg (24lb) for bitches, but soundness must not be sacrificed to smallness.

Exercise
Short, regular walks, and off-the-lead scampers.

Grooming
Normal daily brushing.

Feeding
One to 1½ cans (376g, 13.3oz size) of a branded meaty product, with biscuit added in equal part by volume; or 3 cupfuls of a dry food, complete diet, mixed in the proportion of 1 cup of feed to ½ cup of hot or cold water.

Origin and history
Credit must go to the French for the development of this breed. It is, however, uncertain whether it derives from small English Bulldogs taken to France by Nottingham laceworkers in the 19th century, or from crossings with dogs imported to France from Spain. In any event, this delightful breed is clearly the descendant of small Bulldogs, and by the beginning of this century it had found favour in both Britain and the United States. 28▸

Below: The charming French Bulldog excels as a friendly house pet and an obedient show dog.

AMERICAN COCKER SPANIEL

Good points

- *Adaptable to town or country living*
- *Beautiful*
- *Excellent family pet*
- *Intelligent*
- *Obedient*

Take heed

- *Needs lots of grooming*
- *Appreciates plenty of exercise*

The American Cocker Spaniel is an excellent hunter, and excels in flushing out and retrieving birds. It is also extremely popular as a household pet and is a beautiful, affectionate breed that will make an excellent companion in either town or country surroundings.

The Breed Standard states: 'The American Cocker Spaniel's sturdy body, powerful quarters and strong, well-boned legs show it to be a dog capable of considerable speed combined with great endurance. Above all it must be free and merry, sound and well balanced.'

Size

The ideal height at the withers for an adult dog is 38cm (15in), and for an adult bitch 35.5cm (14in). Height may vary 13mm (½in) above or below this ideal. A dog whose height exceeds 39.5cm (15½in), or a bitch whose height exceeds 37cm (14½in), or an adult bitch whose height is less than 34cm (13½in) should be penalized in the show ring.

Exercise

It must be remembered that the Cocker Spaniel was originally bred for hunting and, although it adapts happily to the role of companion and family pet, it will obviously fit in best with families who are prepared to give it two good walks a day and have a garden for it to romp in at its heart's content.

Grooming

The American Cocker, with its luxuriant coat, needs daily brushing and combing, and a bath and trim every 8-10 weeks. It is best to ask the breeder for advice, or to visit a professional dog groomer, because the skull and muzzle hair must be trimmed to precise accepted lengths with electric clippers, the neck and shoulders carefully scissored, and feathering left on the legs, ears and belly. Feet must also be trimmed. Obviously you may wish to attend to this ritual yourself, but it is advisable to be shown the procedure by an expert first.

Feeding

Recommended would be 1-1½ cans of a branded meaty product (376g, 13.3oz size) with biscuit added in equal part by volume; or 3 cupfuls of a dry food, complete diet, mixed in the proportion of 1 cup of feed to ½ cup of hot or cold water.

Origin and history

The American Cocker is smaller than the English Cocker, has a much thicker coat and, although originating from England, has been bred along different lines in the United States. Its elegant trousers and length of coat are the simplest means of clear identification.

An American Cocker was first shown in America at Manchester, New Hampshire, in September 1883, and when permission was given by the American Kennel Club for the two varieties to be shown, there was great enthusiasm for the American Cocker. 30▸

ENGLISH COCKER SPANIEL

Good points
- *Affectionate, gentle nature*
- *Excellent gundog*
- *Good with children*
- *Long lived*
- *Merry temperament*

Take heed
- *Overfeeding will cause weight problems*
- *Keep ears out of feed bowl*

The 'merry' Cocker, as it is called, makes an ideal family pet – a dog for Dad to take out shooting, or for the children to romp with in the garden. It is manageable, intelligent, and a good all-purpose gundog, second to none at flushing out game.

Size
The weight should be about 12.7-14.5kg (28-32lb). The height at the withers should be: dog 39.5-40.5cm (15½-16in); bitch 38-39.5cm (15-15½in).

Exercise
This is an active dog that needs regular exercise. It adores the country and is likely to return from a walk with tail wagging and covered with mud, so it is not perhaps the ideal choice for smart town dwellers; but it does enjoy home comforts, such as a place beside a warm fire.

Grooming
The Cocker requires daily brushing and combing, care being taken that its coat does not become matted. Particular care must be taken that the ears do not become tangled; and watch out that they do not flop into the feed bowl! You might consider taping them back while the dog is eating or using a special 'spaniel' bowl.

Feeding
Recommended would be 1-1½ cans of a branded meaty product (376g, 13.3oz size), with biscuit added in equal part by volume; or 3 cupfuls of a dry food, complete diet, mixed in the proportion of 1 cup of feed to ½ cup of hot or cold water. Obviously rations will need to be stepped up if the dog is taking vigorous exercise. This is a breed that will plead endearingly for titbits, which should be denied if the owner is to avoid an overweight or smelly pet.

With correct diet and exercise the Cocker Spaniel proves to be one of the healthiest and most long-lived of dogs. Its beautiful, appealing eyes make it difficult to refuse it anything, and there are few breeds in the world to challenge its beauty as a pup.

Origin and history
The Cocker Spaniel is particularly popular in Britain, and in the United States it is known as the English Cocker. It is also sometimes referred to as the 'merry' Cocker because of its happy, lively temperament and constantly wagging tail. Other titles bestowed upon it have been the Cocking Spaniel or Cocker, because of its one-time prowess at flushing out woodcock.

The Cocker Spaniel did however originate in Spain – whence the name 'spaniel' – and its ancestry can be traced back to the 14th century. It is believed to have been used in various countries in falconry. Today, however, it is in its element rabbit hunting, flushing out game for its master, then remaining motionless until a shot has been fired. It is also well able to retrieve and is an ideal choice for both working trials and dog training competitions. 30▸

MEXICAN HAIRLESS (Xoloitzcuintli)

Good points
- *Even temperament*
- *Intelligent*
- *Affectionate*
- *No hairs on the carpet*
- *Pride of ownership – they are almost extinct*

Take heed
- *This breed must be kept warm*
- *Cries instead of barking*

The Mexican Hairless Dog is one of the oldest breeds in the world, and in danger of becoming extinct. However, rumour has it that these animals are sometimes seen wandering along the waterfront in Hong Kong, and efforts are now being made to protect the breed in its native Mexico.

Unlike the Chinese Crested, this breed is totally hairless except for a tuft of short, coarse, and not very dense hair on the skull, though this should never be of the length or softness of the mane of the Chinese Crested. It is a quiet, rather reserved animal, growling only under provocation, and is similar in build to a Staffordshire Bull Terrier. It is described as gay and intelligent, yet at the same time dignified and unaggressive. Young pups tend to be snub-nosed and short-legged and do not conform to their adult appearance until late in their development.

The Mexican Kennel Club Standard states that the skin should be 'soft and smooth to the touch, particularly in those areas less exposed to the sun.'

Size
Weight 13.6-15.9kg (30-35lb).
Height about 48cm (19in).

Feeding
Its normal diet is fruit and vegetables, but it can adapt to usual canine fare. This was proved when, some 20 years ago, two Mexican Hairless Dogs were quarantined in London Zoo. Recommended would be 1-1½ cans (376g, 13.3oz size) of a branded meaty product, with biscuit added in equal volume; or 3 cupfuls of a dry, complete diet mixed in the proportion of 1 cup of feed to ½ cup of water.

Health care
The Mexican Hairless sweats through its skin, unlike other breeds, which sweat through the tongue. They need a warm environment, with a heated kennel, and have a body temperature of 105°F (40.5°C) as against the normal canine temperature of 101.4°F (38.5°C).

Origin and history
The Mexican Hairless did not originate in Mexico, but was brought to that country by nomadic tribes of Indians from north-eastern Asia. It may even have come originally from as far away as Turkey, the land of the Turkish Toy Greyhound, another species of naked canine.

The little naked Xoloitzcuintli, as its new owners called it, was considered as a gift from the gods by the Aztecs, because when anyone was sick, the dog could warm the patient with its naked body.

The earliest inhabitants of Mexico, the Toltecs, had kept the blue Chihuahua in their temples for religious purposes. When the Aztecs conquered the Toltecs, dogs of both breeds were kept in luxury inside the temples. However, it is possible that the inevitable inter-breeding of the Mexican Hairless with the Chihuahua may have produced the Chinese Crested breed we know today. 20▸

GLEN OF IMAAL TERRIER

Good points

- *Affectionate*
- *Courageous*
- *Excellent with children*
- *Good working dog*
- *Loyal*
- *Playful*

Take heed

- *Rarely seen in show ring, so not a good choice for showing*

The Glen of Imaal Terrier originates from a valley of that name in the county of Wicklow in Ireland, where it was—and is—used as a working terrier to dispel fox and badger. It is still mainly to be found in Ireland, combining life as a working terrier with the role of pet and children's protector.

Size

Height not more than 35.5cm (14in); weight up to 15.9kg (35lb), less for bitches.

Exercise

Happiest when able to run in open spaces, but an adaptable little dog that will take to normal household life provided it has a garden to play in and is given regular walks.

Grooming

A good daily brushing.

Above: The tough Glen of Imaal Terrier has a thick protective coat that serves the breed well in its role as a working terrier. It is little known outside Eire.

Feeding

Recommended would be 1-1½ cans of a branded meaty product (376g, 13.3oz size), with biscuit added in equal part by volume; or 3 cupfuls of a dry, complete food, mixed in the proportion of 1 cup of feed to ½ cup of hot or cold water.

Origin and history

The Glen of Imaal Terrier is an Irish-bred working terrier and still popular in its area of origin. But although its fame has long spread outside its native Ireland, where it received official breed recognition in 1933, it is not often seen in the show ring. It is also recognized by the British Kennel Club but not by the AKC. 27▸

KROMFOHRLANDER

Good points
- *Lively*
- *Excellent temperament*
- *Good companion*
- *Guarding/hunting instincts*
- *Intelligent*
- *Faithful and friendly*

Take heed
- *No drawbacks known*

This is a faithful and intelligent dog with guarding and hunting instincts. Regrettably it is little known outside Germany.

Size
Height at the withers 38-46cm (15-18in).

Exercise
This is a terrier with plenty of energy to unleash.

Grooming
Normal daily brushing.

Feeding
One to 1½ cans (376g, 13.3oz size) of a branded meaty product, with biscuit added in equal part by volume; or 3 cupfuls of a dry food, complete diet, mixed in the proportion of 1 cup of feed to ½ cup of hot or cold water.

Origin and history
The Kromfohrländer has come into being only since the end of World War II when, legend has it, a group of American soldiers, accompanied by a medium-sized dog, passed through the Siegen area of Germany, where the dog was found a new home with a Frau Schleifenbaum, who already owned an English Wire-haired Terrier bitch. The resultant progeny from the first and subsequent litters were so pleasing that it was decided to develop a specific type, eventually known as the Kromfohrländer, which in 1953 received recognition by the German Kennel Club. 32▸

Below: The Kromfohrländer, hardly known outside its native Germany, makes a lively and affectionate pet and an excellent watchdog.

PUMI

Good points
- *Good watchdog*
- *Intelligent*
- *Pleasant temperament*
- *Useful farm dog*

Take heed
- *Has a somewhat scruffy appearance*
- *Not keen on strangers*
- *Extremely lively*

The Pumi is a pleasant companion and guard. However, it prefers its owner's company and will give noisy warning of intruders. It has an unkempt appearance that is unusually appealing. Not often seen outside its native Hungary, where it is mainly a farm dog.

Size
Weight: 8-13kg (17½-28½lb), height at withers 33-44.5cm (13-17½in).

Exercise
Happiest running out of doors, but easily trained.

Grooming
Brushing will help!

Feeding
One to 1½ cans (376g, 13.3oz size) of a branded meaty product, with biscuit added in equal part by volume; or 3 cupfuls of a dry food, complete diet, mixed in the proportion of 1 cup of feed to ½ cup of hot or cold water.

Origin and history
The Pumi, like the Komondor, Puli and Kuvasz, is a Hungarian sheepdog. However, in recent years it has been employed mainly as an all-purpose farm dog and herder of cattle in its native country. It also excels at police and guard work. Its history is obscure, but undoubtedly the Puli had a hand in its make-up, perhaps with the Poodle. 31▸

Below: The untidy looking Pumi fulfils the role of an all purpose farm dog and cattle herder in its native Hungary. It is faithful to its owner but will deter intruders with a noisy reception.

JAPANESE SPITZ

Good points
- *Courageous*
- *Intelligent*
- *Loyal*
- *Lively*
- *Delightful show dog*
- *Good family pet*

Take heed
- *Tends to be a one-person dog*
- *Distrustful of strangers*

The Japanese Spitz is a close relation of the Norrbotten Spitz, but has developed as a separate breed in Japan, to which it was undoubtedly imported long ago. It has only recently come upon the international scene and is still comparatively rare.

Size
Height: dog, 30-40.5cm (12-16in); bitch, 25-35.5cm (10-14in).

Below: The charming Japanese Spitz, only just now becoming well known outside Japan, makes a rewarding show dog and reliable house pet.

Exercise
This dog is a natural herder, and enjoys its freedom. However, it adapts well to the life of a house pet, with regular walks.

Grooming
Normal daily brushing.

Feeding
One to 1½ cans (376g, 13.3oz size) of a branded meaty product, with biscuit added in equal part by volume; or 3 cupfuls of a dry food, complete diet, mixed in the proportion of 1 cup of feed to ½ cup of hot or cold water. 31▸

NORRBOTTEN SPITZ

Good points
- *Excellent guard*
- *Good with children*
- *Happy nature*
- *Active*
- *Lively*
- *Faithful to family*
- *Strong herding instinct*

Take heed
- *No drawbacks known*

The Norbotten Spitz is named after the northern region of Sweden, Norrbotten, from which it originates. It is Sweden's answer to the Finnish Spitz and the Norwegian Buhund, though smaller and lighter. It makes an excellent companion, house dog and farmyard protector.

Size
Maximum height 40.5cm (16in).

Exercise
This dog is a natural herder that enjoys its freedom. However it adapts well to the life of a house pet, with regular walks.

Grooming
Normal daily brushing.

Feeding
One to 1½ cans (376g, 13.3oz size) of a branded meaty product, with biscuit added in equal part by volume; or 3 cupfuls of a dry food, complete diet, mixed in the proportion of 1 cup of feed to ½ cup of hot or cold water.

Origin and history
The Norrbotten Spitz is little known outside Sweden, having been declared extinct by the Swedish Kennel Club in 1948. Luckily this proved to be untrue, and there was an upsurge of interest in the 1960s, resulting in sufficient registrations for the breed to become re-established. Its Spitz origin probably derives from Finnish Spitz or Norwegian Buhund ancestry. The Norrbotten Spitz is not yet recognized in either the United Kingdom or the USA. 31▸

Below: The Norrbotten Spitz has a naturally cheerful nature that endears the breed to its owner's family.

FINNISH SPITZ (Suomenpystykorva)

Good points
- *Beautiful*
- *Brave*
- *Excellent guard/housedog*
- *Faithful*
- *Good with children*
- *Home-loving*
- *Sociable*

Take heed
- *No drawbacks known*

The Finnish Spitz is Finland's national dog. It is popular in Scandinavia as both a hunter (mainly of birds) and a show dog. It also has devotees in Great Britain, where it is kept mainly as a pet and show dog. It is a beautiful animal with the habit of cleaning itself like a cat.

Size
Height: dog 44.5cm (17½in), bitch 39.5cm (15½in).

Exercise
This is a real outdoor dog, which likes to run free whenever possible. However, it also relishes its place by the fireside, so it should not be kept kennelled.

Health care
Although a hardy, healthy dog in adulthood, it can prove delicate as a pup, and this Spitz type is not the easiest to breed.

Grooming
Normal daily brushing.

Above: The lively Finnish Spitz makes an attractive guard dog.

Feeding
Recommended would be 1-1½ cans (376g, 13.3oz size) of a branded meaty product, with biscuit added in equal part by volume; or 3 cupfuls of a dry food, complete diet, mixed in the proportion of 1 cup of feed to ½ cup of hot or cold water.

Origin and history
Known for centuries in its own country prior to official recognition when the Finnish Kennel Club gained acceptance by the FCI. It originates from the Eastern zone of Finland and is mentioned in the country's epic the *Kalevala*.

Called the 'Finkie' by Lady Kitty Ritson, who pioneered the breed in Britain in the 1920s, it is related to the Russian Laika breed, a member of which was to orbit the Earth in an early space flight. It is a descendant of the earliest hunter dogs of Lapland and Scandinavia. 31▸

HUNGARIAN PULI (Puli; Hungarian Water Dog)

Good points
- *Easily trained*
- *Fine guard*
- *Highly intelligent*
- *Loyal*
- *Healthy*
- *Weather-resistant coat*
- *Adaptable*

Take heed
- *Tends to be a one-person dog*

The Hungarian Puli is a loyal, obedient dog, and perhaps the best-known of the Hungarian sheepdogs outside its homeland. It is easily distinguishable by its long, dark, corded coat, which is not so difficult to groom as might be believed.

Size
Height: dog 40.5-46cm (16-18in); bitch 35.5-40.5cm (14-16in).
Weight: dog 13.1-15kg (29-33lb); bitch 10-13.1kg (22-29lb).

Exercise
Plenty of exercise is preferable, but this adaptable dog will fit in with city life, as long as it is at its owner's side.

Grooming
The coat hangs in long black cords, which in the adult dog reach to the ground, giving a tousled, unkempt look. The cords have to be separated by hand and regularly brushed and combed. Cleanliness is essential.

Feeding
One to 1½ cans (376g, 13.3oz size) of a branded meaty product, with biscuit added in equal part by volume; or 3 cupfuls of a dry food, complete diet, mixed in the proportion of 1 cup of feed to ½ cup of hot or cold water.

Origin and history
The Puli is better known than other Hungarian sheepdogs, such as the Pumi, the Komondor and the Kuvasz, probably because in its native land it directs the flock by jumping on or over the sheeps' backs. It is said to have existed for 1000 years, being a descendant of the sheepdogs brought to Hungary by the Magyars. It has proved itself as a fine water retriever, and has done well in obedience and police work. Hungarian shepherds favour their dark colour, which is easily picked out among the flock. 31▸

Below: The distinctive Hungarian Puli will make a loyal companion.

STAFFORDSHIRE BULL TERRIER

Good points
- *Excellent guard*
- *Fearless*
- *First-class ratter*
- *Good with children*
- *Very friendly to people*

Take heed
- *Needs discipline in youth*
- *Stubborn*
- *Liable to fight with dogs*

The Staffordshire Bull Terrier is a sound breed and excellent family dog derived from the crossing of a Bulldog with a terrier breed sometime in the 1800s. Probably the partner of the Old English Bulldog in this match was the Old English Black and Tan Terrier, which preceded the Manchester Terrier. It is, of course, an English breed, recognized by the British Kennel Club in 1935.

The Staffordshire Bull Terrier, in common with its close relation, the Bull Terrier, is a surprisingly gentle dog beneath a somewhat fearsome exterior. It is a good guard dog but adores its family and is utterly reliable with young children.

Size
Weight: dog 12.7-17.2kg (28-38lb); bitch 11-15.4kg (24-34lb). Height (at shoulder): 35.5-40.5cm (14-16in).

Exercise
The Staffordshire Bull Terrier can't resist a fight with another dog if given the chance, so keep this breed on the lead when walking on a public thoroughfare. It is a first-class ratter and a good companion in the field but will adapt to life in a normal-sized house and garden as long as regular walks are given.

Grooming
This breed requires little attention other than a good daily brushing.

Feeding
Recommended would be 1-1½ cans per day of a branded meaty

Above: The Staffordshire Bull Terrier is gentle with children.

product (376g, 13.3oz size), with biscuit added in equal part by volume; or 3 cupfuls of a dry, complete food mixed in the proportion of 1 cup of feed to ½ cup of hot or cold water.

Origin and history
The Staffordshire Bull Terrier has a bloody history, for it was evolved for the purpose of the once popular sport of bull and bear baiting, and later for dog fighting. Fortunately, however, with the banning of these sports the Staffordshire was developed as a companion dog and in the mid-1930s it was recognized by the Kennel Club as a pure breed, the standard being drawn up and a Breed Club formed in Cradley Heath, South Staffordshire. 30▸

AMERICAN STAFFORDSHIRE TERRIER

Good points
- *Affectionate*
- *Loyal to owner*
- *Excellent guard*
- *Fearless*
- *Skilful ratter*
- *Good with children*

Take heed
- *Needs discipline in youth*
- *Stubborn*

The American Staffordshire Terrier is not to be confused with the English Staffordshire Bull Terrier, which is a lighter dog with smaller bones. At one time the American Kennel Club was allowing the American Staffordshire Terrier to be shown with the Staffordshire Bull and, indeed, crossbreeding of the two was allowed. However, although the American Staffordshire's ancestry does originate in England, it has evolved as a quite independent breed.

The Breed Standard states: 'Should give the impression of great strength for his size, a well put-together dog, muscular, but agile and graceful.'

Size
Height and weight should be in proportion. A height of about 46-48cm (18-19in) at shoulders for the male and 43-46cm (17-18in) for the female.

Exercise
Appreciates plenty of exercise, but will adapt to town living if given long regular walks.

Grooming
This breed requires little attention other than a good daily brushing.

Feeding
Recommended would be 1-1½ cans per day of a branded meaty product (376g, 13.3oz size), with biscuit added in equal part by volume; or 3 cupfuls of a dry, complete food mixed in the proportion of 1 cup of feed to ½ cup of hot or cold water.

Above: With cropped ears, the American Staffordshire Terrier looks forbidding, but it makes a devoted pet as well as a fearless guard.

Origin and history
The American Staffordshire Terrier is of British origin derived from the traditional English Bulldog and an English terrier. The result was the Staffordshire Terrier, also known as the Pit Bull Terrier and later the Staffordshire Bull Terrier. Once it found its way to the United States, in 1870, it became known variously as a Pit Dog, Yankee Terrier and American Bull Terrier. The breed was recognized by the American Kennel Club in 1935 under the name of Staffordshire Terrier, which was revised on January 1, 1972, to American Staffordshire Terrier. 30▸

BULL TERRIER

Good points

- *Affectionate*
- *Excellent with children*
- *First-class guard*
- *Hardy*

Take heed

- *Best suited to country life*
- *Needs disciplining when young*
- *Powerful dog: you must be strong enough to hold lead!*

The Bull Terrier, despite its somewhat fierce appearance, is a gentle dog and utterly reliable with children, especially the bitch, which will literally let them climb all over her. However, if provoked by another dog, this terrier will happily fight to the death. The Bull Terrier never lets go! It is also a fine guard. It may let an intruder into your house, but one thing is certain: it won't let him out again!

Size

The standard has no height or weight limits: the Bull Terrier could be 31.75kg (70lb) or half that.

Exercise

The Bull Terrier is a powerful dog, with boundless energy, and should not be confined to apartment life, with a run in the back garden. More suitable would be a happily controlled country life with plenty of opportunity to run free.

Grooming

Normal daily brushing.

Feeding

If the dog is 9-22.7kg (20-50lb) give it 1-1½ cans (376g, 13.3oz size) of a branded meaty product, with biscuit added in equal part by volume; or 3 cupfuls of a dry food, complete diet, mixed in the proportion of 1 cup of feed to ½ cup of hot or cold water.

If it is 22.7-45.4kg (50-100lb) in weight, give 1½-2½ cans (376g, 13.3oz size) of a branded meaty product, with biscuit added in equal part by volume; or 5 cupfuls of a dry food, complete diet, mixed in the proportion of 1 cup of feed to ½ cup of hot or cold water.

Health care

The Bull Terrier is a healthy dog. However, don't buy a white one without first checking that it can hear properly; white Bull Terriers are often born deaf.

Origin and history

This terrier began life as a fighting dog and battled on, seemingly impervious to pain, until bull baiting was outlawed by the British Parliament in 1835. Thereafter a dedicated band of fanciers determined to preserve the breed and refine it while preserving its strength and tenacity. They included James Hinks of Birmingham, England, who, by crossing the White English Terrier with the Bulldog and Dalmatian, produced a new strain of white dogs he called English Bull Terriers. Following the Second World War, coloured Bull Terriers made their appearance. However, the breed as a whole has never regained the tremendous popularity it enjoyed in the 1940s as companion and friend. Perhaps this is all to the good, as there are today few except first-class breeders producing sound, attractive stock, though a criticism has been that some animals are too whippety. 30▸

The Miniature Bull Terrier is a replica of its big brother the Bull Terrier in all respects except size. Height should not be more than 35.5cm (14in). Weight should be not more than 9kg (20lb). 28▸

STANDARD SCHNAUZER

Good points
- *Affectionate*
- *Lively and playful*
- *Good with children*
- *Intelligent*
- *Strong and healthy*
- *Excellent watchdog*

Take heed
- *Mistrustful of strangers*
- *Coat needs attention*

The Schnauzer is a good-natured, lively dog that loves both children and games. However, it does not trust strangers. It is terrier-like – thus a great ratter, intelligent and an excellent guard.

Size
Ideal height: bitch 46cm (18in); dog 48cm (19in). Any variation of more than 2.5cm (1in) in these heights should be penalized.

Exercise
Enjoys regular walks and ball games, but will adapt to country or apartment living.

Grooming
The Schnauzer should be brushed every day, and trimmed in spring and autumn.

Feeding
Recommended 1-1½ cans of a branded, meaty product (376g, 13.3oz size), with biscuit added in equal part by volume; or 3 cupfuls, of a dry, complete food, mixed in the proportion of 1 cup of feed to ½ cup of hot or cold water.

Origin and history
As the name implies, the Schnauzer is of German origin, and there is a statue in Stuttgart, dated 1620, depicting a watchman with a dog similar in appearance to the Schnauzer of today.

The breed originated in Bavaria and Württemberg where it was esteemed as a ratter and a cattle driver. However, when cattle driving died out, the breed found its way to the city, where it gained popularity, coming to the attention of serious fanciers about 1900.

Schnauzers were first imported into America in 1905. The Schnauzer Club of America, formed in 1925, allows both the cropped and natural ear to be shown. 32▸

MEDIUM PINSCHER
(German Pinscher)

Good points
- *Alert guard*
- *Elegant appearance*
- *Lively pet*
- *Loyal to owner*

Take heed
- *Aggressive to strangers*
- *Fiery temperament*

The Medium Pinscher, previously known as the German Pinscher, is a very old breed, yet it is virtually unknown outside its homeland. This, the middle-sized of the Pinschers, bears far more similarity to the Dobermann than to the Miniature Pinscher and, like the Dobermann, has its ears cropped in its native country. The tail is docked and the coat is smooth and glossy. Colour usually black with small tan markings or self red. There is also a most attractive and distinctive harlequin Pinscher.

The Medium Pinscher was bred as a ratter, but nowadays is mainly kept as an alert, lively pet. Height is 40.5-48cm (16-19in). 32▸

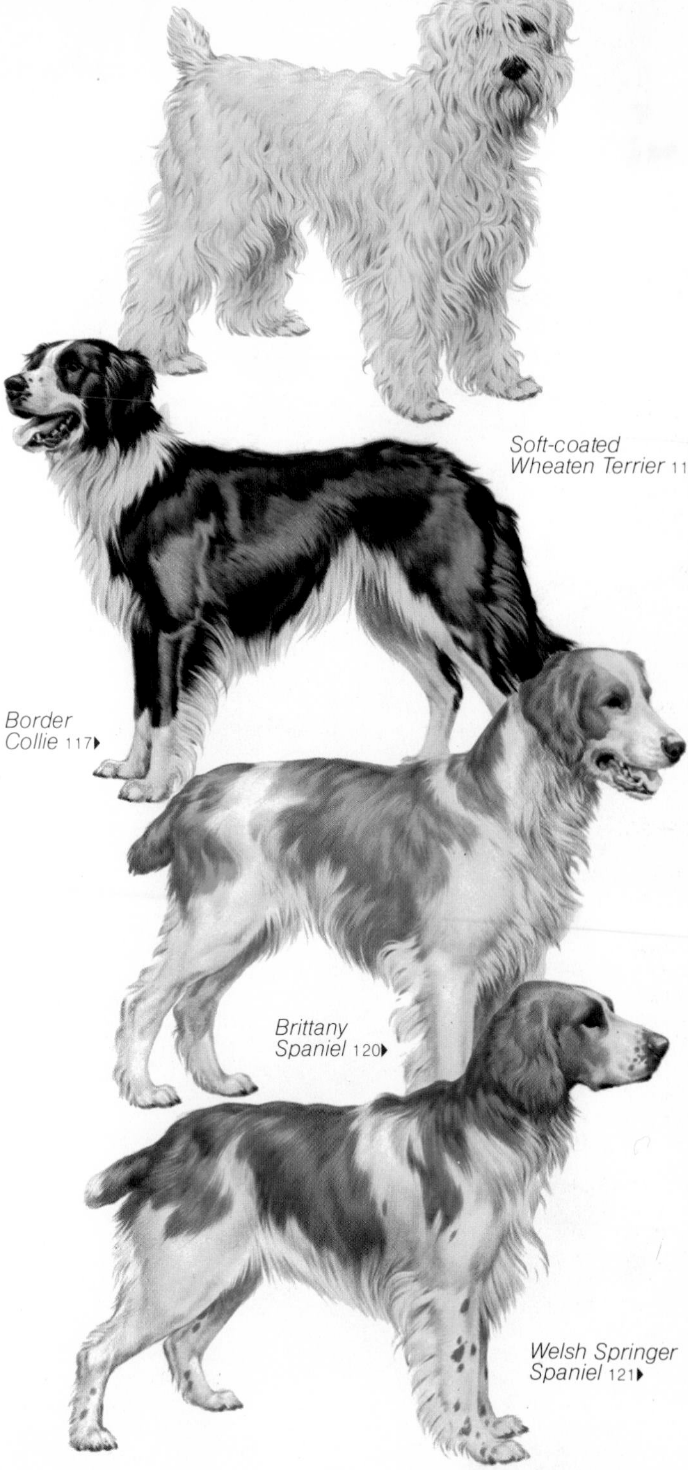

Soft-coated Wheaten Terrier 116▸

Border Collie 117▸

Brittany Spaniel 120▸

Welsh Springer Spaniel 121▸

Bruno de Jura (Swiss Hunting Dog) 125▸

Lucernese (Swiss Hunting Dog) 125▸

Schweizer Laufhund (Swiss Hunting Dog) 125▸

Basset Hound 123▸

Basset Griffon Vendéen 124▸

Basset Artésien Normand 124▸

Lappish Vallhund 130▸
Lapphund 128▸
Iceland Dog 129▸
Norwegian Buhund 126▸
Keeshond 127▸

Field Spaniel 131▸

Sussex Spaniel 133▸

Portuguese Warren Hound (Medio) 134▸

Portuguese Water Dog (Long-coated variety) 135▸

Canaan Dog 136▸

Pointing Wire-haired Griffon 137▸

Shar-Pei 138▸

Bulldog 140▸

Samoyed 142▸
Siberian Husky 141▸
Standard Poodle 143▸
Irish Water Spaniel 145▸
American Water Spaniel 119▸

Elkhound 146▸
Karelian Bear Dog 148▸
Swedish Elkhound 147▸
Beauceron 149▸
English Springer Spaniel 144▸
Clumber Spaniel 150▸

Smalands Hound 155▸
Hygen Hound 157▸
Schiller Hound 156▸
Finnish Hound 156▸
Halden Hound 157▸
Dunker Hound 155▸
English Foxhound 153▸
American Foxhound 154▸
Harrier 151▸

Ibizan Hound 161▸
Pharaoh Hound 160▸
Large Munsterlander 158▸
Drentse Partridge Dog 159▸

Greyhound 166▸

Sloughi 163▸

Saluki 162▸

Afghan Hound 164▸

Airedale 167▸
Dobermann 168▸
Bearded Collie 170▸
Smooth Collie 171▸
Rough Collie 172▸

German
Long-haired Pointer 173▸
German
Wire-haired
Pointer 174▸
German
Short-haired
Pointer 175▸
Pointer 176▸
Irish Setter 185▸
English
Setter 186▸
Gordon
Setter 187▸

German Shepherd Dog 190▸

Belgian
Shepherd Dog
(Groenendael) 188▸

Golden Retriever 196▸

Labrador
Retriever 197▸

Weimaraner 193▸
Dalmatian 192▸
Boxer 194▸
Belgian Shepherd Dog (Malinois) 188▸
Belgian Shepherd Dog (Laekenois) 188▸
Belgian Shepherd Dog (Tervueren) 188▸

Curly-coated Retriever 200▸

Chesapeake Bay Retriever 199▸

Flat-coated Retriever 198▸

Eskimo Dog 206▸

Alaskan Malamute 205▸

Otterhound 207▸
Italian Spinone 208▸
Japanese Akita 204▸
Chow Chow 195▸

WHIPPET

Good points
- *Clean*
- *Elegant*
- *Gentle and affectionate*
- *Good with children*
- *Fine show dog*
- *Excellent watchdog*

Take heed
- *Strong hunting instincts*
- *Needs plenty of exercise*

The Whippet is an excellent choice for those who want a dog that will combine the role of an affectionate and gentle pet with performance on the track and/or in the show ring. It has a peaceful temperament, but can be a little nervous in strange surroundings.

Size
The ideal height for dogs is 47cm (18½in) and for bitches 44.5cm (17½in). Judges should use their discretion and not unduly penalize an otherwise good specimen.

Exercise
The Whippet is a racer, capable of 56-64km (35-40 miles) an hour. It will adapt to life away from the excitement of a track, but make sure that you can give it plenty of vigorous exercise.

Below: Whippets make fine pets; they are clean, elegant and sporty.

Grooming
Generally, the Whippet needs little grooming, but the tail usually needs tidying up for a show. Teeth should be scaled regularly and the nails will need clipping.

Health care
Whippets are hardy, despite their delicate appearance, but should sleep indoors and be kept out of draughts.

Feeding
Recommended would be ½-1 can (376g, 13.3oz size) of a branded meaty product, with biscuit added in equal part by volume; or 1½ cupfuls of a dry food, complete diet, mixed in the proportion of 1 cup of feed to ½ cup of hot or cold water.

Origin and history
The Greyhound obviously had a hand in the Whippet's make-up, but there is some controversy as to whether the cross was with a terrier, a Pharaoh Hound or some other imported hound. The breed has been popular in Britain since the beginning of the century, and was exhibited at Crufts as early as 1897, being recognized by the British Kennel Club five years later. The Whippet is also popular in America, where the standard allows for a slightly larger dog. It was designed for racing and coursing, in which it excels. Many Whippet owners derive immense pleasure from keeping a dog that not only satisfies their sporting interests, but is also a popular show contender and a gentle, affectionate household pet. 32▸

AUSTRALIAN KELPIE / CATTLE DOG

Good points
- *Brave*
- *Equable temperament*
- *Excellent working dogs*
- *Good companions*
- *Loyal*
- *Full of stamina*
- *Intelligent*

Take heed
- *Need plenty of exercise*

The Australian Kelpie is a superb sheepdog descended from working imported Scottish stock. It is famed for the way it runs along the backs of sheep to reach the head of the flock. It is extremely fast and has an almost camel-like ability to go without water for lengthy periods. It is an attractive prick-eared dog with great intelligence and loyalty to its master.

The Australian Cattle Dog is an intelligent dog, amenable and first-rate at its job of driving cattle, sometimes covering vast distances. Like the Kelpie, it has an equable temperament and makes a loyal companion. Both these breeds are seen in the show ring in Australia.

Size
Kelpie. Weight: 13.6kg (30lb). Height: 46-51cm (18-20in) at the shoulder.
Cattle dog. Weight: 15.9kg (35lb). Height: 51cm (20in) at shoulder.

Exercise
The Australian Kelpie and the Australian Cattle Dog are accustomed to plenty of exercise.

Grooming
These breeds will benefit from regular vigorous brushing.

Feeding
One to 1½ cans (376g, 13.3oz size) of a branded meaty product, with biscuit added in equal part by volume; or 3 cupfuls of a dry food, complete diet, mixed in the proportion of 1 cup of feed to ½ cup of hot or cold water.

Above: An Australian Cattle Dog puppy in typically alert pose.

Origin and history
The Kelpie derives from Collies brought to Australia by early settlers. Its ancestry can be traced to a pup named Caesar, later mated to a bitch named Kelpie, whose offspring included the famous King's Kelpie, winner of the first ever sheepdog trials in Australia in 1872. The Scottish writer Robert Louis Stevenson refers to the 'Water Kelpie' in his famous adventure story *Kidnapped,* giving credence to the suggestion that Kelpies derived from the working Scottish Collie.

The Australian Cattle Dog has emerged from crossings with the Old English Sheepdog (or Bobtail), Scottish Collies, Dingoes and Red Bobtails. 32▸

KERRY BLUE TERRIER (Irish Blue Terrier)

Good points

- *First-class guard*
- *Good sporting dog, but mainly kept as a pet*
- *Excellent with children*
- *Easy to train*
- *Coat does not shed*

Take heed

- *Loves a scrap, and not averse to starting one*

The Kerry Blue Terrier loves children and makes an ideal house pet. It does, however, have a fine Irish temper when aroused, and needs firm but gentle training when young if you don't want to be plagued with other folks' veterinary expenses.

Size

Weight: 15-16.8kg (33-37lb); greater tolerance in America.

Exercise

Bred as a working dog, it needs and deserves plenty of exercise.

Grooming

Daily brushing with a stiff brush and metal comb. You can easily learn to scissor trim the pet yourself. If you plan to show, however, there is a lot of work involved in show preparation.

Feeding

One to 1½ cans (376g, 13.3oz size) of a branded meaty product, with biscuit added in equal part by volume; or 3 cupfuls of a dry food, complete diet, mixed in the proportion of 1 cup of feed to ½ cup of hot or cold water.

Origin and history

The Kerry Blue originates from the county of Kerry in south-western Ireland. The Irish Terrier had a hand in its make-up, to which the Bedlington Terrier and Bull Terrier are also said to have contributed.

The Kerry started life as a hunter of badgers and foxes, and has also done its share of otter hunting, being a keen, strong swimmer. It has guarded livestock and saw Army service during World War II. Now, however, it is predominantly kept as a popular pet and show dog. A Kerry Blue Terrier, Champion Callaghan of Leander, won the Best in Show award at Crufts in 1979. 32▸

Below: Properly trimmed, the Kerry Blue Terrier is a champion show dog.

SOFT-COATED WHEATEN TERRIER

Good points
- *Hardy*
- *Not finicky about food*
- *Intelligent*
- *Excellent guard*
- *Gentle with children*
- *Devoted to owner*

Take heed
- *A family dog, not suited to outdoor kennels*

The Soft-coated Wheaten Terrier is an exceptionally intelligent, medium-sized dog, which is defensive without being aggressive. It is an excellent house guard, but gentle with children. The Wheaten has strong sporting instincts, and some have been trained, with success, for the gun.

Size
Weight: dog approximately 15.9-20.5kg (35-45lb).
Height: dog approximately 46-49.5cm (18-19½in) measured at the withers; bitch slightly less.

Exercise
The Wheaten will relish plenty of exercise. It has excelled in the past as a hunter of rats, rabbits, otters and badgers, and will work any kind of covert, its soft coat being ample protection against the densest undergrowth.

Grooming
The Wheaten's coat does not shed. Daily combing should start from puppyhood, as regular grooming will keep the coat clean and tangle-free.

Fuzziness, not natural to the breed, can be aggravated by the use of a wire or plastic brush, and a medium-toothed metal comb should be used instead.

Bathing should be carried out as necessary; if showing, bathing the dog about three days before the event is recommended to avoid a fly-away appearance.

Ears, tail and feet need to be tidied, also any long, straggly hairs underneath the body.

Feeding
About 1-1½ cans (376g, 13.3oz size) of a branded meaty product with biscuit added in equal part by volume, or 3 cupfuls of a complete dry food, mixed in the proportion of 1 cup of feed to ½ cup of hot or cold water. Meat scraps and non-splintery bones are acceptable.

Origin and history
The origin of the Soft-coated Wheaten, like that of so many breeds, has been lost in the mists of antiquity. However, from old pictures and records, the breed has been traced back at least 200 years in Ireland, where for many generations there was hardly a farm or smallholding that did not boast an attendant Wheaten that was valued for its sterling qualities.

It is recorded that the Soft-coated Wheaten Terrier is the oldest Irish breed of terrier, said to be the progenitor of the Kerry Blue and Irish Terrier. Legend tells us that a blue dog swam ashore from a ship wrecked in Tralee Bay about 180 years ago. This dog mated the native Wheaten and from this originated the Kerry Blue. Wheaten-coloured pups have appeared in Kerry Blue litters from time to time. There is no record of cross-breeding in the Wheaten and it appears today to be much as it always has been.

The breed was recognized by the Irish Kennel Club in 1937 and first registered in Britain in 1971. Although reaching America in 1946, the breed was not given show classification until 1973. 97▸

BORDER COLLIE

Good points

- *Intelligent*
- *Loyal*
- *Ideal choice for obedience competitions*
- *Good family or working dog*

Take heed

- *This breed will herd anything, people included, if sheep and cattle are not available*

The Border Collie is a first-class, everyday working dog, famed for herding cattle and rounding up sheep. This is the star of sheepdog trials, the persistent winner of obedience competitions, the breed favoured by those who want a 'working' dog.

The Border Collie (the name refers to the English-Scottish border) was bred for speed, stamina and brains. It makes a first-class companion, is good with children, and is one of the most trainable dogs.

Size

Dog about 53cm (21in); bitch slightly less.

Exercise

This is essentially a working dog that enjoys being out of doors, whether trotting at its master's heels on a routine walk, doing exercises at a dog training class, or working on a farm. It will adapt to whatever role you have for it, but is not ideally suited to town life.

Grooming

Brush regularly with a good pony dandy brush and comb. Inspect the ears for signs of canker, and the ears and feet for foreign matter. Dead fur should be removed when grooming.

Feeding

About 1-1½ cans (376g, 13.3oz size) of a branded meaty product with biscuit added in equal part by volume, or 3 cupfuls of a complete dry food, mixed in the proportion of 1 cup of feed to ½ cup of hot or cold water. Meat scraps and non-splintery bones are acceptable.

Above: The keen expression of a Border Collie eager for work.

Origin and history

The present-day Border Collie is a modern strain descended from Collies of the Lowland and Border counties of England and Scotland. They are working sheepdogs of a distinct, recognizable type, which have been exported to many countries of the world where sheep are farmed, and they are also excellent as guide dogs for the blind.

It was not until July 1976 that a standard for the breed was approved by the British Kennel Club from a combination of several proposed standards submitted to them by interested bodies, including the recognized one from the Australian KC. 97▸

STABYHOUN

Good points
- *Affectionate*
- *Easily trained*
- *Excellent guard dog*
- *Fine all-purpose sporting dog*
- *Hardy*
- *Has great stamina*
- *Good with children*

Take heed
- *No drawbacks known*

The Stabyhoun is one of the most popular dogs in its native Holland, but is little known elsewhere.

This is an excellent all-purpose sporting dog, nowadays kept mainly as a companion house dog. It is reliable with children, has an affectionate nature, is easily trained, and has an equable temperament. It is a splendid retriever, with a good nose.

Size
Dog up to 49.5cm (19½in) at the withers, bitch somewhat smaller.

Exercise
The Stabyhoun excels at working in the field as a retriever, doing the job for which it was bred. It adapts well to town life as long as it has ample opportunity to run free.

Below: The sturdy Stabyhoun is a popular retriever in Holland.

Grooming
Regular brushing will keep the coat in good condition.

Feeding
About 1-1½ cans (376g, 13.3oz size) of a branded meaty product with biscuit added in equal part by volume, or 3 cupfuls of a complete dry food, mixed in the proportion of 1 cup of feed to ½ cup of hot or cold water. Meat scraps and non-splintery bones are acceptable.

Origin and history
The Stabyhoun was recognized by the Dutch Kennel Club in 1942, but it has existed in the Netherlands since as long ago as 1800, when it was bred in the Friesland district as an all-purpose gundog, but primarily as a dispeller of vermin. Crossed with the Wetterhoun it made a formidable ratter!

AMERICAN WATER SPANIEL

Good points
- *Equable temperament*
- *Excellent working dog*
- *Hardy*
- *Strong swimmer*
- *Easy to train*
- *Efficient watchdog*
- *Adapts to family life*

Take heed
- *No drawbacks known*

The American Water Spaniel is little known outside its country of origin, where it has found great favour as a working gundog. It is a strong swimmer, an excellent water-fowler and retriever.

Size
Height: 38-46cm (15-18in). Weight: dog 12.7-20.5kg (28-45lb); bitch, 11.3-18.1kg (25-40lb).

Exercise
Needs plenty of exercise.

Grooming
Daily brushing and weekly combing. Seek advice on stripping of unwanted hair. Take care to clear mud caked in the toes.

Feeding
One to 1½ cans (376g, 13.3oz size) of a branded meaty product, with biscuit added in equal part by volume; or 3 cupfuls of a dry food, complete diet, mixed in the proportion of 1 cup of feed to ½ cup of hot or cold water.

Origin and history
The American Water Spaniel is believed to have originated through the crossing of an Irish Water Spaniel with a smaller spaniel breed and/or with a Curly-coated Retriever.

In some parts of America it is still known as the Boykin Spaniel, after Whit Boykin, one of the pioneers of the breed in Boykin, South Carolina. It was recognized by the American Kennel Club in 1940, but, at the time of writing, has still to be recognized in the United Kingdom. 102▸

Below: The American Water Spaniel, an eager and accomplished worker.

BRITTANY SPANIEL

Good points
- *Affectionate*
- *Intelligent*
- *Excellent pointer*
- *Good nose*
- *Tireless*
- *Loyal*

Take heed
- *A devoted, sensitive dog that needs kind handling*

The Brittany Spaniel combines well the roles of hunter and companion. It has a natural talent for pointing and has been described as more like a setter than a spaniel. It has an excellent nose, and can cope with difficult terrain. It is, however, a sensitive animal that expects, and deserves, every consideration from its master. It is easily distinguishable by its short, stumpy tail. This breed is relatively unknown in the United Kingdom, but has been successful in Field Trials in the USA.

Size
Height: maximum 52cm (20½in), minimum 46.5cm (18¼in); ideal for dog 49-51cm (19¼-20in), for bitch 47.5-50cm (18¾-19¾in).

Exercise
Relishes plenty of exercise.

Grooming
Daily brushing. Take care that ears, eyes and paws are clean.

Feeding
One to 1½ cans (376g, 13.3oz size) of a branded meaty product, with biscuit added in equal part by volume; or 3 cupfuls of a dry food, complete diet, mixed in the proportion of 1 cup of feed to ½ cup of hot or cold water.

Origin and history
The Brittany probably originated either in Spain or in the Argoat Forests of Brittany. There is also a story that one of the red and white English Setters of a Breton count mated with a Breton bitch, thus starting the Brittany Spaniel. 97▸

Below: the Brittany Spaniel, a fine pointer and companion.

WELSH SPRINGER SPANIEL

Good points

- *Loyal*
- *Willing*
- *Fine gundog*
- *Excellent nose*
- *Good water dog*
- *Makes a good pet*

Take heed

- *Needs training or could become a destructive hunter*

The Welsh Springer Spaniel is a lively dog with plenty of enthusiasm and endurance. It is somewhere between the little Cocker Spaniel and the English Springer in stature. It is a tireless breed, and, in common with most spaniels, provided it is given plenty of exercise and correct feeding it will live to a ripe old age.

The Breed Standard states: 'A symmetrical, compact, strong, merry very active dog; not stilty (i.e. stiff in appearance); obviously built for endurance and hard work. A quick and active mover displaying plenty of push and drive.'

Size
Dog up to 48cm (19in) in height at shoulder, and bitch 46cm (18in) approximately.

Exercise
Like most spaniels the Welsh Springer is essentially a working animal and is not ideally suited for apartment life or for those with insufficient time to take it for lengthy walks.

Grooming
Similar care to other spaniels, with regular brushing and combing to maintain smartness.

Feeding
Recommended would be 1-1½ cans (376g, 13.3oz size) of a branded meaty product, with biscuit added in equal part by volume; or 3 cupfuls of a dry, complete diet mixed in the proportion of 1 cup of feed to ½ cup of hot or cold water.

Origin and history
A dog that would seem to be a forerunner of the Welsh Springer Spaniel is mentioned in the earliest records of the Laws of Wales, circa AD 1300, and indeed it appears that even before that time a similar white spaniel with red markings had been associated with the region. The Welsh Springer Spaniel is, in fact, very similar to the Brittany Spaniel, and makes a first-class gundog and household pet. 97▸

Below: The hard-working and very willing Welsh Springer Spaniel.

WETTERHOUN (Dutch Water Spaniel)

Good points
- *Excellent watchdog*
- *Fearless*
- *Hardworking*
- *Impervious to weather conditions*
- *Intelligent*

Take heed
- *Somewhat aggressive – needs firm handling*

The Wetterhoun, or Dutch Water Spaniel, was registered in Holland in 1942. However, it was known for many years before that, although then, as now, almost exclusively in Holland. It is an intelligent and fearless hunter, and is now often kept as a household companion. However, its somewhat aggressive nature, inherited from years of hunting, makes firm early training necessary.

Size
Height at withers: dog about 54.5cm (21½in); bitch should be slightly smaller.

Exercise
Needs plenty of exercise.

Grooming
Regular brushing will be sufficient.

Feeding
One to 1½ cans (376g, 13.3oz size) of a branded meaty product, with biscuit added in equal part by volume; or 3 cupfuls of a dry food, complete diet, mixed in the proportion of 1 cup of feed to ½ cup of hot or cold water.

Origin and history
Bred from dogs used for otter hunting, the Wetterhoun has evolved as a strong and fearless hunter, much prized as a guard dog. It has in the past been crossed with the Stabyhoun, but is a larger, sturdier dog.

Below: The Wetterhoun is a popular guard and farm dog in its native Holland; its dense curly coat is impervious to bad weather. It is also kept as a household companion.

BASSET HOUND

Good points
- *Distinctive appearance*
- *Equable temperament*
- *Good with children*
- *Ideal family pet*
- *Successful show dog*

Take heed
- *Needs lots of exercise*
- *Likes to wander*
- *Has a will of its own!*

The Basset Hound is an affable dog that gets on with most people and makes the ideal family pet. It does, however, retain strong hound instincts and will wander miles if a gate is left conveniently open. Basset owners are always telling folk about their Basset's roamings, often quite far afield, but it is up to them to see that their properties are adequately fenced. Like the Beagle, the Basset has a mind of its own; it is eminently lovable, but not always obedient.

Size
Height: 33-38cm (13-15in).

Exercise
Most important. If you can't give a Basset Hound plenty of exercise, don't have one.

Grooming
Daily brushing and combing. Pay attention to ears and toe-nails.

Feeding
One to 1½ cans (376g, 13.3oz size) of a branded meaty product, with biscuit added in equal part by volume; or 3 cupfuls of a dry food, complete diet, mixed in the proportion of 1 cup of feed to ½ cup of hot or cold water. Careful feeding in puppyhood is advocated for this fast-growing breed.

Health care
Choose the specimen with the straightest limbs, even if those knobbly knees seem attractive.

Origin and history
The Basset Hound is of French origin, being derived from the French Basset Artésien Normand, which was imported to England and crossed with the Bloodhound. It is a slow but sure tracker, still used in Britain to hunt hare. Primarily, however, it is kept as a popular household pet. French sources maintain that the first Bassets appeared in a litter of normal long-legged hounds, and that in breeding from these the Basset (which means 'dwarf') Hound appeared. 98▸

Above: The friendly Basset Hound is renowned for its appealing but definitely soulful expression.

BASSET GRIFFON VENDEEN

Good points
- *Excellent family pet*
- *Friendly*
- *Likes human company*
- *Voice will deter unwelcome callers*

Take heed
- *Needs plenty of exercise*
- *Not suitable for apartments or tiny gardens*

The Basset Griffon Vendéen (Petit) is an ancient French hunting breed. As its name implies, it is a short-legged (basset) rough-coated (griffon) hound, originating in the district of Vendée, and is one of the four breeds of Basset Hounds found in France, the others being the Basset Artésien Normand, the Basset Bleu de Gascogne, and the Basset Fauve de Bretagne.

The Basset Griffon Vendéen (Petit) is a cheerful, active, busy little hound, intelligent and inquisitive. Its friendly nature and liking for human companionship make it an excellent family pet, and its deep resonant voice is a deterrent to unwelcome callers.

Size
Height: 34-38cm (13½-15in). A tolerance of 1cm (²⁄₅in) is allowed.

Exercise
The Basset Griffon Vendéen (Petit) is an active, energetic breed needing plenty of exercise, and is not recommended for life in small apartments or houses with tiny gardens unless great care, time and trouble can be given to its needs and well-being.

Grooming
Its rough coat needs little attention.

Feeding
Recommended would be ½-1 can (376g, 13.3oz size) of a branded, meaty product, with biscuit added in equal part by volume; or 1½ cupfuls of a dry food, complete diet, mixed in the proportion of 1 cup of feed to ½ cup of hot or cold water.

Origin and history
The Griffon Vendéen (Petit) [to quote Monsieur P. Doubigne, an expert on the breed] is a miniature Basset reduced in size and proportions, while retaining all the qualities of the breed: the passion for hunting, fearlessness in the densest coverts, activity and vigour. It was bred down from a larger variety, the Basset Griffon Vendéen (Grand), which was originally used for wolf hunting and is now used, in France, for hunting wild boar. 98▸

BASSET ARTESIEN NORMAND

The Basset Artésien Normand is virtually identical to the Basset Hound and has the same feeding and grooming requirements and general characteristics. It is of ancient French origin, descended from the old French Bloodhound and the St Hubert Hound.

This breed found favour as a hunting dog in France, but was adopted by the British, who crossed it with the Bloodhound to develop the Basset Hound.

The breed stands 25-33cm (10-13in) high. Colours are white or white and orange. A tricoloured dog must be widely marked, with tan on the head and a mantle of specks of black or badger colour. 98▸

SWISS HUNTING DOGS (Schweizer Laufhund, Bruno de Jura, Lucernese, Bernese)

Good points

- *Active*
- *Friendly*
- *First-rate hunting dogs*

Take heed

- *Not really suitable as household companions because of their lively disposition and hunting instincts*

Schweizer Laufhund

There are some four varieties of the Swiss Hunting Dog (not to be confused with smaller types), all of which, with the exception of the Jura, have the same standard in their country of origin. They are friendly, active and powerfully built. They predominantly hunt hare and are speedy and excellent trackers with a good nose. Their lively disposition and strong hunting instincts do not equip them for the role of household companion.

Size

Minimum height: 44.5cm (17½in) all types, but varies considerably.

Exercise

Need plenty of vigorous exercise for full fitness.

Grooming

Regular brushing.

Feeding

One to 1½ cans (376g, 13.3oz size) of a branded meaty product, with biscuit added in equal part by volume; or 3 cupfuls of a dry food, complete diet, mixed in the proportion of 1 cup of feed to ½ cup of hot or cold water. This should be increased when the hound is in hard exercise.

Origin and history

The Swiss Hound, particularly the Laufhund, is a breed previously little known, but now gaining recognition internationally. To trace the origin of the Swiss Hounds we must go back to the pre-Christian era, when similar hunting dogs were introduced into

Above: A powerfully built Bernese Swiss Hound, one of the four types of Swiss Hunting Dogs. All are excellent hunters, with a keen sense of smell and a lively enthusiasm for the hunt.

Egypt by the Phoenicians and the Greeks, eventually finding their way to Switzerland when it was under Roman rule. The antiquity of the breed is verified by illustrations made during the 12th century, which can be seen in Zurich Cathedral. The heaviest of the four is the Jura, which is of the St Hubert type and similar to the French Ardennes Hound. When it gets the scent, it will brief with a drawn-out note that can be heard for many miles around: in fact it is rather like the English Bloodhound. The Bruno type of Jura is about the same size but appears sleeker and faster. 98▸

NORWEGIAN BUHUND (Norsk Buhund)

Good points
- *Alert and active*
- *Intelligent*
- *Full of stamina*
- *Friendly*
- *Gentle with children*
- *Good guard*

Take heed
- *Natural herder*
- *Needs plenty of exercise*

The Norwegian Buhund is a lively and alert dog, but a natural herder that will, like the Border Collie, round up anything, be it poultry, cattle or people. It needs lots of exercise and makes the ideal playmate for children.

Size
Dog not more than 45cm (17¾in); bitch somewhat less.

Exercise
Needs plenty of exercise to unleash its boundless energy.

Grooming
Regular brushing and combing. Easy breed to prepare for showing.

Feeding
One to 1½ cans (376g, 13.3oz size) of a branded meaty product, with biscuit added in equal part by volume; or 3 cupfuls of a dry food, complete diet, mixed in the proportion of 1 cup of feed to ½ cup of hot or cold water.

Origin and history
The Buhund is one of Norway's national dogs and was developed as an all-purpose farm dog to control sheep and cattle. It is, however, only since the 1920s that the breed has become known and appreciated outside its homeland, particularly in the United Kingdom, where it is gaining in popularity. The word buhund is Norwegian for 'farm dog', the Norwegian Buhund being a true farm dog, still occasionally used for herding. 99▸

Below: Norwegian Buhund puppies, safe and friendly with children.

KEESHOND

Good points
- *Equable temperament*
- *Good watchdog*
- *Long-lived*
- *Adapts well as house pet*
- *Very loyal to owner*

Take heed
- *Needs lots of grooming*
- *One-person dog*
- *Loud bark*

The Keeshond, Holland's national dog, began life as a barge dog, and still has the knack of finding an out-of-the-way corner for itself. It is a loyal dog, of sound temperament, but needs a lot of grooming and tends to favour one member of the family. It is an excellent watchdog and generally has a very long life.

Size
Height: dog 46cm (18in), bitch 43cm (17in).

Exercise
Average requirements.

Grooming
Regular attention with a stiff brush. A choke chain should not be used on this breed or it will spoil the ruff.

Feeding
Recommended would be 1-1½ cans (376g, 13.3oz size) of a branded meaty product, with biscuit added in equal part by volume; or 3 cupfuls of a dry food, complete diet, mixed in the proportion of 1 cup of feed to ½ cup of hot or cold water.

Origin and history
The Keeshond (plural Keeshonden), pronounced Kayshond, has a romantic history. During the period of uncertainty that preceded the French Revolution, the patriots were led by a man named Kees de Gyselaer, a dog lover who owned a little dog of this breed. The dog, named Kees, became the symbol of the patriots, and gave the breed its name.

Above: For a fairly large dog, the Keeshond adapts well as a house pet, being happy to curl up in a corner. Its acute hearing and loud bark make it an excellent watchdog.

The Keeshond has never become very popular outside Holland, despite Mrs I. Tucker's Champion Volkrijk of Vorden being Best in Show at Crufts in 1957. It has, however, a staunch band of devotees who breed for soundness and quality. In common with other Spitz varieties, the Keeshond must originally have evolved in the Arctic Circle, and it has the traditional Spitz tail tightly curled over the back. 99▸

LAPPHUND (Lapland Spitz)

Good points
- *Easy to train*
- *Friendly*
- *Lively*
- *Courageous*
- *Intelligent*
- *Good guard dog*

Take heed
- *Suspicious of strangers*

The Lapphund was bred to hunt reindeer, but since the need for this type of work has ceased, the breed has been used not only as a cattle dog, but also as a household pet, a role into which it has fitted happily, being both friendly and easy to train.

Size
Height: dog 44.5-49.5cm (17½-19½in) at the shoulder; bitch 39.5-44.5cm (15½-17½in).

Exercise
Needs regular walks and off-the-lead runs for full fitness.

Grooming
Regular brushing will keep the coat in good condition.

Feeding
One to 1½ cans (376g, 13.3oz size) of a branded meaty product, with biscuit added in equal part by volume; or 3 cupfuls of a dry food, complete diet, mixed in the proportion of 1 cup of feed to ½ cup of hot or cold water.

Above: The Lapphund, popular in its native Sweden, was once a herder of reindeer but has now become a pet and guard dog.

Origin and history
The Lapphund was produced as a hunter and herder of reindeer. When the reindeer became a farm animal, the Lapphund was given a new role as a cattle dog, but a larger number found their way to the south of Sweden, where they began to be kept as family pets. The breed is slowly but surely becoming very popular in its country of origin. 99▸

ICELAND DOG (Icelandic Sheepdog)

Good points
- *Beautiful appearance*
- *Hardy*
- *Faithful*
- *Intelligent*
- *Trustworthy*
- *Excellent guard dog*

Take heed
- *No drawbacks known*

The Iceland Dog has been known since the last century and is a reliable sheepdog. It is similar in appearance to the Finnish Spitz and Norwegian Buhund.

Size
Height about 48cm (19in).

Exercise
Needs plenty of exercise.

Grooming
Normal daily brushing.

Feeding
One to 1½ cans (376g, 13.3oz size) of a branded meaty product, with biscuit added in equal part by volume; or 3 cupfuls of a dry food, complete diet, mixed in the proportion of 1 cup of feed to ½ cup of hot or cold water.

Origin and history
A standard was introduced for the Iceland Dog in Denmark in 1898. It is also recognized in the United Kingdom but not in the USA; registrations are very low, however, and the breed is rarely exhibited. It would seem that the role of the Iceland Dog, like that of the Buhund, is a reliable, all-purpose farm animal. 99▸

Below: The beautiful Iceland Dog is a sheepdog and farm animal.

LAPPISH VALLHUND (Laplandic Herder)

Good points

- *Fine herder/guard*
- *Alert*
- *Very hardy*
- *Full of stamina*
- *Willing worker*
- *Makes a good pet*

Take heed

- *No drawbacks known*

The Lappish Vallhund is similar to the Swedish Lapphund. It is, however, a Finnish Spitz, mainly used for herding reindeer. It also makes a good pet and companion.

Size

Height: dog 48-54.5cm (19-21½in); bitch 43-48cm (17-19in).

Exercise

Provide liberal amounts of vigorous exercise for good health.

Grooming

Regular brushing will keep the coat looking healthy.

Feeding

Recommended would be 1½-2½ cans (376g, 13.3oz size) of a branded meaty product, with biscuit added in equal part by volume; or 5 cupfuls of a dry food, complete diet, mixed in the proportion of 1 cup of feed to ½ cup of hot or cold water.

Origin and history

Writing in *Dogs of the World*, Bo Bengtson and Ake Wintzell suggest that, when communications between the native peoples of Lapland in northern Scandinavia increased, their dogs interbred with various southern breeds. This resulted in southern breeders preserving the pure strain of the original Lapphund while the Laplanders' own dogs were ruined for their task of reindeer herding through crosses with unsuitable dogs of other breeds. Subsequently they set about breeding out imported, undesirable traits, the result becoming known as the Laplandic Herder. 99▸

Below: The Lappish Vallhund, a versatile, hardy Scandinavian breed.

FIELD SPANIEL

Good points
- *Sensible*
- *Intelligent*
- *Excellent in the field*
- *Affectionate*
- *Docile temperament*
- *Good house pet*

Take heed
- *Needs exercise in open spaces for full health*

The Field Spaniel is of similar origin to the Cocker, and it was not until 1892 that they were categorized as separate breeds, after which the Cocker Spaniel improved dramatically and the Field Spaniel did not, becoming, in fact, extremely long bodied and short legged. However, the Field Spaniel Society was reformed in the United Kingdom in 1948 and —thanks to tremendous work and enthusiasm—a standard type has evolved that is breeding true; but it is little known, although recognized, in the United States. The passing of the Field Spaniel would be a tragedy, as it is an extremely docile animal, excellent in the field and a fine house pet. It is intelligent and also has a very steady temperament.

Size
Weight: about 15.9-22.7kg (35-50lb). Height: about 46cm (18in) to the shoulder.

Exercise
It would be a great pity to keep a Field Spaniel in an apartment or a city environment where it would not get the lengthy walks and runs that it needs and deserves.

Grooming
A daily brushing and comb will suffice, taking care that the coat does not become tangled or matted and that nothing becomes lodged between the toes.

Feeding
Recommended would be 1-1½ cans (376g, 13.3oz size) of a branded meaty product, with biscuit added in equal part by volume; or 3 cupfuls of a dry, complete diet mixed in the proportion of 1 cup of feed to ½ cup of hot or cold water.

Above: The docile Field Spaniel, saved from extinction by dedicated enthusiasts, is a tireless working dog and an affectionate house pet ideally suited to country living.

Origin and history
The history of the Field Spaniel runs parallel with that of the Cocker, and until the breeds were separated in 1892 they were shown as Field Spaniels under and over 11.3kg (25lb). The breed is recognized in the United States, but there are few registrations. 100▸

WACHTELHUND (German Spaniel; German Quail Dog)

Good points
- *Excellent nose*
- *Good in water*
- *Fine retriever/gundog*
- *Hardy*
- *Fine sporting companion*
- *Good guard dog*

Take heed
- *No drawbacks known*

The Wachtelhund is a hardy breed bearing some resemblance to the English Springer Spaniel. It is little known outside Germany, where it has a sound reputation as a gundog and retriever.

Size
Height: 39.5-49.5cm (15½-19½in).

Exercise
Needs plenty of exercise.

Grooming
Normal daily brushing.

Feeding
One to 1½ cans (376g, 13.3oz size) of a branded meaty product, with biscuit added in equal part by volume; or 3 cupfuls of a dry food, complete diet, mixed in the proportion of 1 cup of feed to ½ cup of hot or cold water.

Origin and history
The Germans, when they produced the Wachtelhund, wanted to create a breed that could cope with waters and forest and also flush out and retrieve game. The breed was produced by the crossing of a number of small dogs. However, Harrap's *Champion Dogs of the World* credits the old German Stöber with the Wachtelhund's excellent nose, the Stöber having had tracking ability similar to the Bloodhound.

The Wachtelhund, which is not recognized in either the United Kingdom or the USA, is usually dark brown in colour and there can be white marks on chest and toes. It can also be white with brown spots, white and brown, or solid white in colour.

Below: The Wachtelhund, or German Spaniel, is at home in the fields flushing out and retrieving game.

SUSSEX SPANIEL

Good points

- *Loyal*
- *Tireless worker*
- *Intelligent*
- *Alert*
- *Excellent nose*
- *Easily trained*

Take heed

- *Tends to be a one-person dog.*

The Sussex Spaniel has been known in southern England for more than a century; it was very popular with Sussex farmers and thus its name was derived. The breed was first recognized by a Mr Fuller in 1795, when the breed was very much larger than at the present time; later, another strain, called the Harvieston, appeared, which had something of the Clumber and the Bloodhound about it. It is a pity that suddenly the Sussex Spaniel is in danger of extinction, for it is a breed that makes a loyal companion, is active and alert, and has an extremely good nose. This dog has a rich liver-coloured coat, which strangely loses something of its golden hue and darkens if the animal is kept indoors as a pet.

Below: Strongly built for work in the country, the Sussex Spaniel is, sadly, becoming less common.

Size

Ideal weight: dog 20.5kg (45lb); bitch 18.1kg (40lb). Height: 38-40.5cm (15-16in).

Exercise

Like most spaniels the Sussex is essentially a working animal and is not ideally suited for apartment life or for those with insufficient time to take it for long walks.

Grooming

A daily brush and comb is necessary, taking care—as with other spaniels—that the ears do not become tangled and that mud does not become caked between the paws or elsewhere in the coat.

Feeding

Recommended would be 1-1½ cans (376g, 13.3oz size) of a branded meaty product, with biscuit added in equal part by volume; or 3 cupfuls of a dry, complete diet, mixed in the proportion of 1 cup of feed to ½ cup of hot or cold water.

Origin and history

The Sussex is essentially an English breed and has been shown since 1862, when breed members were exhibited at Crystal Palace, London. The breed was kept going between the wars by Mrs Freer of Fourclovers Kennels, who is owed tremendous credit for the survival of the breed. In the mid-1950s fresh blood was introduced by crossing the Sussex with the Clumber, which seems to have resulted in improved bone size and temperament. 100▸

PORTUGUESE WARREN HOUND

Good points
- *Attractive*
- *Choice of size*
- *First-class hunter*
- *Affectionate*
- *Intelligent*
- *Alert*
- *Good watchdog*

Take heed
- *No drawbacks known*

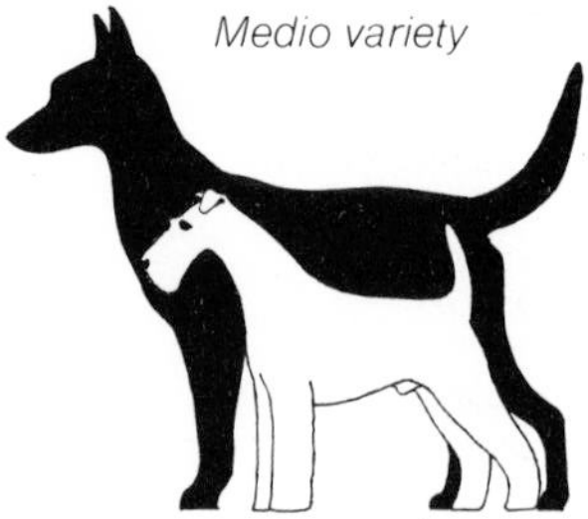
Medio variety

In its native land, the Portuguese Warren Hound is known as the Podengo. It is fairly rare, although by no means unknown, outside Portugal, where it is popular both as a companion and as a hunter of rabbits, hares and even deer. It comes in three sizes, the Podengo Pequeno, which resembles a rather large, smooth-coated Chihuahua, a larger (Medio) variety, and the biggest, which more closely resembles the Spanish Ibizan Hound, the Podenco Ibicenco.

Size
The Podengo Pequeno (small) stand 20-30cm (8-12in) high at the shoulder, the Podengo Medio (medium) stand 51-56cm (20-22in), and the Podengo Grande (large) stands 56-68.5cm (22-27in) high.

Exercise
Happiest when given plenty of exercise.

Grooming
Regular brushing is needed. A velvet pad will also improve the appearance of the coat.

Feeding
For the small Podengo ½-1 can (376g, 13.3oz size) of a branded meaty product with biscuit added in equal part by volume; or 1½ cupfuls of a dry food, complete diet, mixed in the proportion of 1 cup of feed to ½ cup of hot or cold water. For the medium-sized Podengo, 1-1½ cans of a branded meaty product of similar dimensions, with biscuit added in equal part by volume; or 3 cupfuls of a dry food, complete diet, mixed in the proportion of 1 cup of feed to ½ cup of hot or cold water. The large variety should receive 1½-2½ cans of a branded meaty product, of similar dimensions, with biscuit added in equal part by volume; or 5 cupfuls of a dry food, complete diet, mixed in the proportion of 1 cup of feed to ½ cup of hot or cold water.

Origin and history
The Podengo is well established in its own country, where the small variety, the Pequeno, is used for rabbiting and also for hunting hares; the medium variety also hunts rabbits and hares while the larger dog is used for hunting deer. There is an infusion of blood from a number of gazehounds and although the Pequeno is closely allied to the Chihuahua, the larger variety resembles the Ibizan Hound.

This dog is not currently recognized by the AKC, the UK KC or the FCI. However, it is usually fawn in colour and can be rough- or smooth-coated. Other coat colours are yellow, brown, grey-black or sooty, with or without white spots.

The breed is shown at Portuguese dog shows, but is rarely seen in other countries. Very popular with the country people of Portugal, the Warren Hound may be owned as a single dog or kept in a pack for hunting purposes. The larger varieties are usually hunted singly or in pairs, while the small variety is taken out in a pack. 100▸

PORTUGUESE WATER DOG (Cão d'Agua)

Good points
- *Strongly built*
- *Active*
- *Excellent retriever*
- *First-rate swimmer*
- *Good watchdog*
- *Loyal*

Take heed
- *Suspicious of strangers*

The Portuguese Water Dog is most commonly found in the Algarve area of its native Portugal where it is a true fisherman's dog, acting virtually as a member of the crew and tackling a variety of tasks ranging from guarding the nets to diving and retrieving; it will actually catch an escaping fish in its jaws and swim back with it safely to the boat. It is loyal to its master, but not very trustworthy with strangers.

Size
Height: dog 51-57cm (20-22½in); bitch 43-52cm (17-20½in).
Weight: dog 19-25kg (42-55lb); bitch 15.9-22kg (35-48½lb).

Exercise
Revels in an active, outdoor life.

Grooming
The Portuguese Water Dog comes in two coat types, but as this is the only difference there is only one standard for the breed. There is a long-coated variety, which has a lion show trim reminiscent of the Poodle; and a short curly-coated variety, which gives the animal an appealingly scruffy appearance, particularly as it is so often in water. Regular brushing is advised to maintain smartness.

Feeding
One to 1½ cans (376g, 13.3oz size) of a branded meaty product, with biscuit added in equal part by volume; or 3 cupfuls of a dry food, complete diet, mixed in the proportion of 1 cup of feed to ½ cup of hot or cold water.

Above: The Portuguese Water Dog is now mainly found in the Algarve.

Origin and history
This unusual dog, which is not only a fine fisherman but can also catch rabbits, has been known for centuries around the Iberian Peninsula, where it was bred for its task of retrieving fish and guarding nets. Formerly used throughout Portugal, it is almost limited today to the region of the Algarve, where fishing traditions continue very much as in the past. It is little known outside its country of origin. This breed should not be confused with the Portuguese Warren Hound (or Podengo), which is mainly found in Northern Portugal, where it is used for hunting rabbits and other animals. 100▸

CANAAN DOG

Good points
- *Alert*
- *Excellent guard*
- *Intelligent*
- *Courageous*
- *Easy to train*
- *Devoted to family*

Take heed
- *Distrusts strangers*

This dog is a native of Israel, where it is used as a guard and protector of livestock. It is alert, intelligent and home-loving. Although distrustful of strangers, it does not look for trouble.

Size
Weight: 18.1-25kg (40-55lb).
Height: 49.5-60cm (19½-23½in).

Exercise
Regular walks will be sufficient.

Grooming
Normal daily brushing.

Feeding
Recommended would be 1-1½ cans (376g, 13.3oz size) of a branded meaty product, with biscuit added in equal part by volume; or 3 cupfuls of a dry food, complete diet, mixed in the proportion of 1 cup of feed to ½ cup of hot or cold water.

Origin and history
The Canaan Dog is indigenous to Israel, where it is used as a guard and protector of livestock. During the Israeli war it was used as a messenger and guard, and created sufficient interest for breed members to be exported to the United States and elsewhere. It is recognized by the FCI and the American Kennel Club but not, as yet, in the United Kingdom. 101▸

Below: The Canaan Dog from Israel makes a sturdy, reliable watchdog.

POINTING WIRE-HAIRED GRIFFON

Good points
- *Strongly built*
- *Easy to train*
- *Equable temperament*
- *Good companion*
- *Intelligent*

Take heed
- *A reliable and careful, rather than speedy, gundog*

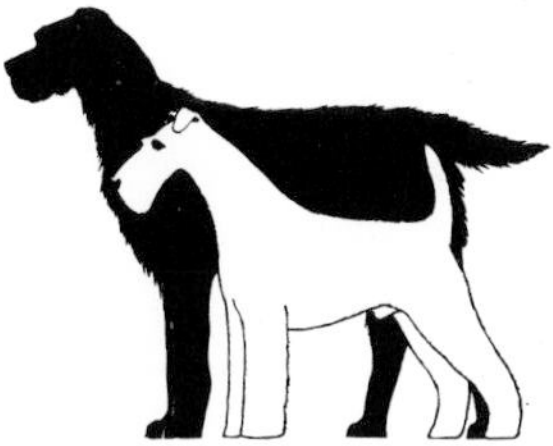

The Pointing Wire-haired Griffon is an intelligent, companionable dog that not only points, but also works well in water. It is an attractive, good-natured animal, which performs its task slowly but surely. It is easily trained.

Size
Height: dog 54.5-60cm (21½-23½in), bitch 49.5-54.5cm (19½-21½in).

Exercise
Needs plenty of vigorous exercise.

Grooming
Regular brushing will keep the coat in good condition.

Feeding
One to 1½ cans (376g, 13.3oz size) of a branded meaty product, with biscuit added in equal part by volume; or 3 cupfuls of a dry food, complete diet, mixed in the proportion of 1 cup of feed to ½ cup of hot or cold water.

Origin and history
The Pointing Wire-haired Griffon was developed around 1874 by a Dutch sportsman named Edward Korthals. Korthals was a man of considerable breeding experience, who had managed the kennels of a German prince for many years, and it was his resolve to produce a dog with both courage and hunting ability. He achieved this by experimental crossings with French, Belgian and German gundogs until the Pointing Wire-haired Griffon was established – a pointer that was at home in water and, although not as swift a worker as other gundogs, a reliable and plucky worker. Some say that it is the ideal gundog for the older sportsman. It was first shown in the United Kingdom in 1888. 101▸

Below: The slow but reliable Pointing Wire-haired Griffon. It is known in the USA as the Wire-haired Pointing Griffon.

SHAR-PEI (Chinese Fighting Dog)

Good points

- *Excellent watchdog*
- *Loyal to owner*
- *Amiable unless provoked*
- *Highly intelligent*
- *Good with children*

Take heed

- *May be more susceptible to disease than other imports, which have built up immunity*

The Chinese Shar-Pei currently has the distinction of being listed in the *Guinness Book of Records* as the rarest dog in the world, but interest in the breed is steadily rising.

What does it look like? Descriptions vary from a dog that looks as if its skin is several sizes too big for it, to a Bloodhound, but with wrinkles all over.

The Shar-Pei has small, rectangular ears that point towards the eyes, a tail that forms a circle, its tip touching its base, and stiff short hair that stands up. It is likely that its rarity will be short-lived, for at a recent reckoning 14 Shar-Peis were in the kennels of Mr Ernest Albright of California, the man largely responsible for saving the Shar-Pei from extinction. There are also now a handful of Shar-Peis scattered throughout the United States and Canada, the owners of which will doubtless perpetuate the breed, the future of which was put in peril when, in 1947, the tax on dogs in the People's Republic of China rose so steeply that few people could afford to keep them and many were utilized as food. The Shar-Pei may have escaped this fate simply because it did not make a sufficiently tasty meal!

It is an extremely intelligent dog,

Below: The extraordinary head of the extremely rare Shar-Pei.

an excellent guard, and amiable unless provoked, and it enjoys human companionship; it is also most affectionate, an added advantage being that Shar-Pei pups are said to house-train themselves!

Size
Weight: 18.1-22.7kg (40-50lb). Height: 46-51cm (18-20in) at the withers.

Exercise
The Shar-Pei – or, to give it its former name, the Chinese Fighting Dog – was used to hunt wild boar and to herd flocks. It is a breed more suited to those with large gardens, or living near areas where it may unleash its energies, and it needs good daily walks and off-the-lead runs.

It will interest obedience enthusiasts to learn that 'Chin', a Shar-Pei trained by Ernest Albright in the United States, has won three ribbons in obedience trials.

Feeding
In their land of origin these dogs are undoubtedly fed on rice, a diet that has resulted in instances of rickets and other ailments associated with malnutrition. The Shar-Pei is a hardy dog and, if fed correctly, should have few health problems. The branded canned food requirement for a dog of its size is approximately 1½ cans (376g, 13.3oz size) per day, with the usual biscuit supplement.

Health care
The breed is susceptible to entropion, an eye disease that can cause blindness if the lashes penetrate the cornea. The disease is curable, and a veterinarian should be consulted at any sign of eye irritation.

A unique feature of this breed is that heat in the female can be at irregular intervals, and with some females the season may not occur until she is 15 months of age or more. Also, when the Shar-Pei is in season, she will not attract the attention of males of other breeds, and only of certain members of her own breed, so planned mating calls for vigilant surveillance.

Origin and history
Works of art depicting a likeness to the Shar-Pei survive from the Han Dynasty (206 BC to AD 220).

It is possible that the Shar-Pei originated in Tibet or the Northern Province of China about 20 centuries ago, when it was probably a much larger dog than it is now, weighing 38.6-74.8kg (85-165lb). Other sources maintain that the Shar-Pei is a descendant of the Service Dogs that, for thousands of years, lived in the Southern Province near the South China Sea.

Certainly, for hundreds of years it lived up to its name of Chinese Fighting Dog; it was provoked, and then matched against other dogs for the owner's profit, the loose skin of the Shar-Pei making it difficult for its opponent to get a firm grip on its body. It is said that drugs were used to heighten the breed's aggression, for it is basically a loving and gentle animal. 101▶

BULLDOG

Good points
- *Courageous and intelligent*
- *Good tempered*
- *Loves children*

Take heed
- *Best suited to a temperate climate—excessive heat causes heart attacks*
- *Snores*
- *Not built for strenuous exercise*

The Bulldog, despite its somewhat ferocious appearance, has a docile temperament and generally adores children. It is quick to learn and will enjoy taking part in games. However, its build precludes any fast running, and it must never be allowed to rush about in hot weather, as its nose does not equip it for rapid breathing. It should never be shut in a car or other confined space unless plenty of fresh air is available.

This breed is not renowned for longevity. It can, however, be warmly recommended as a loyal guard and lovable family pet.

Size
Dog: 25kg (55lb). Bitch: 22.7kg (50lb).

Exercise
The Bulldog will benefit from a good daily walk on a loose lead. If the owner lives in a safe, rural area, or has a nearby enclosed park, the dog will enjoy being allowed off the lead so that it may amble at its own pace. But please don't drag it, or let it over-exert itself as a pup. Experience will show how much exercise it enjoys without tiring.

Grooming
A daily brushing with a fairly stiff brush and a rub-down with a hound glove will keep the Bulldog in good condition. Choose a warm summer's day for its annual bath!

Feeding
The Bulldog needs a full can (376g, 13.3oz) of branded dog food or 454g (1lb) of raw meat daily, with the addition of biscuit meal. A daily teaspoonful of cod liver oil is recommended in winter as a body builder. It is best to feed after exercise so that the meal may digest while the dog sleeps.

Origin and history
This breed can be traced back to the Molossus, the fighting dog of the ancient Greek tribe at Athens called the Molossi. However, the Mastiff would seem to resemble this powerful breed more faithfully, which suggests that the Mastiff, Bulldog and Boxer may have a common ancestor. Certainly they were all fighting dogs: the Mastiff fought against both gladiators and wild beasts in the arenas of Rome, and the Boxer was known in Germany as 'Bullenbeisser' or bull-baiter.

It is, however, the Bulldog that is generally associated with the unpleasant 'sport' of bull-baiting—seizing the bull by the nose and holding it until it fell. The sport was promoted by a certain Earl Warren of Stamford, Lincolnshire, who, after enjoying the spectacle of two dogs fighting bulls in 1209, sought to bring such a sight to a wider audience.

When bull-baiting became illegal in 1838, the Bulldog was in danger of extinction, for it appeared to have served its purpose. However, a Mr Bill George continued to breed Bulldogs, and to him a debt of gratitude is due in that the breed, despite its fearsome countenance, has developed into a much esteemed, reliable pet. 101▸

SIBERIAN HUSKY

Good points
- *Healthy*
- *Adaptable*
- *Friendly*
- *Good with children*
- *Intelligent*
- *Reliable*
- *Good guard dog*

Take heed
- *Needs lots of exercise*

The Siberian Husky is perhaps the most friendly of all Arctic Spitz breeds, having a long history of friendship with man, combining the roles of household companion with work-mate, hauling the sled or herding. It is faithful and reliable.

Size
Height at the withers: dog 53-60cm (21-23½in); bitch 51-56cm (20-22in). Weight: dog 20.5-27.2kg (45-60lb); bitch 15.9-22.7kg (35-50lb). Weight should be in proportion to height.

Exercise
Famed for sled racing, remarkable endurance and great powers of speed, this is not a dog to keep confined in a small back yard.

Grooming
Regular brushing will keep the coat in good condition.

Feeding
Recommended would be 1½-2½ cans (376g, 13.3oz size) of a branded meaty product, with biscuit added in equal part by volume; or 5 cupfuls of a dry food, complete diet, mixed in the proportion of 1 cup of feed to ½ cup of hot or cold water.

Origin and history
The Siberian Husky was bred by the nomadic Chukchi tribes of north-east Asia. Their purpose in breeding the Husky, from other local dogs, was to produce a hardy animal of great endurance, that would combine the roles of companion and hunter with that of a speedy sled dog which, at times, would be their only means of transport.

More recently, the Siberian Husky has been recognized as a show dog. It performed creditably as a Search and Rescue dog for the American Air Force in World War II, and has popularized the sport of sled racing in America and elsewhere in the world. 102▸

Below: The Siberian Husky, a legend for its speed and endurance.

SAMOYED

Good points
- *Beautiful appearance*
- *Devoted to owner*
- *Obedient*
- *Intelligent*
- *Very hardy*
- *Good show dog*

Take heed
- *Slightly independent*
- *That white coat sheds*

The Samoyed, or 'Sammy' as it is often called, is a beautiful, somewhat independent breed that should, according to its standard, show 'marked affection for all mankind'. These dogs adore the snow and are happiest in the wide open spaces. But having said that, I know of some living happily in semi-detached houses, and one that has become a TV star.

Size
Height at the shoulder: dog 51-56cm (20-22in); bitch 46-51cm (18-20in). Weight should be in proportion to size.

Below: The handsome Samoyed, a strong and faithful working dog.

Exercise
Needs a liberal amount of exercise and, if possible, some obedience work, even if this is only weekly attendance at a dog training club – which, after all, is recommended for all breeds.

Grooming
Regular brushing and combing, and a towelling after getting wet. The under-coat sheds once a year: at such times it is best to comb out as much surplus hair as one can. Bathing helps, as this tends to loosen the hair.

Feeding
Recommended would be 1½-2½ cans (376g, 13.3oz size) of a branded meaty product, with biscuit added in equal part by volume; or 5 cupfuls of a dry food, complete diet, mixed in the proportion of 1 cup of feed to ½ cup of hot or cold water.

Origin and history
The Samoyed is a beautiful Spitz-type that takes its name from the Siberian tribe of the Samoyedes. It is a sled dog in its native country, and is also used as a guard and herder of reindeer. Some Sammies were used by the explorer Nansen on his journey to the North Pole.

The breed came to Britain in 1889, and much of the present-day stock can be traced to the original pair. British stock has done much to popularize the breed in other countries of the world. 102▸

STANDARD POODLE

Good points
- *Good temperament*
- *Intelligent*
- *Splendid retriever*
- *Usually good with children and other dogs*

Take heed
- *Do not make a clown or fashion model out of a fundamentally outdoor type*

The Poodle has a character full of fun. It is intelligent and obedient. In the United Kingdom it has proved a useful competitor in obedience competitions. It has a fondness for water, if the owner permits, but is much favoured for the show ring where, exhibited in the traditional lion clip, it is a beauty to behold. It is also, debatably, the most difficult breed to prepare for the ring, involving the handler in a day's canine beauty treatment.

The Breed Standard states: 'A very active, intelligent, well-balanced and elegant-looking dog with good temperament, carrying itself very proudly.'

Size
Height: 38cm (15in) and over. Present day Standard Poodles may be seen measuring 63.5cm (25in) or more at the shoulder.

Exercise
This is a robust, healthy dog that loves the outdoors, has plenty of stamina and has lost none of its retrieving sporting instincts. It will enjoy plenty of exercise.

Grooming
Use a wire-pin pneumatic brush and a wire-toothed metal comb for daily grooming. The lion clip is an essential for the show ring, but pet owners generally resort to the more natural lamb clip with the hair a short uniform length. It is possible to clip your own dog with a pair of hairdressers' scissors. However, if, despite the help which is usually available from the breeder, you find the task tedious, there are numerous pet and poodle parlours to which you should take your dog every six weeks. Bath regularly.

Feeding
About 1½ cans (376g, 13.3oz size) of a branded, meaty product, with biscuit added in equal part by volume; or 3 cupfuls of a dry, complete food, mixed in the proportion of 1 cup of feed to ½ cup of hot or cold water.

If you are using your Poodle as a working dog then these amounts may need to be increased.

Origin and history
The Poodle was originally a shaggy guard, a retriever and protector of sheep, with origins similar to the Irish Water Spaniel and, no doubt, a common ancestor in the French Barbet and Hungarian Water Hound.

The Poodle may not be, as many suppose, solely of French origin. It originated in Germany as a water retriever; even the word poodle comes from the German 'pudelnass' or puddle. From this fairly large sturdy dog, the Standard Poodle, the Miniature and the Toy have evolved.

The breed has been known in England since Prince Rupert of the Rhine, in company with his Poodle, came to the aid of Charles I in battle. The breed was favoured also by Marie Antoinette who, rumour has it, invented the lion clip by devising a style which would match the uniform of her courtiers. It is also popular in the United States. 102▸

ENGLISH SPRINGER SPANIEL

Good points
- *Excellent with children*
- *Good worker in the field*
- *Intelligent*
- *Loyal*
- *Good house pet*

Take heed
- *Could develop skin trouble and/or put on weight, if under-exercised*

The English Springer Spaniel makes an excellent dual-purpose gundog and pet. It gives a good account of itself in obedience competitions and excels as a happy, efficient retriever.

Size
The approximate height should be 51cm (20in). The approximate weight should be 22.7kg (50lb).

Exercise
Needs plenty of exercise, or is likely to put on weight. Lack of exercise often leads to skin troubles, too.

Grooming
Daily brushing. Take care that mud does not become caked in the paws, and make sure that the ears are kept clean and tangle-free to prevent infection.

Feeding
One to 1½ cans (376g, 13.3oz size) of a branded meaty product, with biscuit added in equal part by volume; or 3 cupfuls of a dry food, complete diet, mixed in the proportion of 1 cup of feed to ½ cup of hot or cold water.

Above: The English Springer Spaniel needs regular grooming and plenty of long energetic walks.

Origin and history
The English Springer is the oldest of the British spaniels except for the Clumber, but it has never gained the popularity of the smaller Cocker Spaniel, tending to be favoured, in the main, by those with an interest in shooting and/or field trials. Incidentally, the English Springer was appreciated by the Americans as a 'bird' dog before it had even been recognized by the Kennel Club in London. There is some controversy as to whether the dog, originally called a Norfolk Spaniel, came from the county of Norfolk, England, or took its name from the famous Norfolk family. Certainly the name 'springer' is derived from its early task of 'springing' game for the hunter's nets. 103▸

IRISH WATER SPANIEL

Good points
- *Brave*
- *Easily trained*
- *Excellent retriever*
- *Strong swimmer*
- *Equable temperament*
- *Intelligent*
- *Loving*

Take heed
- *No drawbacks known*

The Irish Water Spaniel is a most attractive animal, loyal, intelligent and with a deeply affectionate nature. It is an excellent retriever and a strong, fearless swimmer, most useful for wildfowling.

Size
Height: dog 53-58.5cm (21-23in); bitch 51-56cm (20-22in).

Exercise
Needs plenty of exercise.

Grooming
Daily brushing and weekly combing. Seek advice on stripping of unwanted hair. Take care that mud does not become caked in the toes.

Feeding
One to 1½ cans (376g, 13.3oz size) of a branded meaty product, with biscuit added in equal part by volume; or 3 cupfuls of a dry food, complete diet, mixed in the proportion of 1 cup of feed to ½ cup of hot or cold water.

Origin and history
It is not surprising that there is some resemblance between the Standard Poodle and the Irish Water Spaniel, because they are, or were, both water retrievers. This dog was developed in Ireland from several spaniel breeds towards the end of the 19th century. Unfortunately, perhaps, it has never gained immense popularity. 102▸

Below: As happy in the water as on the land, the strong and intelligent Irish Water Spaniel excels in retrieving wildfowl.

ELKHOUND (Norwegian Elkhound)

Good points

- *Intelligent and alert*
- *Good household pet*
- *Lacks doggy odour*
- *Reliable with children*
- *Sensible guard*

Take heed

- *Needs firm but gentle discipline in puppyhood*
- *Thrives on vigorous exercise*

The Elkhound is a happy breed, loyal and devoted to its master and reliable with children. It has a great love of the outdoors, is energetic, and is not recommended for those unable to provide exercise.

Size
Height at shoulder: dog 52cm (20½in); bitch 49.5cm (19½in). Weight: dog 22.7kg (50lb); bitch 19.5kg (43lb).

Exercise
Needs plenty of exercise in open spaces to stay healthy.

Grooming
Daily brushing and combing.

Feeding
One to 1½ cans (376g, 13.3oz size) of a branded meaty product, with biscuit added in equal part by volume; or 3 cupfuls of a dry food, complete diet, mixed in the proportion of 1 cup of feed to ½ cup of hot or cold water.

Origin and history
The job of the Elkhound was to seek out the elk and hold it at bay until its master moved in for the kill. It has existed in Norway for centuries, but was not considered a show prospect until 1877, the year in which the Norwegian Hunters' Association first held a show.

Today's Elkhound has been tailored to meet the ideal decided upon by various Scandinavian clubs and societies, whereby other Spitz breeds fell by the wayside, a Norwegian breed standard emerging for the dog that has become its national breed. 103▸

Below: The Elkhound, a hardy and lively breed from Scandinavia.

SWEDISH ELKHOUND (Jämthund)

Good points
- *Brave*
- *Intelligent*
- *Equable temperament*
- *Excellent hunter*
- *Good guard dog*

Take heed
- *No drawbacks known, but remember it is essentially a hunter*

The Swedish Elkhound is little known outside its native country, where its popularity surpasses that of the Norwegian Elkhound. It has great stamina and makes a bold and energetic hunter. It is also an excellent guard. It is loyal to its master, of a calm temperament, and extremely agile.

Size
Dog 58.5-63.5cm (23-25in), bitch 53-58.5cm (21-23in).

Exercise
Needs plenty of exercise.

Grooming
Daily brushing and combing.

Below: The Swedish Elkhound, the largest of the Elkhound types.

Feeding
One to 1½ cans (376g, 13.3oz size) of a branded meaty product, with biscuit added in equal part by volume; or 3 cupfuls of a dry food, complete diet, mixed in the proportion of 1 cup of feed to ½ cup of hot or cold water.

Origin and history
The Swedish Elkhound is similar to the Norwegian Elkhound, but despite continuing popularity in its country of origin it is little known elsewhere – unlike the Norwegian Elkhound, which has had universal success in the show ring.

The breed was evolved by Swedish huntsmen who considered their local Spitz breeds superior to the Norwegian Elkhound for hunting. 103▸

KARELIAN BEAR DOG

Good points
- *Striking appearance*
- *Brave*
- *Fine hunter*
- *Hardy*
- *Loyal to its owner*

Take heed
- *Does not get on with other dogs*
- *Unsuitable as a family pet*

The Karelian Bear Dog is a sturdy hunter of bear and elk. It is a brave dog, and loyal to its master. It does not get on with other dogs and can not, ideally, be recommended as a family pet.

Size
Height at shoulder: 53-61cm (21-24in) for dogs, 48-53cm (19-21in) for bitches.

Exercise
Needs plenty of exercise in open spaces to stay healthy.

Grooming
Daily brushing will keep the coat in good condition.

Feeding
One to 1½ cans (376g, 13.3oz size) of a branded meaty product, with biscuit added in equal part by volume; or 3 cupfuls of a dry food, complete diet, mixed in the proportion of 1 cup of feed to ½ cup of hot or cold water.

Origin and history
The Karelian Bear Dog is a Spitz belonging to the Russian breed of Laikas, but this type evolved in Finland. It is known throughout Scandinavia as a fearless hunter of bear and elk. (The Russians decreed, in 1947, that only four distinct types of Spitz should in future be referred to as Laikas, and these are neither known nor exported outside the USSR.) 103▸

Below: The tenacious Karelian Bear Dog – hardy but fierce.

BEAUCERON (Beauce Shepherd, Bas-rouge, French Short-haired Shepherd, Berger de la Beauce)

Good points
- *Brave*
- *Faithful*
- *Easily trained*
- *Fine guard*
- *Intelligent*

Take heed
- *Ferocious if roused*
- *Needs a job to do*

Above: The powerful Beauceron makes an effective guard dog.

The Beauceron is a guard and herder of supreme intelligence and loyalty. It resembles the Dobermann in appearance.

Size
Height at shoulder: dog 63.5-71cm (25-28in); bitch 61-68.5cm (24-27in).

Exercise
Happiest when working or exercising in the wide open spaces.

Grooming
Regular brushing will keep the coat in good condition.

Feeding
Recommended would be 1½-2½ cans (376g, 13.3oz size) of a branded meaty product, with biscuit added in equal part by volume; or 5 cupfuls of a dry food, complete diet, mixed in the proportion of 1 cup of feed to ½ cup of hot or cold water.

Origin and history
The Beauceron belongs to the four best-known herding breeds of France, all of which derive from different areas, the others being the Briard, Picardy and Pyrenean Mountain Dog. The Beauceron resembles the Dobermann in both colour and appearance. It has come down from an old, less refined shepherd dog, probably used also for hunting, and has been established in its present form only since the end of last century. It is a natural herder, and in recent years its temperament has been greatly improved. 103▸

CLUMBER SPANIEL

Good points

- *Striking appearance*
- *Even temperament*
- *Intelligent*
- *Reliable*
- *Excellent nose*
- *Easy to train*

Take heed

- *Slow but sure worker*
- *Prefers the outdoor life*

The Clumber is the heaviest of the spaniels and is thought to be of French origin, brought about by crossing the Basset Hound with the Alpine Spaniel (which is now extinct).

It is a brave, attractive and reliable dog; a slow but sure worker that excels for rough shooting and is an excellent retriever.

Size

Dog about 25-32kg (55-70lb); bitch about 20.5-27kg (45-60lb).

Exercise

This is essentially a working dog, best suited to country life and needs plenty of exercise and off-the-lead runs in open spaces.

Grooming

Routine brushing. Keep coat tangle free and take care that mud does not become lodged between the toes.

Feeding

Recommended would be 1½-2½ cans of a branded meaty product (376g, 13.3oz size), with biscuit added in equal part by volume; or 5 cupfuls of a dry food, complete diet, mixed in the proportion of 1 cup of feed to ½ cup of hot or cold water. Rations should be stepped up or decreased, according to the amount of work the dog is asked to do.

Origin and history

The Clumber Spaniel was fostered and promoted by the Duc de Noailles in the years before the

Above: Clumber Spaniels are massively built dogs with a thoughtful expression and a characteristic rolling gait. They make slow but reliable working dogs as beaters and retrievers.

French Revolution. The breed became renowned as beaters and retrievers in the field.

With the advent of war, the Duc de Noailles brought his dogs to England and entrusted them to the Duke of Newcastle at Clumber Park, from which the name is derived. The Duc de Noailles was killed in the revolution, but fortunately he left the legacy of his spaniels in England. 103▸

HARRIER

Good points
- *Strongly built*
- *First-rate hunter*
- *Lively*
- *Hardy*

Take heed
- *Noisy*
- *This breed does not make a suitable pet*

The Harrier bears some similarity to the Beagle but more closely resembles the Foxhound, with which it has been so interbred that few purebred Harriers exist today. It is slower than the Beagle and Foxhound and is generally used to hunt the hare on both foot and horseback, although it is also used for foxhunting.

Size
Height varies from 46 to 56cm (18-22in).

Exercise
Needs liberal amounts of exercise.

Grooming
Use a hound glove.

Below: Like the Foxhounds, which it resembles, the Harrier is not really suitable as a family pet. It is essentially a hunting breed.

Feeding
As for Foxhounds (see page 153).

Origin and history
The Harrier is extremely popular in the United States but is, in fact, an ancient British breed, the first pack of which was recorded in the year 1260. This pack, the Penistone, was established by Sir Elias de Midhope and existed for over five centuries. The word 'harrier' is Norman French for 'hunting dog', and at one time all hunting dogs in Britain were known as Harriers. The breed is similar in appearance to the Foxhound. Primarily used for fox and rabbit hunting, it has an additional, unexpected chore in South America and Ceylon, where it is used for leopard hunting. Harriers are exhibited in dog shows in the United States. It is also popular with the American drag hunt. 104▸

HAMILTON HOUND (Hamiltonstövare)

Good points

- *First-rate scent hound*
- *Lively*
- *Affectionate*
- *Intelligent*
- *Good companion dog*

Take heed

- *Has a loud resonant bay in common with other hunting dogs*
- *Needs lots of exercise*

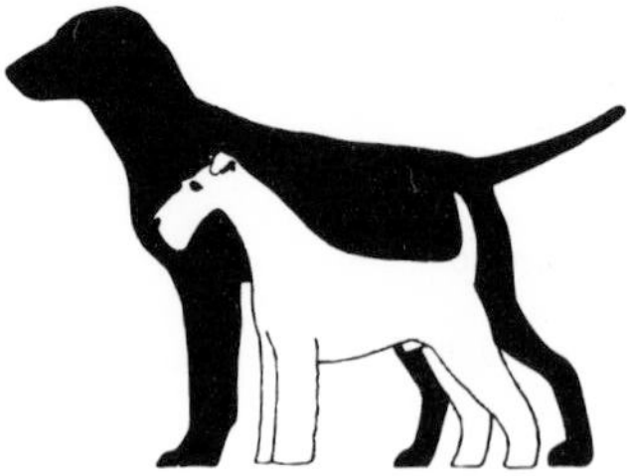

The Hamilton is not a pack dog, but is kept singly or in pairs in the homes of its owners. It is used to flush game for the guns in Sweden's large coniferous forests. It is intelligent, trainable, and a good companion and house dog.
This medium-sized hound was named after Count Hamilton, who created the breed by crossing the English Foxhound with the best German hounds, including the Holstein Hound and the Hanoverian Haidbracke. It is the most popular hunting hound in Sweden. Count Hamilton was the founder of the Swedish Kennel Club.

Below: The Hamilton Hound, an elegant hunter from Sweden.

Size
Height at the shoulder: dog 49.5-58.5cm (19½-23in); bitch 46-57cm (18-22½in).

Exercise
Requires plenty of strenuous exercise to stay in good condition.

Grooming
Use a hound glove.

Feeding
One to 1½ cans (376g, 13.3oz size) of a branded meaty product, with biscuit added in equal part by volume; or 3 cupfuls of a dry food, complete diet, mixed in the proportion of 1 cup of feed to ½ cup of hot or cold water.

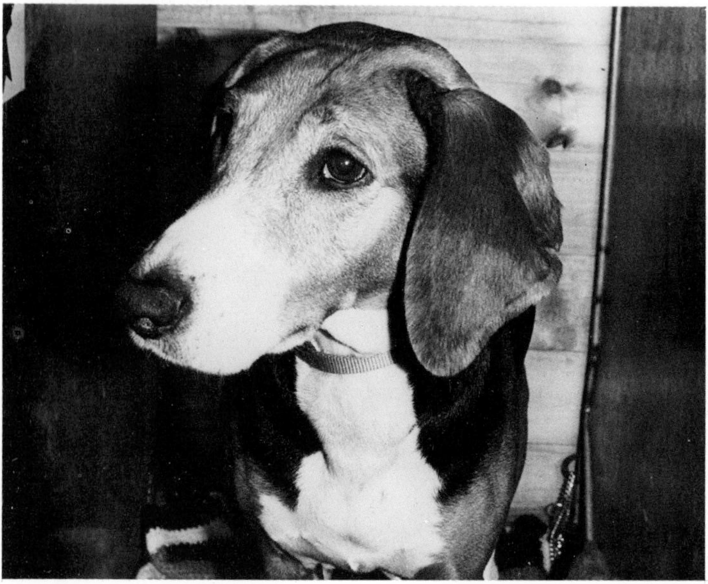

ENGLISH FOXHOUND

Good points
- *Strongly built*
- *First-rate hunter*
- *Lively*
- *Full of stamina*

Take heed
- *Noisy*
- *This breed does not make a suitable pet*

The Foxhound is not suitable as a household pet. It is almost always the property of a foxhunting pack. Hunt supporters often take on the role of puppy walker, in order to accustom a young hound to road hazards and livestock before returning it to its pack. Hounds are attractive, vivacious pups, but far too active and destructive for the average household. It is not possible in the United Kingdom to purchase a Foxhound as a pet. Hounds are always counted by the pack in couples: the huntsman will talk of having 30 couples.

Size
Height: dog 58.5cm (23in); bitch just a little less.

Exercise
Vigorous exercise is necessary. Foxhounds should have the stamina to spend all day running foxes with the hunt.

Below: A pack of English Foxhounds waiting for the hunt to begin.

Grooming
Use a hound glove.

Feeding
Foxhounds are not fed as household pets, pack members being trencher-fed with horse flesh and an oatmeal mash called a 'pudding' The leaner hounds are led to the trough first, so that they may eat their fill, and then the remainder are led in. They are not fed the day before a hunt.

Origin and history
The Foxhound is descended from the heavier St Hubert Hounds, brought to England by the Norman invaders, and from the now extinct Talbot Hounds. The Ardennes Hounds derived their name of Hubertus Hounds from the Bishop of Liege who later became St Hubert, patron saint of all hunters.

The Foxhound is never exhibited at ordinary dog shows, but has its own events under the auspices, in the United Kingdom, of the Association of Masters of Foxhounds. 104▸

AMERICAN FOXHOUND

Good points
- *First-rate hunter*
- *Lively*
- *Full of stamina*
- *Friendly*

Take heed
- *Noisy*
- *Inclined to be disobedient*
- *This breed does not make a suitable pet*

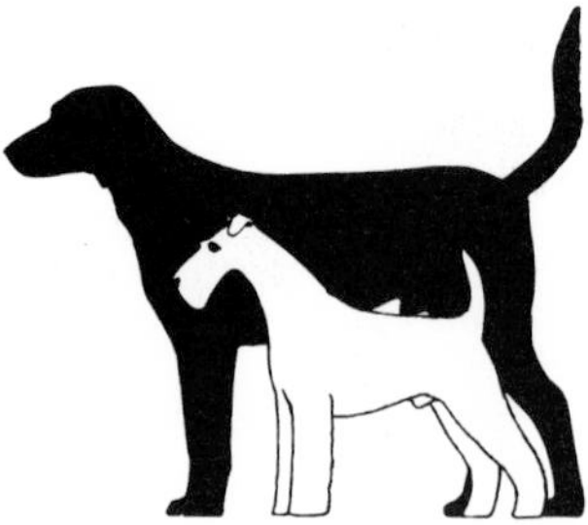

The American Foxhound is a lighter, racier-looking dog than the English Foxhound. It is seen in the show ring in the USA.

Size
Height: dogs should not be under 56cm (22in) nor over 63.5cm (25in); bitches should not be under 53cm (21in) nor over 61cm (24in).

Exercise
Needs plenty of vigorous exercise.

Grooming
Use a hound glove.

Feeding
Foxhounds are not fed as household pets, pack members being trencher-fed with horse flesh and an oatmeal mash called a 'pudding'. The leaner hounds are led to the trough first, so that they may eat their fill, and then the remainder are led in. They are not fed the day before a hunt.

Below: The American Foxhound, an agile and powerfully built hunter.

Origin and history
The American Foxhound is believed to have been derived from a pack of Foxhounds taken from Britain to America by Robert Brooke in 1650. They are very fast, their quarry – the American red fox – being a speedier prey than its English counterpart. In about 1770, George Washington also imported Foxhounds from Great Britain and received the gift from Lafayette of some excellent French specimens in 1785. The French and English breeds were crossbred, producing the Virginia Hounds, which form today's American Foxhound. 104▸

Smalands Hound

Dunker Hound

SMALANDS HOUND

(Smålandsstövare)

Good points

- *Keen hunting instinct*
- *Strong and sturdy*

Take heed

- *Not suitable as pet*

The Smalands Hound is, in company with the Hamilton Hound and Schiller Hound, one of the three oldest hunting varieties in Sweden. It is somewhat smaller than the other hunting varieties, strong, sturdy and able to cope with the dense forest that covers a large area of Smaland in southern Sweden. It is a born hunter of considerable strength and is not recommended as a house pet.

Size

About 49.5cm (19½in).

Grooming

Use a hound glove daily.

Feeding

One to 1½cans (376g, 13.3oz size) of a branded meaty product, with biscuit added in equal part by volume; or 3 cupfuls of a dry food, complete diet, mixed in the proportion of 1 cup of feed to ½ cup of hot or cold water.

Origin and history

This breed, although well known throughout Scandinavia, is little known elsewhere and is not recognized by the British or American Kennel Clubs. There are, however, numerous historical references to the breed in its country of origin, many of which refer to the breed's naturally short tail; it is never docked.

Baron von Essen is credited with perfecting the breed at the beginning of the 20th century through crossing the best of Swedish hounds with the Schiller Hound. The Smalands Hound was recognized by the Swedish KC in 1921.

DUNKER HOUND

(Norwegian Hound)

Good points

- *Excellent hunting dog*

Take heed

- *Not suitable as pet dog*

The Dunker Hound is a Norwegian variety, has considerable trekking ability and is a good retriever. It is popular in Sweden and throughout Scandinavia but is not recognized by the British or American Kennel Clubs. It has staying power rather than speed and is used to hunt the hare. The Dunker Hound is a strong dog, with a deep chest and long legs. It is both affectionate and trustworthy, but is not, however, recommended as a household pet.

Size

Height: 47-56cm (18½-22in).

Grooming

Use a hound glove. 104▸

SCANDINAVIAN HOUNDS

Schiller Hound

Finnish Hound

Feeding
One to 1½ cans (376g, 13.3oz size) of a branded meaty product, with biscuit added in equal part by volume; or 3 cupfuls of a dry food, complete diet, mixed in the proportion of 1 cup of feed to ½ cup of hot or cold water; or hound diet (see Foxhounds, page 153).

Origin and history
The Dunker takes its name from Wilhelm Dunker who, around the middle of the last century, mated his hound, renowned as a trekker and retriever, with the best bitches in order to perpetuate these hunting qualities. It is understood that crossing with the Hygen Hound took place at one time and an effort was made to register the progeny as Norwegian Beagles. However, the suggestion was rejected and the breeds have since gone their separate ways, both retaining considerable tracking ability. 104▸

SCHILLER HOUND (Schillerstövare)

Good points
- *Excellent hunting dog*

Take heed
- *Not recommended as a pet*

The Schiller Hound, like the Hamilton Hound, is one of Sweden's most popular hunting dogs, but is slightly shorter. It was evolved through crossing with hounds from Germany, Austria and Switzerland. The Schiller Hound is possibly the fastest of the Scandinavian hounds. It is also used for tracking.

Size
About 49.5-61cm (19½-24in).

Feeding
One to 1½ cans of a branded meaty product (376g, 13.3oz size), with biscuit added in equal part by volume; or 3 cupfuls of a dry food, complete diet, mixed in the proportion of 1 cup of feed to ½ cup of hot or cold water.

Grooming
Use a hound glove daily. 104▸

FINNISH HOUND

(Suomenajokoira)

Good points
- *Excellent hunting dog*

Take heed
- *Not recommended as a pet*

The most popular dog in Finland, used in its native land for hunting not only hare and fox, but also moose and lynx. The breed was established in the 19th century by a goldsmith named Tammelin, by careful crossing of English, German, Swiss and Scandinavian hounds. The Finnish Hound is good-natured and friendly but has a strong streak of independence.

Size
Height: dog, 54.5-61cm (21½-24in); bitch, 51-57cm (20-22½in).

Hygen Hound

Halden Hound

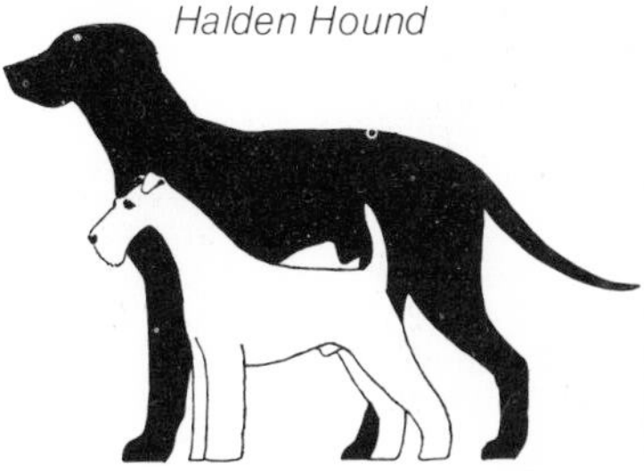

Feeding
As for other Scandinavian hounds.

Grooming
Use a hound glove daily. 104▸

HYGEN HOUND

(Hygenhund)

Good points
- *Excellent hunting dog*

Take heed
- *Not recommended as a pet*

The Hygen Hound excels in trekking and retrieving. It is a fine hunting dog, dignified and of equable temperament. It is, however, little known outside Scandinavia.

Size
About 61cm (24in).

Grooming
Used a hound glove daily.

Feeding
As for other Scandinavian hounds.

Origin and history
The breed takes its name from a Norwegian named Hygen who, in 1830, bred the now extinct Ringerike Hounds. The Hygen Hound emerged as a separate variety, and was then crossed with the Dunker, and an attempt was made to register the progeny under the name of Norwegian Beagles. This venture failed, and the breeds have gone their separate ways. Similarities in appearance remain but the Hygen Hound is heavier and less poised than the Dunker, and it also retains the colour of the Ringerikes. 104▸

HALDEN HOUND

(Haldenstövare)

Good points
- *Excellent hunting dog*

Take heed
- *Not recommended as a pet*

This is a medium-sized hound, of considerable stamina, little known outside Scandinavia. It is a Norwegian breed named after the town of Halden. This gentle and affectionate hound has evolved through the crossing of Norwegian hounds by careful selection with hounds imported from Britain, Germany, France and, it is suggested, Russia.

Size
About 63.5cm (25in).

Feeding
As for other Scandinavian hounds.

Grooming
Use a hound glove daily. 104▸

NB. The Scandinavian hounds are not usually kept in packs. They hunt in forests, in countryside calling for a tallish hound with a good nose and able to give tongue loud and clear for the benefit of the following huntsmen.

LARGE MUNSTERLANDER

Good points
- *Affectionate*
- *Easily taught*
- *Good multi-purpose gundog*
- *Good house pet*
- *Loyal*
- *Trustworthy*

Take heed
- *Needs plenty of space for exercise*

The Large Munsterlander is officially recorded as the youngest pointing retriever gundog breed, but has been known in Germany for as long as all the other German gundog breeds. It resembles a setter in both build and coat, and has a head like that of a spaniel. It is a multi-purpose gundog, ideal for the rough shoot: it has an excellent nose and staying power, and works equally well on land or in water. It also makes an intelligent and likeable family pet.

Size
Height: dog approximately 61cm (24in); bitch approximately 58.5cm (23in). Weight: dog approximately 25-29.5kg (55-65lb); bitch approximately 25kg (55lb).

Exercise
This is an energetic dog needing plenty of exercise.

Below: The alert expression of the intelligent Large Munsterlander

Grooming
A daily brushing will be sufficient.

Feeding
One and a half to 2½ cans of branded dog food (376g, 13.3oz size) supplemented by biscuit in equal part by volume; or, if you prefer, 5 cupfuls of a dry food, complete diet, mixed as 1 cup of feed to ½ cup of hot or cold water.

Origin and history
In bygone days, the best working dogs were mated to the best working bitches, with little regard to colour, breeding or coat texture. Early in the 19th century, however, people became breed- and colour-conscious and records of the best dogs were kept. So it was with the Large Munsterlander, which was then classed as a Long-haired German Pointer.

When the German Kennel Club was founded and the general stud book came into operation, only brown and white Long-haired German Pointers were permitted registration. The litters containing 'odd-coloured' puppies were frequently given away, finding their way into the hands of farmers and gamekeepers, who were delighted to have such well-bred dogs that would work. They were not bothered by the dogs' lack of colour or of registration. This was fortunate, for it resulted in the saving of the breed now known as the Large Munsterlander.

The Small Munsterlander (or Moorland Spaniel) is a lighter dog, 43-56cm (17-22in) tall. 105▸

DRENTSE PARTRIDGE DOG *(Drentse Patrijshond, Dutch Partridge Dog)*

Good points
- *Affectionate*
- *Equable temperament*
- *Excellent gundog*
- *Easy to train*
- *Intelligent*
- *Good house pet*

Take heed
- *No drawbacks known*

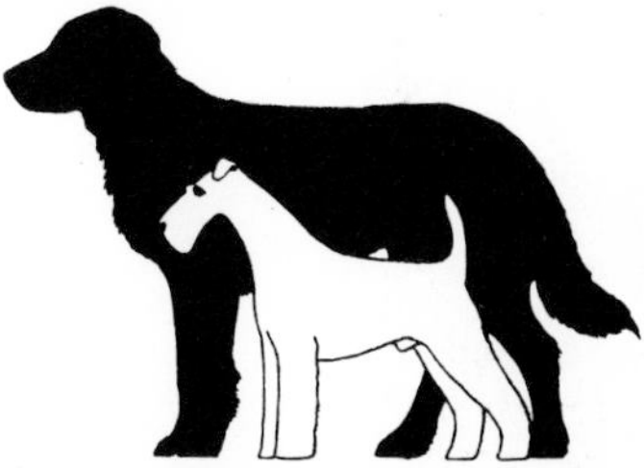

The Drentse Partridge Dog is little known outside Holland. This is a pity, because not only is it an attractive dog – something like the Springer Spaniel in appearance – but it also admirably combines the role of all-purpose gundog with that of an affectionate family pet. It will point and retrieve, and has been a successful competitor in Field Trials in its homeland.

Size
Height about 58.5-61cm (23-24in).

Exercise
Needs plenty of exercise in open spaces to stay healthy.

Grooming
Regular brushing will maintain the coat in good condition.

Above: The Drentse Partridge Dog is an all-purpose worker and pet.

Feeding
About 1½-2½ cans (376g, 13.3oz size) of a branded meaty product, with biscuit added in equal part by volume; or 5 cupfuls of a dry food, complete diet, mixed in the proportion of 1 cup to ½ cup of water.

Origin and history
The Drentse Partridge Dog, or Patrijshond, comes from the Drentse district of north-east Holland, where it has existed for some 300 years, no doubt having evolved through early crossings with long-haired German sporting breeds. It is an accomplished wildfowler, and obviously justifies more widespread popularity. 105▸

PHARAOH HOUND

Good points
- *Striking appearance*
- *Affectionate*
- *Intelligent*
- *Excellent hunter*
- *Full of fun*
- *Good with children*

Take heed
- *Not suitable for town life*
- *Wary of strangers*

The Pharaoh Hound is the oldest domesticated dog in recorded history. Two hounds hunting gazelle are depicted on a circular disc dating back to around 4000 BC, certainly before the First Dynasty.

The dog, and particularly the hunting dog, played an intimate part in the daily life of kings and nobles in Ancient Egypt. It is therefore not surprising to find them frequently depicted in the reliefs carved on the tomb walls of these men.

The Pharaoh Hound is a medium-sized hound, elegant, powerful and swift. It is intelligent, affectionate and full of fun; also very good with children, but a little diffident at first with strangers. Out hunting it is keen and fast. Unlike the Greyhound it hunts by both scent and sight.

Size
Height: dog ideally 56-63.5cm (22-25in); bitch ideally 53-61cm (21-24in). Overall balance must be maintained.

Exercise
This is a breed that needs plenty of exercise. It is unsuitable for town or apartment living.

Grooming
The silky, smooth coat needs little attention for a smart appearance.

Feeding
This is a hardy and healthy breed, yet on the island of Gozo (near Malta), to which it is believed the Pharaoh Hound was brought by Phoenicians, it was fed almost entirely on a meat-free diet of soup and goat's milk. Nowadays it enjoys a more traditional canine diet, but care must be taken that it does not become over-weight.

Recommended would be 1-1½ cans of a branded, meaty product (376g, 13.3oz size), with biscuit added in equal part by volume; or 3 cupfuls of a complete, dry food, mixed in the proportion of 1 cup of feed to ½ cup of hot or cold water. Increase rations if working.

Origin and history
It is thought that the Phoenicians took these hounds with them when they settled on Malta and Gozo, and that the preservation of the breed, which has changed little in 5000 years, can be accredited to Malta, where it is known to have existed for over 2000 years. In Malta, Pharaohs are bred for rabbit hunting and are known by the Maltese as 'kelb-tal-fenek' (rabbit dog).

In 1935 the Harvard-Boston expedition, under Dr George Reisner, working in the great cemetery west of the Pyramid of Cheops at Giza, found an inscription recording the burial of a dog named Abuwtiyuw. The burial was carried out with all the ritual ceremonies of a great man of Egypt, by order of the kings of Upper and Lower Egypt.

Like other Egyptian nobles, the dog was in constant attendance, a daily fact in the life of the king; and when it died, the monarch ordered that it be buried ceremonially in a tomb of its own. 105▶

IBIZAN HOUND

Good points
- *Excellent with children*
- *Good gundog*
- *Kind disposition*
- *Seldom fights*
- *Wonderful house pet*

Take heed
- *Has acute hearing so must not be shouted at*
- *Sensitive and easily hurt*

The Ibizan Hound is a kind dog loved by children, in whom it seems to inspire confidence. It is easily hurt, however, and due to its acute hearing must not be shouted at or its spirit can be crushed. It has great stamina and can, according to the natives of Ibiza, hunt by day or by night, singly or in pairs. But it is not a dog to go off on its own and not return. These dogs seldom fight, and have to be pushed to do so. They willingly retrieve and are often taken hunting on the island without guns. It is said that a pair can catch 1000 rabbits in a day. They are useful as gundogs, and make wonderful house pets.

Size
Weight 22.2-22.7kg (49-50lb); height 56-71cm (22-28in), for a dog, less for a bitch.

Exercise
It would be unkind to keep this hound in a confined space, for it is a tireless dog, able to retrieve and to jump great heights. It is an excellent companion for a sportsman. It must not be kennelled; ideally it should be kept as a companion in the home.

Grooming
The Ibizan needs a good brush every day but is not difficult to maintain in good condition.

Feeding
Recommended would be 1-1½ cans (376g, 13.3oz size) of a branded meaty product, with biscuit added in equal part by volume; or 3 cupfuls of a dry food, complete diet, mixed in the proportion of 1 cup of feed to ½ cup of hot or cold water. The addition of raw fish and fruit to the diet of the Ibizan is beneficial.

Origin and history
We known that hounds like the Ibizan were owned by the ancient pharaohs of Egypt, because hunting dogs of this type were drawn on rock, stone and papyrus as early as 3000 BC. Indeed, bones of similar hunting dogs have been found from about 4770 BC. The dogs of the pharaohs probably spread through trade to neighbouring lands. On the invasion of Egypt by the Romans, their neighbours the Carthaginians and the Phoenicians were driven out to the island of Ibiza in the 9th century BC, where they lived for about a century; but the hounds that they brought with them remained on Ibiza for the next 3000 years. Although some fine hounds have recently been taken from Ibiza to Majorca, the purest hounds are still found on Ibiza, retaining all the colours shown in the Egyptian drawings, i.e. spotted red and lion on white, or any of these as a single colour.

The Ibizan Hound is a relative newcomer to America. The offspring of imports made in 1956, together with the pups of subsequent imports, formed the basis of a thriving breeding population. The aim of all breeders is to maintain the fine qualities of the original island dogs. The AKC approved the breed for showing purposes in 1979. 105▸

SALUKI (Gazelle Hound)

Good points
- *Excellent guard*
- *Good companion*
- *Healthy*
- *Intelligent*
- *Odour-free*
- *Reliable with childen*

Take heed
- *Strong hunting instincts*
- *Needs plenty of exercise*

The Saluki and the horse are prized Arab possessions, the Saluki being capable of great speed and able to keep pace with the fleet-footed Arab stallions. It is still used in the Middle East for hunting the gazelle, but in the West it is kept mainly as an elegant companion, pet and show dog. It is intelligent and somewhat aloof, but is a faithful, gentle companion and trustworthy with children. Care must be taken, particularly in country areas, that the Saluki is kept under control; despite its domestic role, it retains very strong hunting instincts.

Size
Height of dog should average 58.5-71cm (23-28in), bitch slightly smaller.

Exercise
Salukis need plenty of exercise, and ownership should not be contemplated by those without a large garden or other exercise area.

Grooming
Brush daily with a soft brush, and use a hound glove. Combing of ear and tail fringes may also be necessary, especially if the owner intends to enter the beautiful Saluki for a dog show.

Feeding
One to 1½ cans (376g, 13.3oz) of a branded meaty product, with biscuit added in equal part by volume; or 3 cupfuls of a dry food, complete diet, mixed in the proportion of 1 cup of feed to ½ cup of hot or cold water.

Above: The Saluki has strong hunting instincts and must be kept under control in country areas.

Origin and history
The Saluki is one of the most ancient breeds of dog and, like the Afghan and Greyhound, is a sight hound that derives from the Middle East. The Saluki is said to take its name from Saluk in the Yemen, but its likeness is portrayed on the tombs of the Egyptian Pharaohs.

The breed did not gain recognition by the American Kennel Club until 1927. In Britain it was known long before, for a litter bred in London Zoo in 1836 was shown as the 'Persian Greyhound'; but it was another 60 years before the Amherstia foundation kennels were started from two imported hounds. The breed was recognized by the British Kennel Club in 1922 and has excelled as a show dog. 10

SLOUGHI

Good points
- *Excellent guard*
- *Good companion*
- *Healthy*
- *Intelligent*
- *Odour-free*
- *Reliable with children*

Take heed
- *Has strong hunting instincts*
- *Needs plenty of exercise*

The Sloughi is one of the rarest sighthounds (hounds that hunt by sight) known in the West and – like the Saluki, which it closely resembles – is capable of great speed. In the East, it is used for hunting the gazelle.

This is an intelligent, gentle dog, which, although retaining strong hunting instincts, adapts well to life as a domestic companion.

Size
Height 56-76cm (22-30in).

Exercise
Ownership should not be contemplated by those unable to provide a large garden or suitable exercise area.

Grooming
Brush daily with a soft brush, and also use a hound glove.

Feeding
Recommended would be 1½-2½ cans (376g, 13.3oz.size) of a branded meaty product, with biscuit added in equal part by volume; or 5 cupfuls of a dry food, complete diet, mixed in the proportion of 1 cup of feed to ½ cup of hot or cold water.

Origin and history
The Sloughi is frequently mistaken for a smooth-coated Saluki but is a heavier dog, often with characteristic black markings around the eyes. It evolved in Morocco and shares with the Saluki the distinction of being the only other dog recognized by the Arabs as purebred. They call it 'el hor', the aristocrat. It is said that its sandy colour assists the Sloughi in hunting gazelle because, in the desert, its quarry is unable to distinguish it until the danger is at hand. This breed is recognized by the FCI. 106▸

Below: The elegant Sloughi can be kept as a domestic pet as long as it is given plenty of exercise in wide open spaces.

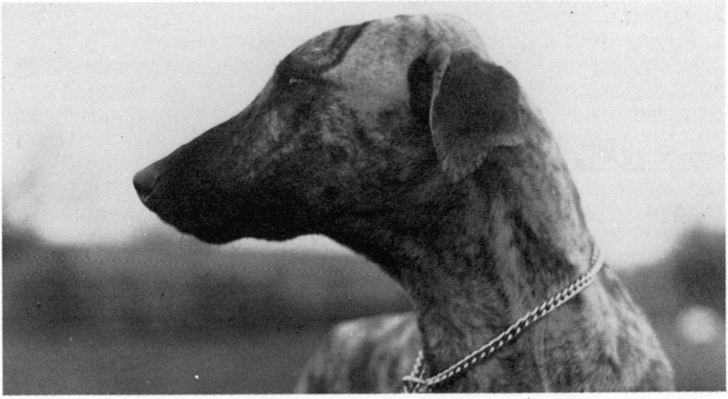

AFGHAN HOUND

Good points
- *Loyal and affectionate*
- *Good with children who do not tease*

Take heed
- *Must have space – not suitable for apartments*
- *Needs daily grooming*
- *Must have firm, loving handling*
- *Can be fiery tempered*

The Afghan is dignified, aloof and fond of comfort. Though it enjoys nothing more than surveying the scene from a cosy armchair, the Afghan is not the ideal choice for apartment dwellers or even those with a small house and garden. For despite its beautiful house manners, the Afghan is basically a hunting dog, warmly affectionate to its owners and usually trustworthy with children, but independent in character and often quite fiery in temper, particularly in adolescence.

It is impossible to show an Afghan too much affection, and it shouldn't be bullied. But it is important to maintain superiority from the first, especially during showing and training sessions, or later you may suffer the indignity, and physical near-impossibility, of publicly wrestling with a powerful creature armed with a mouthful of large teeth.

Size
Ideal height: dog 68.5-73.5cm (27-29in), bitch approximately 5-7.5cm (2-3in) smaller.

Exercise
Afghans need free running to keep fit and happy; their original task was to hunt wolves and gazelles in the deserts of Afghanistan, so a stroll in the park or a run up and down a suburban garden will not be enough to subdue their boundless energy. A puppy, from the first should be allowed unrestricted exercise in its waking hours. This should be in a safe enclosed place. An adult should have a minimum of half an hour's free galloping a day, as well as disciplined walking on the lead.

Grooming
Daily grooming is vitally importan to prevent the dog's thick coat from matting; the well-groomed Afghan is a delight to behold, the neglected specimen an abomination. Indeed, this breed is definitely not for those with little time on their hands for grooming and exercising.

The only type of brush capable of getting through an Afghan's coat is one with an air cushion behind the tufts. The best of all is a Mason Pearson real bristle – made for humans, and expensive. The nylon version is cheaper but remember to use a coat lubricant with this, otherwise static electricity will build up and cause the hair to become brittle. An air-cushioned brush with steel pins is excellent, and is not expensive.

Feeding
Recommended would be 1½-2½ cans (376g, 13.3oz size) of a branded meaty product, with biscuit added in equal part by volume; or 5 cupfuls of a dry food, complete diet, mixed in the proportion of 1 cup of feed to ½ cup of hot or cold water.

Origin and history
The Afghan is an ancient breed reputed to have been among those creatures taken into the Ark by Noah, and, to quote the book

Above: The Afghan Hound must surely be the most elegant and glamorous dog in the world.

Champion Dogs of the World, 'even if one rejects this claim it still remains virtually certain that some sort of Afghan existed thousands of years ago in the Middle East'. Present-day experts believe that it was crossed with the Saluki.

A papyrus found in Sinai dated *c.* 3000 BC was, from early translations, thought to refer to a Cynocephalus, or monkey-faced hound; this could have been the forerunner of the Afghan, which because of its facial resemblance is often called a 'monkey dog'. However, later work on the translation confirmed belief that it referred not to a dog but to a hound-faced baboon.

At any rate a Greyhound-like dog was destined to find its way, perhaps through Persia, to Afghanistan, where it grew a long, shaggy coat for protection against the harsh climate and found favour with the royal and aristocratic families of that land.

The first Afghan Hound Breed Club was formed in the United Kingdom in 1926. The AKC adopted a breed standard in the same year, but a totally new and original one was accepted in 1948. 106▸

GREYHOUND

Good points
- *An aristocrat, built for speed*
- *Affectionate*
- *Good with adults and children – rarely snaps unless teased*

Take heed
- *It is the Greyhound's instinct to chase moving objects!*
- *Has a tendency to rheumatism and arthritis*

One of the most ancient breeds and, some say, the most misunderstood, for although built for speed and used for racing and coursing, the Greyhound is basically lazy. It adapts well to life as a family pet, and will enjoy nothing better than lazing on a settee or mattress, which is what it will have done for many hours when living in racing kennels. It is a good-natured, friendly and affectionate dog, and is very gentle with children.

Size
Dog 71-76cm (28-30in); bitch 68.5-71cm (27-28in). There is no standard desired weight.

Exercise
Three or four short walks every day will be sufficient. Although the Greyhound must never be exercised off the lead in a public place, it will enjoy the opportunity to run free in open country, away from sheep and other livestock. It is a highly sensitive creature, and will learn to respond quickly to the tone of voice, which helps greatly in obedience training.

Grooming
Daily use of a hound glove will keep the coat shining.

Feeding
A retired Greyhound is like every other dog in that it responds best to a regular routine, especially where feeding and exercise are concerned. During their racing careers they are fed twice daily, in the early morning and in mid-afternoon, and exercised four times a day. There is no need to continue this routine once the Greyhound has settled in a new home, but it is kind to allow it to adapt gradually to its new lifestyle.

The canned food requirement for a Greyhound is between 1½ and 2½ cans of branded dog food (376g, 13.3oz size) per day and this, or 340-454g (12-16oz) of minced or chopped meat, should be mixed with 284-454g (10-16oz) of biscuit meal and moistened with bone stock, for Greyhounds are used to sloppier food than most breeds. They should also be pampered with a thick slice of brown bread crumbled into 0.28l (½pt) of milk at breakfast time, and have a small drink of milk with two large-sized dog biscuits at bedtime.

Health care
A retired Greyhound may at first be restless in its new surroundings. It must be remembered that the home is a very different environment from a racing track, and it is unlikely that a retired racing Greyhound, when it leaves the track, will have seen home appliances such as television sets.

Origin and history
The Greyhound is a pure breed: that is, it has not evolved from crossings with other types. Indeed, it seems unlikely that this breed has altered materially since early Egyptian times, as proved by a carving of a Greyhound in an Egyptian tomb in the Nile Valley, circa 4000 BC. 106▸

AIREDALE

Good points
- *Attractive, sporty appearance*
- *Faithful (if formidable) guard*
- *Good with children*

Take heed
- *That hard, wiry coat ought to be hand stripped*
- *If it gets into a fight, you could end up with the other chap's veterinarian's bill!*

The Airedale is the king of the terriers and the largest of the terrier group. It is a splendid-looking animal with plenty of stamina, and combines ideally the roles of family pet and guard.

Prior to the First World War, the Airedale worked as a patrol dog with dock and railway police. It served during the war in the Russian Army and the British Army. It also worked for the Red Cross, locating the wounded and carrying messages. Indeed, at that time its abilities as a messenger and guard were considered superior to those of the German Shepherd Dog.

Size
Approximately 25kg (55lb). Height: dogs 61cm (24in) at the shoulder, bitches slightly less.

Exercise
One of the useful features about this dog is that although large it will adapt easily to living in a reasonably confined space, provided that it has at least two good 20-minute walks and an off-the-lead run every day. Alternatively, it will be in its element running with horses in the country and squelching, with wagging tail, through muddy fields.

Grooming
The Airedale needs a daily grooming with a stiff brush, and if you plan to enter the dog in the show ring it is essential that its coat is regularly hand stripped. Ask the breeder to show you how this is done and don't be ashamed if you eventually resort to having the job done by a skilled canine beautician. If you do not plan to show, you need have your Airedale stripped only in spring and summer for coolness and neatness, but allow it to keep its thick coat for winter protection.

Feeding
The Airedale needs at least 1-1½ cans (376g, 13.3oz size) of a branded meaty dog food, or the fresh meat equivalent, every day, plus a generous supply of biscuit meal. It will also appreciate the occasional large dog biscuit.

Watch the Airedale's weight and, if it shows signs of becoming too heavy, reduce the supply of biscuit meal. Its girth will depend on how active a life the dog leads.

Origin and history
The Airedale is named after the valley of Aire in Yorkshire from which its ancestors came. It was originally called the Waterside, or working terrier. The forerunner of the present-day Airedale was kept for vermin control by Yorkshire gamekeepers and it was probably crossed with the Otterhound.

In the late 1800s the Fox Terrier enjoyed immense popularity, and much thought and care went into the breeding and development of this bigger terrier as an attractive and, at the same time, useful dog. It was soon adopted as a companion, but—when given the chance—can still prove itself as an expert ratter and ducker. It can also be trained to the gun. 107▶

DOBERMANN (Dobermann Pinscher; Doberman)

Good points

- *Brave*
- *Loyal*
- *Ideal guard*

Take heed

- *Stands aloof from those outside the family circle*
- *Likely to win any battle*
- *If kennelled outside, needs heated, draught-proof kennels*

The Dobermann is a strong, alert guard that will enjoy the comforts of its master's fireside and protect him and his family with its life. It is unlikely to have to give its life, however, for the Dobermann generally gets the better of any opponent and is one of the best guard dogs in the world. It is an aloof animal that takes its responsibilities seriously, is skilled at tracking, and makes a fine police dog.

Size

Ideal height at withers: dog 68.5cm (27in); bitch 65cm (25½in). Considerable deviation from this ideal to be discouraged.

Exercise

Certainly at least 40 minutes each day, which must include a 10-minute off-the-lead run in an unrestricted open space.

Grooming

The Dobermann, with its short coat, needs little grooming other than a daily rub down with Turkish towelling to remove loose hairs.

Feeding

Recommended would be 1½-2½ cans (376g, 13.3oz size) of a branded, meaty product, with biscuit added in equal part by volume; or 5 cupfuls of a dry food, complete diet, mixed in the proportion of 1 cupful of feed to ½ cupful of hot or cold water. Yeast tablets are beneficial at meal-times, especially during winter; also cod liver oil. These dogs fare well on raw meat, which keeps them in excellent condition.

Above: The Dobermann—a noble breed renowned as a guard dog.

Origin and history

Louis Dobermann of Apolda, in Thuringia, Germany, was a tax collector during the 1880s. Having a penchant for fierce dogs, he decided to breed the ideal animal to accompany him on his rounds. It was a relatively easy task for him, as he was keeper of the local dog pound, with access to numerous strays. He had in mind a medium- to large-sized dog, which must be short-coated (thus easily maintained).

The existing German Pinscher was considered to be both aggressive and alert, so it was around this breed that Louis Dobermann founded his stock, introducing the the Rottweiler—a dog with great stamina and tracking ability—and, it is believed, the Manchester Terrier, which at that time was a much larger animal; no doubt it is from the Manchester that the Dobermann obtained its gleaming coat and black and tan markings. Possibly the Pointer was also used. 107▸

HUNGARIAN VIZSLA

Good points
- *Distinguished appearance*
- *First-class gundog*
- *Clean*
- *Steady temperament*
- *Intelligent*
- *Easy to train*
- *Makes an excellent family pet*

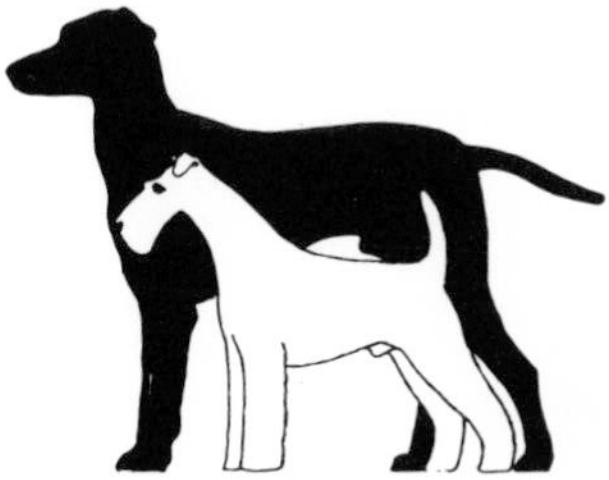

Take heed
- *No drawbacks known*

The Vizsla is Hungary's national dog and one of the purest breeds in the world. It is an excellent all-purpose gundog, with a keen nose, and well able to point, set and retrieve. Despite its hunting abilities it adapts happily to life as a family pet, and its temperament is sound.

Size
Height at withers: dog 57-63.5cm (22½-25in); bitch 53-60cm (21-23½in). Weight: 22-30kg (48½-66lb).

Exercise
Needs plenty of vigorous exercise.

Grooming
Regular brushing will keep the coat in a healthy condition.

Feeding
Recommended would be 1½-2½ cans (376g, 13.3oz size) of a branded meaty product, with biscuit added in equal part by volume; or 5 cupfuls of a dry food, complete diet, mixed in the proportion of 1 cup of feed to ½ cup of hot or cold water.

Origin and history
The Hungarian Vizsla was no doubt developed by the Magyar nobles and great care has been taken to avoid introducing new blood. It is a pure breed of outstanding ability and quality. 178▸

Below: The Hungarian Vizsla is a pure breed of distinguished appearance that makes an excellent gundog and sound family pet.

BEARDED COLLIE

Good points
- *Devoted pet*
- *Good with children*
- *Intelligent*
- *Natural herder*
- *Playful*
- *Easily trained*
- *Beautiful show dog*

Take heed
- *Needs plenty of exercise*

The Bearded Collie is not so well known as other Collies in Britain, and was almost extinct after the Second World War. Now, however, numbers of this delightful breed are increasing. It is a lovable dog, ideally suited for family life, but retaining its herding capabilities. It is easily trained and reliable with children, and proves a willing, lively playmate.

Size
Ideal height at the shoulder: dog 53-56cm (21-22in), bitch 51-53cm (20-21in).

Exercise
Not suitable for a confined existence. Needs plenty of exercise, including off-the-lead runs.

Grooming
Daily brushing. Bathing and chalking are necessary for show.

Feeding
One to 1½ cans (376g, 13.3oz size) of a branded meaty product, with biscuit added in equal part by volume; or 3 cupfuls of a dry food, complete diet, mixed in the proportion of 1 cup of feed to ½ cup of hot or cold water.

Origin and history
The lovable Beardie bears a keen resemblance to the Old English Sheepdog, or Bobtail, and is reckoned to be one of the oldest herding dogs in Scotland. It is said to be of Polish origin, being derived from purebred Polish Lowland Sheepdogs – two bitches and a dog were exchanged on a trading

Above: The Bearded Collie makes an obedient and lovable family pet.

voyage to Scotland in 1514, for a ram and a ewe. It has also been said to have Hungarian blood.

Luckily the survival of the breed was assured when Mrs G. Willison, of the former Bothkennar Kennels, acquired a Beardie bitch puppy (then without pedigree) in 1944, and, after a fruitless search for a Beardie dog, found one playing with its owners on the beach at Hove, Sussex. They were willing to sell and from this pair, 'Jeannie' and 'Bailie', all to-day's Beardies are descended.

A dog that bears a fairly strong resemblance to the Beardie is the Dutch Schapendoes, which has Beardie blood in its veins, as well probably as that of the Bergamasco, Puli and Briard. It is a popular sheepdog, guard and house-dog in Holland, but is little known in other countries. 107▸

SMOOTH COLLIE (Smooth-haired Collie)

Good points
- *Affectionate*
- *Easily trained*
- *Excellent pet*
- *Loves children*
- *Loyal*
- *Intelligent*
- *Simple to groom*

Take heed
- *Not too keen on strangers*

The Smooth Collie is like the Rough Collie in temperament. It makes an ideal family pet, and is hardy and simple to groom. It is identical to the Rough-hair except in coat.

Size
Height at shoulder: dog 56-61cm (22-24in); bitch 51-56cm (20-22in). Weight: dog 20.5-29.5kg (45-65lb); bitch 18.1-25kg (40-55lb).

Exercise
Normal daily exercise, with off-the-lead runs when possible.

Grooming
Daily brushing will keep the coat shining and in good condition.

Below: The striking Smooth Collie, an affectionate pet for children.

Feeding
Recommended would be 1½-2½ cans (376g, 13.3oz size) of a branded meaty product, with biscuit added in equal part by volume; or 5 cupfuls of a dry food, complete diet, mixed in the proportion of 1 cup of feed to ½ cup of hot or cold water.

Origin and history
Every Smooth Collie and Rough Collie can trace its origin to a tricolour dog called 'Trefoil', born in 1873; and until 1974 the Smooth-coat did not have a separate standard in Britain, except for the coat. However, while the Rough-coat has maintained international popularity, the Smooth-coat is seldom seen and might have become extinct were it not for the determined efforts of a number of dedicated breeders. 107▸

ROUGH COLLIE (Rough-haired Collie)

Good points
- *Attractive appearance*
- *Affectionate*
- *Easily trained*
- *Excellent pet*
- *Loves children*
- *Loyal*
- *Good guard dog*

Take heed
- *Not too keen on strangers*

No breed causes so much consternation to buyers and those giving breed information as the Collie. People tend to have a fixed idea of the type of Collie they want, be it Rough, Smooth, Border, Old English or Bearded; and, having written to enquire about a Collie, they expect the recipient of their letter to be on the same wavelength. If it's a dog like the film star 'Lassie' that you want, you *are* thinking of a Rough Collie, sometimes erroneously called a Scottish Collie; the Sheltie, or Shetland, is a 'Lassie' in miniature.

The Rough Collie makes an ideal family pet, being biddable, affectionate and loyal. It is hardy and, despite its thick coat, relatively simple to groom.

Size
Height at shoulder: dog 56-61cm (22-24in); bitch 51-56cm (20-22in). Weight: dog 20.5-29.5kg (45-65lb); bitch 18.1-25kg (40-55lb).

Exercise
Normal daily exercise with off-the-lead runs when possible.

Grooming
Daily brushing. Don't be afraid to vacuum clean with the smallest brush, if it gets muddy. But get the dog accustomed to the noise of the machine first.

Feeding
Recommended would be 1½-2½ cans (376g, 13.3oz size) of a branded meaty product, with biscuit added in equal part by volume; or 5 cupfuls of a dry food, complete diet, mixed in the proportion of 1 cup of feed to ½ cup of hot or cold water.

Origin and history
The Rough Collie is generally spoken of as a Scottish breed. In fact, its ancestors were introduced into England and Scotland from Iceland 400 years ago. But it was as guardians of the flock that they acquired their name in Scotland, where sheep with black faces and legs were known as colleys. Queen Victoria kept a Rough Collie at Balmoral in 1860, and in the same year a breed member was exhibited in a Birmingham show. 107▸

Below: The beautiful Rough Collie, an aristocratic-looking breed with a friendly nature, lively spirit and hardy constitution.

GERMAN LONG-HAIRED POINTER

Good points
- *Easily trained*
- *Equable temperament*
- *Excellent gundog*
- *Good with children*
- *Makes a good household pet*
- *Obedient*
- *Loyal*

Take heed
- *Needs plenty of exercise*

The German Long-haired Pointer (or Langhaar) is, alas, almost extinct. It is a healthy dog, with a good temperament, much endurance and the swimming and hunting ability of all pointers. It is energetic and immensely loyal to its master.

Size
Height: 61-63.5cm (24-25in) at the shoulder.

Exercise
Should be allowed plenty of off-the-lead runs in open spaces.

Grooming
Brush the coat regularly to keep it in good condition.

Feeding
Recommended would be 1½-2½ cans (376g, 13.3oz size) of a branded meaty product, with biscuit added in equal part by volume; or 5 cupfuls of a dry food, complete diet, mixed in the proportion of 1 cup of feed to ½ cup of hot or cold water.

Origin and history
This type varies in appearance from other pointers, in that it resembles the setter in appearance. This is not surprising, because it evolved as the result of crossing Dutch and French spaniels and local German breeds with the Gordon Setter, which at the time was greatly favoured by German huntsmen. It is an attractive dog, of great endurance, but its numbers are sadly dwindling in favour of the Wire-haired Pointer. 108▶

Below: The elegant but rarely-seen German Long-haired Pointer.

GERMAN WIRE-HAIRED POINTER

Good points
- *Easily trained*
- *Equable temperament*
- *Excellent gundog*
- *Good with children*
- *Obedient*

Take heed
- *Needs plenty of exercise*
- *Slightly more aggressive than other pointer types*

In its native country the German Wire-haired Pointer is known as the Drahthaar (literally translated, this means 'wire hair') and is perhaps more spirited and aggressive than its fellow pointers, with stronger guarding instincts and a hardy physique. It is an excellent gundog.

Size
Dog 61-66cm (24-26in), bitch smaller, not less than 56cm (22in).

Exercise
Needs plenty of exercise.

Grooming
Brush the coat regularly.

Feeding
Recommended would be 1½-2½ cans (376g, 13.3oz size) of a branded meaty product, with biscuit added in equal part by volume; or 5 cupfuls of a dry food, complete diet, mixed in the proportion of 1 cup of feed to ½ cup of hot or cold water.

Origin and history
The German Wire-haired Pointer is identical to the Short-hair except in coat. There are, however, some differences in background, and although the English Pointer undoubtedly contributed to its development, the Wire-hair was also derived from other hunting breeds. It is mentioned in German medieval documents. 108▸

Below: A first-class gundog, the German Wire-haired Pointer, will also make a spirited pet. Very harsh hair covers its skin.

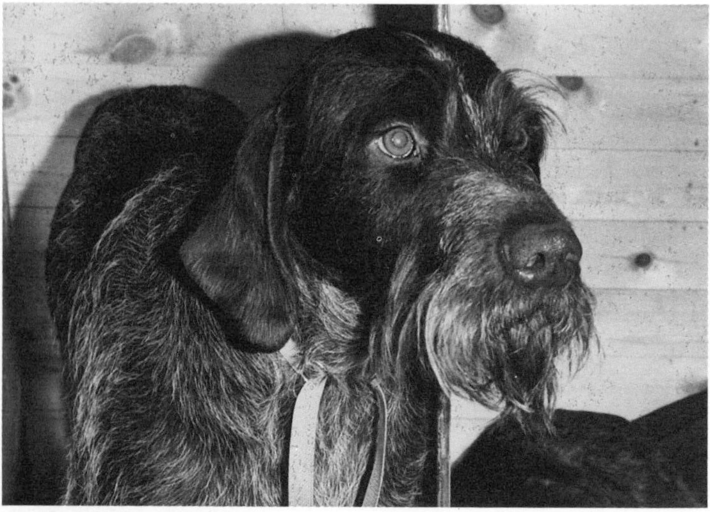

GERMAN SHORT-HAIRED POINTER

Good points

- *Easily trained*
- *Equable temperament*
- *Excellent gundog*
- *Good with children*
- *Makes a good household pet*
- *Obedient*
- *Good watchdog*

Take heed

- *Needs plenty of exercise*

The German Short-haired Pointer is a good all-round sporting dog, and affectionate and good with children. It is, however, happiest when in the wide open spaces, and is excellent at working wildfowl and most types of game. It is a first-rate swimmer.

Size
Dog 58.5-63.5cm (23-25in); bitch 53-58.5cm (21-23in).

Exercise
Needs plenty of exercise.

Grooming
Brush the coat regularly.

Feeding
Recommended would be 1½-2½ cans (376g, 13.3oz size) of a branded meaty product, with biscuit added in equal part by volume; or 5 cupfuls of a dry food, complete diet, mixed in the proportion of 1 cup of feed to ½ cup of hot or cold water.

Origin and history
The German Short-haired Pointer is of Spanish origin, bred from dogs imported into Germany and crossed with local hounds and, probably, with the English Foxhound for speed, the Bloodhound for nose, and the English Pointer to retain its pointing ability. 108▸

Below: A noble, steady dog showing power, endurance and speed, the German Short-haired Pointer can work in the water as well as on land. Given plenty of exercise, it will adapt to a family life at home.

POINTER

Good points
- *Equable temperament*
- *Obedient*
- *Good with children*
- *Easily trained*
- *Excellent gundog*
- *Makes a good household pet*
- *Successful show dog*

Take heed
- *Needs plenty of exercise*

The Pointer is famed for its classic pose 'pointing' with its nose and tail in the direction of the game that has been shot. It is a friendly dog, and makes an ideal household pet, getting on well with other animals. and children. But it does need a generous amount of exercise to really thrive.

Size
Desirable height: dog 63.5-68.5cm (25-27in); bitch 61-66cm (24-26in).

Exercise
Needs plenty of exercise.

Grooming
Brush the coat regularly.

Feeding
Recommended would be 1½-2½ cans (376g, 13.3oz size) of a branded meaty product, with biscuit added in equal part by volume; or 5 cupfuls of a dry food, complete diet, mixed in the proportion of 1 cup of feed to ½ cup of hot or cold water.

Origin and history
There is some controversy as to whether the Pointer originated in Spain, or was produced in Britain through crossings of Bloodhounds, Foxhounds and Greyhounds. A great authority on the breed, William Arkwright of Sutton Scarsdale, England, spent his life travelling the world to check on the history and development of the breed. He believed that it originated in the East, found its way to Italy, then to Spain (where it developed its classic head) and thence to England and South America. *Arkwright on Pointers* is still the bible of the breed. 108▸

Below: The Pointer conveys the impression of strength and endurance.

Bouvier des Flandres 212▸

Briard 213▸

Rottweiler 209▸

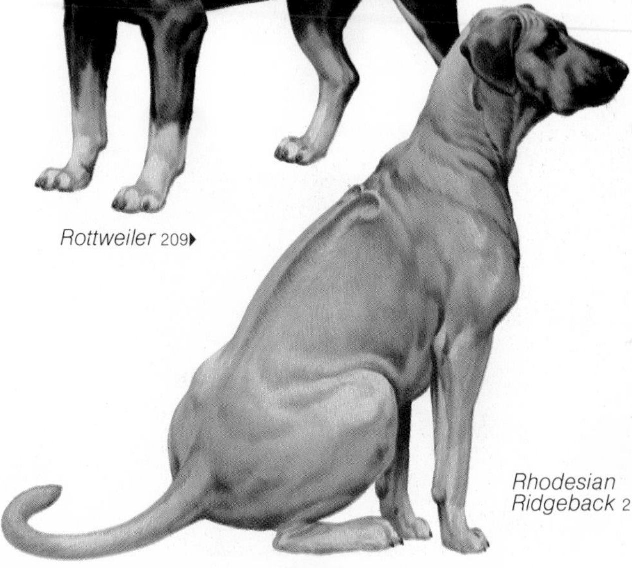

Rhodesian Ridgeback 202▸

Hungarian Vizsla 169▸

Slovakian Kuvasz (Tsuvatch) 216▸

Hungarian Kuvasz 217▸

Great Swiss Mountain Dog 218▸

Bernese Mountain Dog 218▸

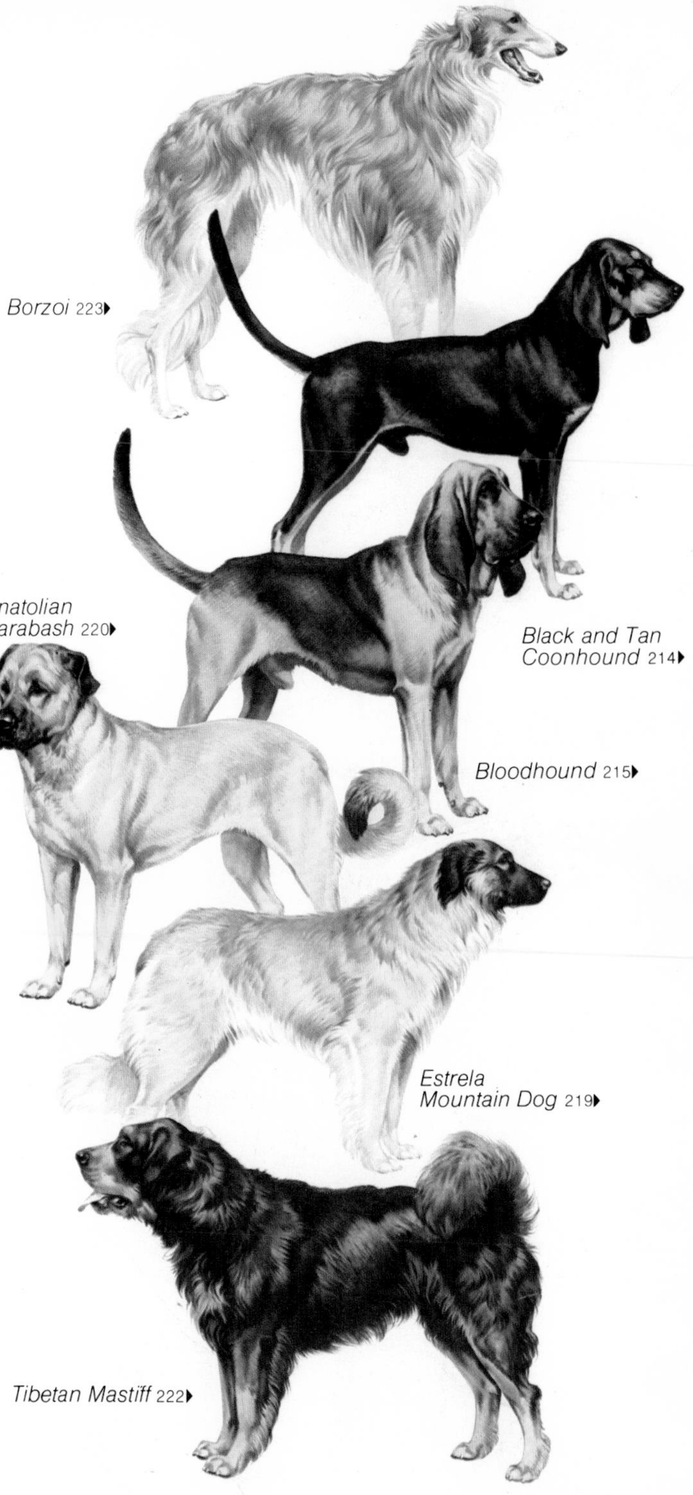
Borzoi 223▸
Anatolian Karabash 220▸
Black and Tan Coonhound 214▸
Bloodhound 215▸
Estrela Mountain Dog 219▸
Tibetan Mastiff 222▸

Irish Wolfhound 225▸

Deerhound 224▸

Polish Sheepdog (Lowlands) 210▸

Old English Sheepdog 211▸

Leonberger 226▸

Pyrenean Mountain Dog 227▸

Komondor 229▸

Maremma Sheepdog 228▸

Bullmastiff 230▸

Neapolitan Mastiff 231▸

Mastiff 232▸

Giant Schnauzer 233▸

Great Dane 234▸

St Bernard 235▸

Newfoundland 236▸

Below: A young St Bernard needs regular exercise but should not be taken for long, tiring walks.

IRISH SETTER (Red Setter)

Good points
- *Affectionate*
- *Beautiful*
- *Excellent with children*
- *Hunting ability*
- *Successful show dog*

Take heed
- *Lively*
- *No good as a guard; it loves everybody!*

The Irish Setter is a first-class gundog that combines this work admirably with the role of family pet. It is happiest as a housedog and has great need of affection, which it returns a hundredfold. It is intelligent and utterly reliable with children. It is, however, high spirited and lively and should not be confined in close quarters or kept by those who cannot provide adequate exercise. It often strikes up a good relationship with horses.

Size
The Americans look for a tall dog, 63.5-68.5cm (25-27in) high, but in Britain no height is specified.

Exercise
An exuberant dog that needs lots of exercise, either working or running in the wide open spaces.

Left and below: Supremely elegant, the Irish Setter is a champion pet, show breed and working gundog.

Grooming
That luxurious coat will need regular brushing to keep it looking glossy. Keep the ears clean.

Feeding
Recommended would be 1½-2½ cans (376g, 13.3oz size) of a branded meaty product, with biscuit added in equal part by volume; or 5 cupfuls of a dry food, complete diet, mixed in the proportion of 1 cup of feed to ½ cup of hot or cold water.

Origin and history
The Irish Setter has evolved from the crossing of Irish Water Spaniels, Springer Spaniels, the Spanish Pointer and English and Gordon Setters, its name being settled by the Ulster Irish Setter Club in 1876. Synonymous with the breed is the name of Edward Laverack who, prior to his death in 1877, spent almost a lifetime improving the breed. 108▸

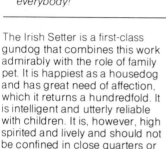

ENGLISH SETTER

Good points
- *Adaptable*
- *Beautiful*
- *Can live in house or kennel*
- *Reliable gundog*

Take heed
- *Not a loner; thrives in company of humans or of other dogs*
- *Needs plenty of exercise*

The English Setter is the most distinctive of the three Setter varieties, Irish, Gordon and English. It has a gentle nature that makes it the ideal companion for children, at the same time being an excellent gundog. As it needs lots of exercise, it is not a suitable companion for a flat dweller. It also requires a fair amount of grooming.

Size
Weight: dog 27.2-30kg (60-66lb); bitch 25.4-28.1kg (56-62lb). Height: dog 65-68.5cm (25½-27in); bitch 61-63.5cm (24-25in).

Exercise
Needs at least 10 minutes of exercise a day as a 3-month-old pup and a hour in adulthood to keep it in top condition.

Grooming
You will need trimming scissors and a fine steel comb for daily grooming, also a good stiff brush for the coat. Take care that the feathering on the legs does not become tangled. The silky hair under the ears should be removed and also hair under the throat and below the ear down to the breast bone. Care must also be taken to remove hair that forms between the dog's pads. Any straggly hairs have to be plucked from the body before the dog goes into the show ring. The English Setter is always bathed before a show, and the coat combed flat when it is dry. American competitors are trimmed more heavily than those exhibited in the United Kingdom.

Origin and history
It is generally agreed that the English Setter evolved from spaniels. Credit for the breed is given to Edward Laverack (1815-1877) who in his work *The Setter* wrote: 'this breed is but a Spaniel improved'. The Setting Spaniel, accepted by many modern authorities as the forerunner of the English Setter, was used as far back as the 16th century for setting partridges and quails. Through interbreeding, Laverack affected the strain so that it acquired not only the standard of excellence in the 19th century but that on which the present-day English Setter was built. To quote Sylvia Bruce Wilmore writing in *Dog News* magazine: 'About the time the Laverack strain of English Setter was at its zenith, Mr R.L. Purcell Llewellin purchased a number of Mr Laverack's best Show dogs of the pure Dash-Moll and Dash-Hill Laverack blood. He crossed these with entirely new blood which he obtained in the North of England represented by Mr Slatter's and Sir Vincent Corbet's strain, since referred to as the Duke-Kate-Rhoebe. The Llewellin strain of English Setter became immensely popular at the turn of the century, their reputation spreading to the United States and Canada where they dominated field trials for a quarter of a century, thus firmly establishing the line of breed in America.' 108▸

GORDON SETTER

Good points
- *Affectionate*
- *Intelligent*
- *Equable temperament*
- *Tireless worker*
- *Excellent gundog*
- *Good with children*

Take heed
- *Not suitable for a guard dog*
- *Needs plenty of exercise*

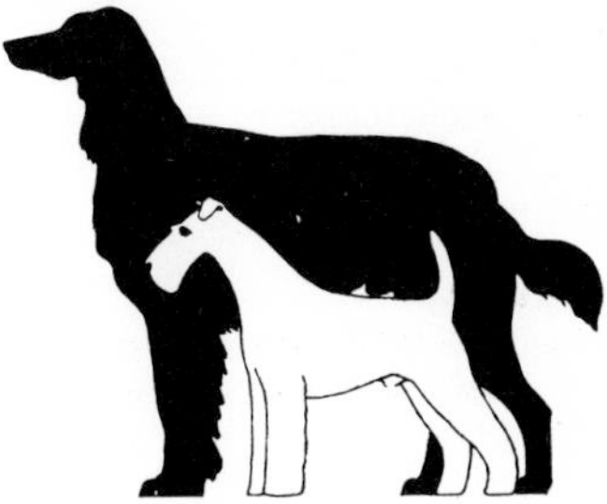

The Gordon Setter is a fine gundog, a bird-finding dog, used to silent trekking. It does not fit the role of guard, although it will not accept strangers as readily as the Irish Setter, which could well lick the face of a burglar while presenting him with some item 'retrieved' from its mistress's wardrobe.

The Gordon makes an excellent family pet and is trustworthy with children. It does enjoy an active working life, however, and is not really suitable for apartments.

Size
Shoulder height for dog, 66cm (26in), weight about 29.5kg (65lb); bitch, 62cm (24½in), weight about 25.4kg (56lb).

Exercise
Ensure that it has plenty of exercise.

Below: The Gordon Setter is a strong gundog and friendly pet.

Grooming
Regular brushing, and monthly nail clipping.

Feeding
Recommended would be 1½-2½ cans (376g, 13.3oz size) of a branded meaty product, with biscuit added in equal part by volume; or 5 cupfuls of a dry food, complete diet, mixed in the proportion of 1 cup of feed to ½ cup of hot or cold water.

Origin and history
The Gordon is a true Scot, bred at Gordon Castle, Banffshire, the seat of the Duke of Richmond and Gordon. It is the only native Scottish gundog and was originally known as the Gordon Castle Setter. Credit must go to the 4th Duke of Richmond and Gordon for establishing the breed in the late 1770s, using probably the Collie and the Bloodhound. 108▸

BELGIAN SHEPHERD DOG

Good points

- *Alert and agile*
- *Excellent guard*
- *Intelligent*
- *Physically robust*

Take heed

- *Best suited to the open spaces, so won't take kindly to apartment living*
- *Needs firm but kind handling*

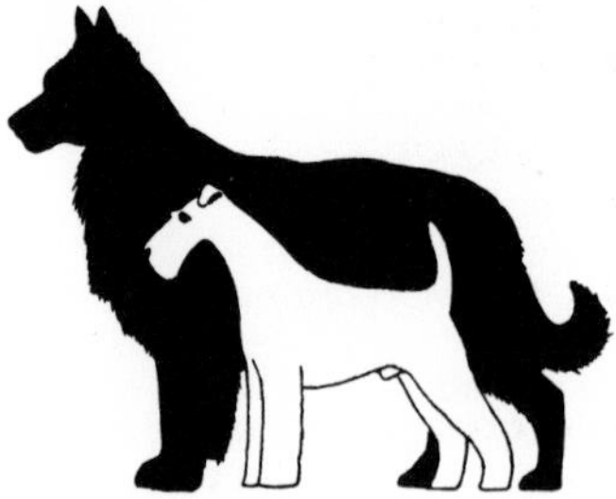

There are four types of Belgian Shepherd Dog – the Groenendael, the Laekenois, the Malinois and the Tervueren – all of which are similar to the German Shepherd.

Basically, they are hunting and herding dogs, but they have also served as Red Cross messengers in war-time, are vigilant guards and kindly protectors of children.

Size

The desired height for the dog is 61-66cm (24-26in) and for the bitch 56-61cm (22-24in). This applies to all four types.

Exercise

The Belgian Shepherd Dog is a working dog that excels in defending master and property. It is oblivious to bad weather, and enjoys being out of doors, so adequate exercise is vital.

Grooming

Little grooming is needed other than a good surface brushing. Bathing is not recommended, even for exhibition, unless the dog has got its coat into a filthy condition. As it has a double coat, combing out the under-coat will result in a dog with only half a coat.

Feeding

The Belgian Shepherd Dog should be fed similarly to other dogs of its size. Daily rations might be 1½ to 2 cans of branded dog food (376g, 13.3oz side), with an equal volume of biscuits, or 5 cupfuls of a dry food, complete diet, mixed in the proportion of 1 cup to ½ cup of hot or cold water.

Origin and history

At the end of the 19th century there were Shepherd Dog varieties of all colours and sizes in Belgium, but in about 1890, Monsieur Rose of the Café du Groenendael discovered a black, long-coated bitch among one of his litters. Later, he bought a similar dog from a Monsieur Bernaert and, by selective breeding and strict culling, eventually produced the Groenendael.

The origin of the modern Belgian Shepherd Dog dates from 1891, when a collection of shepherd dogs of all colours and sizes was gathered at the Brussels Veterinary University. It was decided to recognize three varieties: the rough-coated black; the smooth-coated fawn with black mask; and the wire-haired darkish grey. Since then there have been various additions to and subtractions from these types, but they have now been settled into four varieties: the Groenendael (long-coated black); the Tervueren (long-coated other than black); the Malinois (smooth-coated); and the Laekenois, or de Laeken (wire-coated).

It should be mentioned that in America only the Groenendael is known as the Belgian Shepherd Dog or Belgian Sheepdog; the Malinois and the Tervueren are registered as separate breeds, and the Laekenois – the rarest of the four – is not recognized. Incidentally, the breeds are known in America as the Belgian Malinois and the Belgian Tervuren, the latter with a different spelling. 109/110▸

HOLLANDSE HERDER (Dutch Shepherd Dog)

Good points
- *Excellent guard*
- *Hardy*
- *Intelligent*
- *Alert and active*
- *Sound temperament*
- *Faithful*
- *Easy to train*

Take heed
- *No drawbacks known*

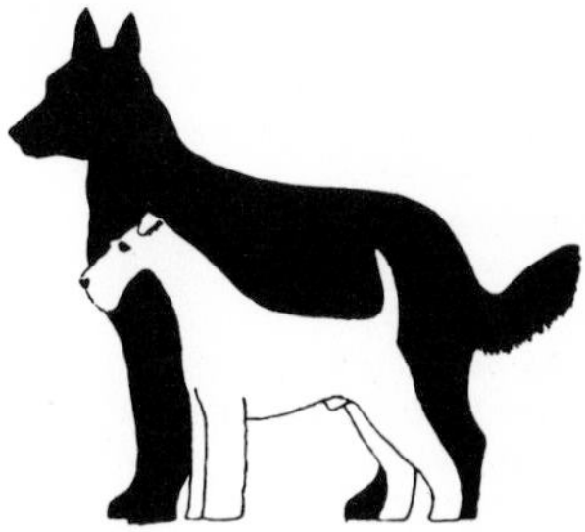

The Hollandse Herder was bred in Holland as a sheepdog, but nowadays is kept mainly as a companion and guard. It is relatively unknown outside its native country, where it is used as a police dog, as a guide dog for the blind (seeing eye dog) and occasionally for farmyard duties. It comes in three coat types: short-hair, long-hair and wire-hair. The long-haired variety is almost extinct and the wire-hair is not commonly seen; the short-hair type is the one most widely known.

Size
Height at the withers: dog 58.5-63.5cm (23-25in); bitch 54.5-62cm (21½-24½in). In the case of the long-hairs only, the minimum is 54.5cm (21½in) for dogs, 53cm (21in) for bitches.

Below: The wire-haired Hollandse Herder, originally a sheepdog.

Exercise
Needs plenty of exercise to keep in good health.

Grooming
Regular brushing will keep the coat in good condition.

Feeding
Recommended would be 1½-2½ cans (376g, 13.3oz size) of a branded meaty product, with biscuit added in equal part by volume; or 5 cupfuls of a dry food, complete diet, mixed in the proportion of 1 cup of feed to ½ cup of hot or cold water.

Origin and history
The Hollandse Herder is closely related to the Belgian Shepherd Dog and they are of similar origin. It has, however, developed as a separate breed in its native Holland, where it has always been extremely popular.

GERMAN SHEPHERD DOG (Alsatian)

Good points
- *Devoted to owner*
- *Excellent worker/herder*
- *Favoured for obedience trials*
- *Supremely intelligent*
- *Protective*

Take heed
- *Tendency to over-guard*
- *Not a lap dog, but a worker that needs a task in life*

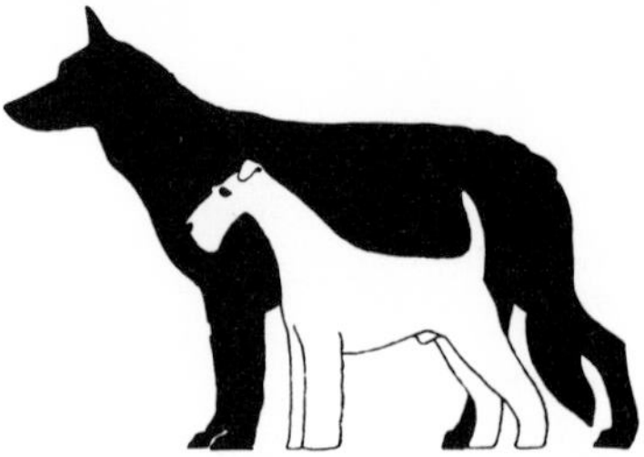

The German Shepherd Dog has one of the largest followings in the world. It is also the breed that rouses the strongest emotions in the public. They either worship the German Shepherd or abhor it. If a smaller breed takes a nip out of the postman's trousers, the misdeed may go unreported; but if a German Shepherd is involved, the headlines are likely to be: 'German Shepherd Dog savages postman!'

The German Shepherd is one of the most courageous and intelligent of dogs, debatably *the* most intelligent. Breed members have fought bravely, and many lost their lives in two World Wars. They have been, and still are, used as guide dogs for the blind (US 'seeing eye dogs'), police dogs, and military dogs. Certainly they are a very popular guard. It is this strong guarding instinct that can be their undoing, however, for a German Shepherd protecting a toddler may menace a stranger at the garden gate. It could also turn nasty through sheer boredom, if acquired as a mere pet dog. The German Shepherd deserves a job to do, whether it be in the public service, or competing eagerly in obedience and working trials.

Below: The German Shepherd Dog, without doubt one of the most intelligent and popular of dogs.

Size
The ideal height (measured to the highest point of the shoulder) is 56-61cm (22-24in) for bitches and 61-66cm (24-26in) for dogs. The proportion of length to height varies between 10:9 and 10:8.5.

Exercise
Needs plenty of exercise, off-the-lead runs and, if possible, obedience exercises. It will excel at the local dog training club in 'scent' and 'retrieve'. Remember that this breed is used to sniff out illegal drug shipments, and to detect the elusive 'black box' amid the wreckage strewn over many miles after airplane crashes.

Grooming
Daily brushing is recommended.

Feeding
Give 1½-2½ cans (376g, 13.3oz size) of a branded meaty product, with biscuit added in equal part by volume; or 5 cupfuls of a dry food, complete diet, mixed in the proportion of 1 cup of food to ½ cup of hot or cold water.

Health care
This is a healthy, hardy breed. However, its popularity in recent years has encouraged indiscriminate breeding, resulting in loss of temperament and form. Take care, when purchasing a German Shepherd Dog, to acquire only from registered HD-free stock. HD is an abbreviation for hip dysplasia, a malformation of the hip joint that can result in the dog being crippled before middle age. Reliable vendors do not breed from affected stock. Many people feel this defect came about through over-emphasis on that desired show dog crouch.

Origin and history
The German Shepherd Dog is attributed by some to the Bronze Age wolf, perhaps an unfortunate suggestion in that it wrongly associates the breed with wolf-like tendencies. Certainly around the 7th century AD a sheepdog of this type, but with a lighter coat, existed in Germany; and by the 16th century the coat had appreciably darkened.

The breed was first exhibited at a dog show in Hanover in 1882. Credit for the formation of the breed is widely assigned to a German fancier named von Stephanitz, who did much to improve its temperament and physical appearance.

The German Shepherd Dog was introduced into Britain following the First World War by a small band of dedicated fanciers who had seen the breed working in Germany. These included the late Colonel Baldwin and Air Commodore Alan Cecil-Wright, President of the Kennel Club. It was thought inappropriate at that time to glorify an animal bearing a German prefix, so, as the breed had come from Alsace, it became known in the United Kingdom as the Alsatian. Only in 1971 did the British Kennel Club relent and agree to the breed being known once more as the German Shepherd Dog. 109▸

DALMATIAN

Good points
- *Equable temperament*
- *Loyal*
- *Easy to train*
- *Intelligent*
- *Makes a good house pet*
- *Reliable with children*

Take heed
- *Needs ample exercise*
- *That coat will shed!*

The Dalmatian has a happy nature, is loyal and devoted to its owners and rarely fights. It is easily trained and fairly simple to present in show. It is generally long-lived, and has a lively youth. Remember that it was bred to run with horse and carriage, and has the need and stamina for plenty of exercise.

Size
Overall balance of prime importance, but the ideal height for a dog is 58.5-61cm (23-24in), for a bitch 56-58.5cm (22-23in).

Exercise
Don't buy a Dalmatian unless you can give it plenty of exercise. It is in its element running behind a horse, but an active, open-air country life will suffice.

Grooming
Daily brushing; occasional bathing.

Health care
Some Dalmatians suffer from deafness. Check that a pup can hear before buying.

Feeding
Recommended would be 1½-2½ cans (376g, 13.3oz size) of a branded meaty product, with biscuit added in equal part by volume; or 5 cupfuls of a dry food, complete diet, mixed in the proportion of 1 cup of feed to ½ cup of hot or cold water.

Origin and history
The Dalmatian is often thought of as a British dog, mainly because of its popularity as a carriage dog in the 18th century, but in fact it originated in Yugoslavia. The breed has enjoyed an upsurge in popularity since 1959, when Walt Disney made a film of Dodie Smith's enchanting book, *A Hundred and One Dalmatians*. It is still shown on the cinema circuits during children's holiday periods, and has a healthy effect on Dalmatian registrations. Mrs E.J. Woodyatt's Champion Fanhill Faune won Best in Show at Crufts in February 1978. 110▸

Above: Capable of great endurance with a fair amount of speed, the lively Dalmatian will make a loyal companion and thrive as a pet, provided it is given plenty of exercise in open countryside.

WEIMARANER

Good points

- *Distinctive appearance*
- *Does not shed*
- *Excels in obedience competitions*
- *Fine gundog*
- *Good temperament*

Take heed

- *Likes to have a job of work to do*
- *Thrives best if kept indoors*

The Weimaraner (or Silver Ghost) is an excellent gundog, which originally hunted big game. It is obedient and eminently trainable, excelling in obedience competitions, and has been used as both police dog and guard. It makes a good pet, but is happiest when given a job to do.

Size

Height at withers: dog 61-68.5cm (24-27in), bitch 56-63.5cm (22-25in).

Exercise

Needs plenty; has boundless energy. No need to rule out town living, but it is essential that the Weimaraner has lots of supervised freedom.

Grooming

Needs very little brushing, if any, for its sleek coat will naturally free itself of mud. Clip nails when necessary.

Feeding

Recommended would be 1½-2½ cans (376g, 13.3oz size) of a branded meaty product, with biscuit added in equal part by volume; or 5 cupfuls of a dry food, complete diet, mixed in the proportion of 1 cup of feed to ½ cup of hot or cold water.

Origin and history.

The Weimaraner burst upon the British scene in the early 1950s, since when it has become popular as a family pet, show dog and contender in obedience competitions. It is also well thought of in the United States, the best stock being available in those two countries. But the Weimaraner is in fact no newcomer, having been purpose-bred as a gundog at the court in Weimar, Germany, towards the end of the 18th century. Bloodhounds, Pointers and the old St Hubert Hounds are said to have assisted in its make-up. Its silver-grey colour is extremely distinctive. 110▸

Below: With its distinctive pale eyes and metallic silver-grey coat, the Weimaraner is as striking in appearance as it is impressive as a first-rate gundog.

BOXER

Good points

- *Brave*
- *Clownish*
- *Good guard*
- *Loves children*
- *Loyal*
- *Impressive show dog*

Take heed

- *Enjoys a scrap and respects opponents smaller than itself!*

The Boxer is a delightful animal that takes longer than most to grow up. It loves children and is a faithful protector of the family. However, it is an exuberant, fairly powerful dog, deserving a reasonable-sized home and garden and owners prepared to spend the necessary time on exercising and training. It has served in the armed forces and as a guide dog for the blind (seeing eye dog). Its tail is docked, and when pleased it tends to wag its whole body with pleasure.

Size

Height at the withers: dog 56-61cm (22-24in); bitch 53-58.5cm (21-23in). Weight: dogs around 58.5cm (23in) should weigh about 30kg (66lb); and bitches of about 56cm (22in) should weigh about 28.1kg (62lb).

Exercise

Good daily walks and off-the-lead runs are recommended.

Grooming

Daily brushing is sufficient.

Feeding

Recommended would be 1½-2½ cans (376g, 13.3oz size) of a branded meaty product, with biscuit added in equal part by volume; or 5 cupfuls of a dry food, complete diet, mixed in the proportion of 1 cup of feed to ½ cup of hot or cold water.

Origin and history

The Boxer is traceable to the old holding dogs of Mollossus or Mastiff type, which the Cimbrians took into battle against the Romans. Like the Bulldog, its jaw is undershot, a trait common in bull-baiters. The Brabant bull-baiter, from which the English Bulldog evolved, also played its part in the evolution of the Boxer, which retains its fighting spirit to this day. 110▸

Below: The Boxer is renowned for its enthusiasm and lively personality.

CHOW CHOW

Good points

- *Beautiful*
- *Loyal*
- *Odour-free*

Take heed

- *Formidable opponent*
- *Needs firm gentle handling*
- *Strong willed*
- *One-man dog (but will accept owner's family)*

The Chow Chow, whose name is perhaps derived from the Chinese Choo Hunting Dog, is a member of the Spitz family known for over 2000 years, lion-like in appearance and famed for its black tongue. It is odour-free and makes an incredibly loyal companion, tending to devote itself to one member of the family though accepting and returning the affection of other household members. It needs quiet but firm handling: with its aloof temperament it is unlikely to deign to walk at your heel without persuasion. It does not take kindly to strangers and is a fearsome fighter if provoked.

The Chow Chow is an extremely successful show dog; its beautiful coat and dignified appearance attract great attention from visitors and fellow competitors.

Size

Minimum height for Chows is 46cm (18in), but in every case balance should be the outstanding feature and height left to the discretion of the judges.

Exercise

Most Chow owners seem to manage with regular on-the-lead walks with runs in permitted areas. However, mindful of the Chow's prowess as a hunter of wolves, game and anything that moves, it seems unfair to keep it in confined surroundings or to deprive it of the open spaces that it relishes.

Grooming

About 5 or 10 minutes' brushing a day and about an hour each weekend with a wire brush should keep the Chow gleaming.

Feeding

One to 1½ cans (376g, 13.3oz size) of a branded meaty product, with biscuit added in equal part by volume; or 3 cupfuls of dry, complete food mixed in the proportion of 1 cup of feed to ½ cup of hot or cold water. Perhaps not surprisingly, they also do well on rice or on tripe, chicken and lean beef.

Origin and history

Although there are other black-mouthed dogs, the Chow is the only dog with a black tongue, although small bears—to which it has some resemblance—share this characteristic. Reputed to be the original Lama's Mastiff, the Chow Chow must be one of the oldest members of the Spitz family and was bred variously for its flesh —which in many parts of Asia is considered a delicacy—and for its fur and as a useful hunter of game. In early Chinese writings, it was known as the Tartar Dog, or Dog of Barbarians. The first breed members imported into England, in 1760, were exhibited in a zoo. Sadly, a reputation for ferocity has come down with the Chow, yet it is an affectionate, devoted animal. It is unlikely to fight unless provoked, but then it will be a formidable opponent. The Chow Chow Club was formed in England in 1895 and today around 600 or 700 breed members a year are registered with the British Kennel Club, and interest in the breed is constantly growing. 112▸

GOLDEN RETRIEVER

Good points
- *Excellent gundog*
- *Gentle with children*
- *Sound temperament*
- *Intelligent*
- *Easy to train*
- *First-class show dog*
- *Good family pet*

Take heed
- *No drawbacks known*

The Golden Retriever cannot be too highly recommended as a breed to suit all the family. It will romp with the children, enjoy a day's shooting with the man of the house, and happily accompany the mistress on a shopping trip, or for a session at the dog training club. This is a trustworthy breed, which can be kennelled, but individuals are happiest sharing the fireside with their family. They love to retrieve and will enjoy nothing better than carrying the newspaper home, or wandering around the house with an old chewed slipper. They are often used as guide dogs (seeing eye dogs) for the blind.

Size
The average weight in good hard condition should be: dog 31.8-36.3kg (70-80lb); bitch 27.2-31.8kg (60-70lb). Height at shoulder: dog 56-61cm (22-24in); bitch 51-56cm (20-22in).

Exercise
Needs at least an hour's exercise every day, and free runs, also an ample garden.

Grooming
Regular brushing will keep the coat in good condition.

Feeding
Recommended would be 1½-2½ cans (376g, 13.3oz size) of a branded meaty product, with biscuit added in equal part by volume; or 5 cupfuls of a dry food, complete diet, mixed in the proportion of 1 cup of feed to ½ cup of hot or cold water.

Origin and history
There is some controversy as to the origin of this breed. Did it, as many like to believe, develop from a troupe of Russian shepherd dogs found by Lord Tweedmouth performing in a Brighton circus in 1860, or did it begin with a litter of golden-haired pups of retriever/spaniel ancestry born on his Scottish estate? Romanticists like to believe the tale that Lord Tweedmouth was so greatly impressed with the Russian shepherd dogs that he bought the entire troupe and bred from them, adding Bloodhound blood to develop the nose. It is a theory that still has enthusiasts arguing. 109▸

Below: The Golden Retriever is second to none as a gentle and trustworthy pet for all the family.

LABRADOR RETRIEVER

Good points
- *Equable temperament*
- *Excellent gundog*
- *Good family pet*
- *Kind with children*
- *Easy to train*
- *Intelligent*
- *First-class showdog*

Take heed
- *No drawbacks known*

Like the Golden Retriever, the Labrador Retriever cannot be too highly recommended as a breed tailor-made to suit the whole family. It is an excellent retriever, can be trusted with the children and will give a good account of itself in obedience training competitions. The Labrador Retriever is a breed much favoured as a guide dog (seeing eye dog) for the blind.

Size
Height: dog 56-57cm (22-22½in); bitch 54.5-56cm (21½-22in).

Exercise
Needs an hour a day at least, with free runs, also an ample garden.

Grooming
Regular brushing will keep the coat in good condition.

Feeding
Recommended would be 1½-2½ cans (376g, 13.3oz size) of a branded meaty product, with biscuit added in equal part by volume; or 5 cupfuls of a dry food, complete diet, mixed in the proportion of 1 cup of feed to ½ cup of water.

Origin and history
The Labrador Retriever came to Britain with fishermen from Newfoundland (not Labrador) in the 1830s, the dog's task in those days being to land the nets of the fishermen; their ability to swim has survived. Among the most popular British gundogs, they are also much sought after as family pets in many parts of the world. 109▸

Below: Three Labrador Retrievers, obedient and intelligent as ever.

FLAT-COATED RETRIEVER

Good points
- *Can live kennelled or as a housepet*
- *Easy to train*
- *Good with children*
- *Hardy*
- *Natural retriever*
- *Good guard dog*

Take heed
- *No drawbacks known*

The Flat-coated Retriever is likely to enjoy renewed popularity since attaining the coveted Best in Show award at Crufts in 1980. It is a natural retriever, used for picking up game; it is hardy and easily trained, and makes a good household companion if you wish, being very good with children.

Size
Should be 27.2-31.8kg (60-70lb).

Exercise
Thrives on plenty of exercise.

Grooming
Regular brushing and tidying up.

Feeding
Recommended would be 1½-2½ cans (376g, 13.3oz size) of a branded meaty product, with biscuit added in equal part by volume; or 5 cupfuls of a dry food, complete diet, mixed in the proportion of 1 cup of feed to ½ cup of hot or cold water.

Origin and history
The Flat-coat probably owes its evolution to the Labrador Retriever, the Collie and certain spaniels. It was at one time known as the Wavy-coated Retriever, and it is thought that Collie blood was introduced to produce the Flat-coat. Prior to the First World War the Flat-coat was perhaps the best-known gundog in Britain, but it was over-shadowed in the post-war era by the Golden Retriever and Labrador Retriever, whose appeal has remained constant, not, however, to the detriment of the quality of the Flat-coat breed. 111▸

Below: The Flat-coated Retriever is a strongly-built working dog that will make a dependable pet.

CHESAPEAKE BAY RETRIEVER

Good points
- *First-class retriever*
- *Sportsman's favourite*
- *Usually good with children*
- *Intelligent*
- *Devoted to owner*

Take heed
- *Occasionally aggressive*
- *Oily coat may be off-putting to some people*

The Chesapeake Bay is a favourite with American sportsmen but has to date few devotees in the United Kingdom. It is an excellent swimmer and an unsurpassed retriever of wild duck. It is generally good with children, but can be a little headstrong and difficult to train. Distinguishing features are the breed's yellow eyes and web feet. Its coat is water-resistant.

Size
Weight: dog 29.5-34kg (65-75lb), bitch 25-29.5kg (55-65lb). Height: dog 58.5-66cm (23-26in), bitch 53-61cm (21-24in).

Exercise
Needs plenty of hard exercise to stay in good condition.

Grooming
Normal brushing is sufficient.

Feeding
Recommended would be 1½-2½ cans (376g, 13.3oz size) of a branded meaty product, with biscuit added in equal part by volume; or 5 cupfuls of a dry food, complete diet, mixed in the proportion of 1 cup of feed to ½ cup of hot or cold water.

Origin and history
This is an American retriever of British origin. An English brig went aground off the coast of Maryland in 1807 and was rescued by an American ship, the *Canton*. Aboard the brig were two pups, which were named 'Canton', after the rescue ship, and 'Sailor'. They were subsequently trained to retrieve duck, and crossed with Otterhounds and the Curly-coated and Flat-coated Retriever. The pups are said to have been Newfoundland in origin. Americans seem to want to retain the breed as a sporting dog, which is why it has not found its way into many homes as a pet. People either rave about the merits of the Chesapeake Bay, or are completely put off by their oily coats, not unpleasant oily odour, and yellow-orange eyes. 111▸

Above: Not widely kept as a household pet, the Chesapeake Bay Retriever has many admirers for its abilities as a sporting dog. Its web feet and oily, water-resistant coat make it well suited for retrieving wild duck.

CURLY-COATED RETRIEVER

Good points

- *Beautiful appearance*
- *Equable temperament*
- *Excellent guard*
- *Fine swimmer*
- *Good nose/retriever*
- *Full of stamina*
- *Intelligent*

Take heed

- *No drawbacks known*

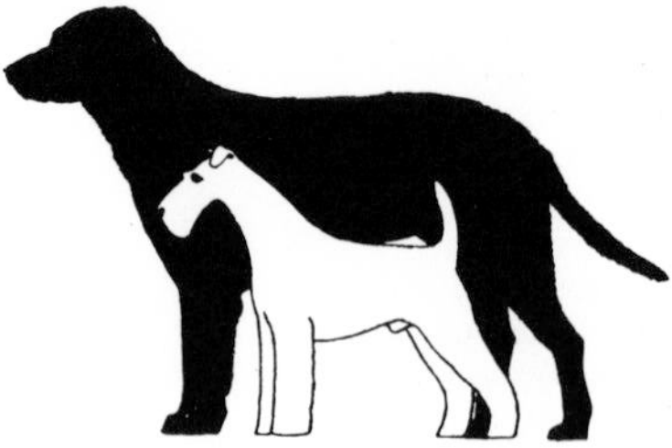

The Curly-coat is an excellent worker on land and in water, and will retrieve any game. It is a hardy dog, of good temperament and fine appearance. One wonders why its numbers have diminished.

Size

Weight: 31.8-36.3kg (70-80lb).
Height: 63.5-68.5cm (25-27in).

Exercise

Thrives on liberal amounts of vigorous exercise.

Grooming

Don't brush and comb this breed Just damp the coat down and massage with circular movements. Seek advice on trimming.

Feeding

Recommended would be 1½-2½ cans (376g, 13.3oz size) of a branded meaty product, with biscuit added in equal part by volume; or 5 cupfuls of a dry food, complete diet, mixed in the proportion of 1 cup of feed to ½ cup of hot or cold water.

Origin and history

The Curly-coat was one of the earliest British retrievers. It was exhibited at dog shows in England as early as 1860 and was depicted in many sporting prints beforehand. Its popularity seems to have waned since the beginning of the First World War and, despite its superb working ability, it has never been in great demand since. The early Labrador obviously played a part in its make-up and, to hazard a suggestion, the Water Spaniel, which, with its tight curly coat, it closely resembles. 111▸

Below: Bred for retrieving game from thick cover and water, the Curly-coated Retriever makes a faithful companion and house pet.

HOVAWART

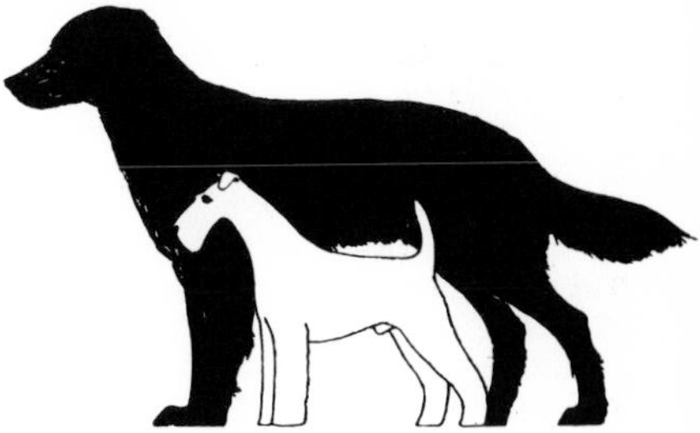

Good points
- *Excellent guard*
- *Home-loving*
- *Fond of children*
- *Loyal*
- *Obedient*

Take heed
- *Slow to mature*
- *Tends to be a one-person dog*
- *Will fight if challenged*

The Hovawart is an old German breed which, like so many of similar origin, was not bred for a specific purpose. It is, and always has been, just a loyal companion dog and protector of the home. The German Kennel Club recognized the breed in 1936.

It is generally obedient, loves children, and has utter loyalty to its master, tending to be a one-person dog, although defending the entire family with its life. It is good natured, but will fight well if put to the test.

Size
Height: 63.5-68.5cm (25-27in); Weight: 29.5-40.8kg (65-90lb): bitches less.

Exercise
Normal regular exercise.

Grooming
Regular brushing will keep the coat shining and in good condition.

Feeding
Recommended would be 1½-2½ cans (376g, 13.3oz size) of a branded meaty product, with biscuit added in equal part by volume; or 5 cupfuls of a dry food, complete diet, mixed as 1 cup of feed to ½ cup of hot or cold water.

Origin and history
The Hovawart was already a popular companion dog in Germany during the Middle Ages. In fact, the name Hovawart means 'house guard'. It resembles the Kuvasz in stature and looks like a large Collie. The breed seems to have suffered a period of unpopularity, but after the First World War such specimens as could be found were crossed with Leonbergers and Newfoundlands to perpetuate a once famous breed.

Below: The loyal Hovawart will instinctively defend its owners.

RHODESIAN RIDGEBACK

Good points
- *Affectionate*
- *Obedient*
- *Good with children*
- *Superior intelligence*
- *Sense of fun*

Take heed
- *Will guard you, and your possessions, with its life!*
- *Deserves a large garden*

The Rhodesian Ridgeback is a handsome, muscular, medium-sized dog of the hound group, with a short tan-coloured coat, pendulous ears and a long, uncropped tail.

The breed is named after the line of hair, shaped like the blade of a broadsword, that grows in the reverse direction along the back, with two crowns at the shoulder and the point towards the tail. This ridge is a very distinctive marking that is not found in any other breed of dog.

Although the ridge may appear to be a superficiality, created for the show ring or as a talking point, in fact it is far from recent and has come down through the centuries by way of the African Hottentot Hunting Dog.

The Rhodesian Ridgeback is of a quiet temperament and rarely barks; it enjoys spending hours curled up lazily in the corner of a room, stretched out in the summer sun, or basking in front of an open fireplace. Although its exploits as a hunter of African game first brought it recognition, the breed was developed as a dual-purpose dog, as a hunter and a gentle guardian of the families of the early white settlers. More and more people are discovering the tranquil temperament of this breed, its affectionate disposition and desire for human companionship. The Ridgeback likes nothing better than to lean against you, or to sit on your feet. And if you own a diamond, this is just the dog to guard it!

Below: The beautiful Rhodesian Ridgeback will adorn its owner's house as well as protect it.

Size

The desirable weight is: dog 36.3kg (80lb), bitch 31.75kg (70lb), with a permissible variation of 2.3kg (5lb) above and below these weights. A mature Ridgeback should be a handsome, upstanding animal; dogs should be of a height of 63.5-68.5cm (25-27in) and bitches 61-66cm (24-26in). Minimum bench standard: dog 63.5cm (25in), bitch 61cm (24in).

Exercise

This large, sleepy and apparently slow-moving animal with its characteristic love of lazing, contrasts sharply with its action when alerted. In a flash, it is converted into a graceful streak of rhythmic motion, a pleasure to watch as it quickly overtakes a rabbit or a squirrel in full flight. This is a pet that should have a large garden to run in, and deserves a master able to give it a good walk every day.

Grooming

Daily grooming with a hound glove, coupled with correct feeding and plenty of exercise, will keep the Ridgeback in healthy and gleaming condition.

Feeding

About 1½-2½ cans of branded dog food (376g, 13.3oz size), supplemented by biscuit, should be sufficient for your Ridgeback. Or, if you prefer, 5 cupfuls of a dry food, complete diet, mixed in the proportion of 1 cup of feed to ½ cup of hot or cold water. And of course, like most breeds, the Ridgeback will enjoy meat scraps and the occasional large bone.

Remember that suggested quantities are only a guide, and should be increased or decreased according to the desired weight of your dog. Watch it carefully, and if it appears to be putting on undue weight, cut down on the biscuit.

Origin and history

Long before Europeans settled in South Africa, the members of the Hottentot tribe had, as a companion who accompanied them on their hunting expeditions, an animal that has since been called the Hottentot Hunting Dog, a distinct characteristic of which was the ridge of hair growing in the reverse direction along its back.

During the 16th and 17th centuries, Dutch, Boers, Germans and Huguenots migrated to South Africa and, as these people were pioneers in a new and uncivilized country teeming with fierce wild animals, they brought with them their own European medium-sized and large working and hunting dogs. Probably by chance, the white settlers' dogs became crossed with the tough Hottentot Hunting Dogs, and the superior quality and vigour of their offspring were quickly recognized, the presence of the ridge identifying the most desirable dogs.

This blending over 200 years of the best qualities of many European breeds with those of the Hottentot Hunting Dog formed the immediate ancestor of today's Ridgeback, which has many of the characteristics usually associated with other hounds. 177▸

JAPANESE AKITA (Akita)

Good points
- *Strong and courageous*
- *Easily trained*
- *First-class guard*
- *Versatile hunter/retriever*
- *Good temperament*
- *Intelligent*
- *Extremely faithful*

Take heed
- *No drawbacks known*

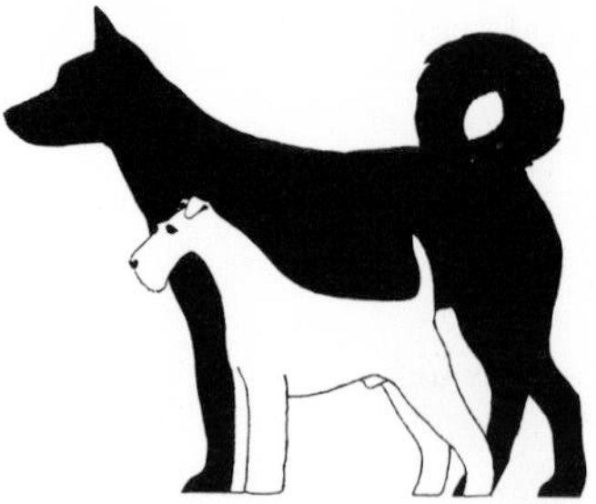

The Japanese Akita is the best-known of the Japanese Spitz breeds but has only recently come on the international scene. The breed has been exhibited in recent years in the United Kingdom and America, and the Japanese are doing all possible to improve their purebred stock. Bred as a hunter of wild boar, deer and even black bear, the Akita is undoubtedly capable of ferocity, but it is easily trained and generally has an equable temperament.

Size
Height: dog 53-61cm (21-24in), some bigger; bitch 48-53cm (19-21in). Weight: 38.6-49.9kg (85-110lb).

Exercise
Does not require a great deal of exercise. Incidentally, it has webbed feet and is a fine swimmer and a good water dog.

Grooming
Normal daily brushing.

Feeding
Recommended would be 1½-2½ cans (376g, 13.3oz size) of a branded meaty product, with biscuit added in equal part by volume; or 5 cupfuls of a dry food, complete diet, mixed in the proportion of 1 cup of feed to ½ cup of hot or cold water.

Origin and history
The Akita resembles a smooth-coated Chow and is the largest of the known Japanese Spitz breeds. It is bred in its native land as a

Above: The Japanese Akita is highly respected for its fearless spirit.

hunter of wild boar and deer, and is obviously related to the Icelandic breeds. However, it has bred true in Japan's Akita Province for more than 300 years, and its exact origin is obscure.

The Akita is revered in Japan for its hunting and retrieving skills, particularly its stamina for working in deep snow and its ability to retrieve waterfowl and even drive fish into fishermen's nets. In 1931 the breed was officially appointed a national treasure and monument of Japan.

American servicemen returning after the Second World War took the Akita home and boosted its popularity in America. 112▸

ALASKAN MALAMUTE

Good points
- *Affectionate*
- *Fast and strong*
- *Fine sled dog*
- *Loves children*
- *Intelligent*
- *Sociable*

Take heed
- *No drawbacks known*

The Alaskan Malamute is an Arctic Spitz-type little known outside Alaska and the United States. It is a sociable dog, capable of being driven in sled races by children. It is highly prized as a sled dog, and capable of immense speed. Don't be put off by the wolfish appearance: the kindly expression is genuine!

Size
Height: dog 63.5-71cm (25-28in); bitch 58.5-66cm (23-26in). Weight: 38.6-56.7kg (85-125lb).

Exercise
Needs plenty of vigorous exercise to stay healthy.

Grooming
Regular brushing will keep the coat in good condition.

Feeding
Recommended would be 1½-2½ cans (376g, 13.3oz size) of a branded meaty product, with biscuit added in equal part by volume; or 5 cupfuls of a dry food, complete diet, mixed in the proportion of 1 cup of feed to ½ cup of hot or cold water.

Origin and history
The Alaskan Malamute is named after a native tribe called the Mahlemuts. The origin of the dogs is obscure, but the breed is obviously closely related to other Spitz-types, such as the Samoyed. 111▶

Below: The Alaskan Malamute combines great strength, stamina and beauty in the shape of a fine working dog and an affectionate companion.

ESKIMO DOG /GREENLAND DOG

Good points
- *Beautiful appearance*
- *Can become devoted*
- *Great endurance*
- *Excellent sled dogs*
- *Strong*
- *Fine guards*

Take heed
- *Rarely live indoors*
- *Suspicious of strangers*

The Eskimo Dog is one of several regional sled dogs of different names, few of which are well known outside the polar area. It is hardy, and accustomed to fending for itself, living outside and often having to find its own food.

The Greenland Dog is so similar that controversy rages as to whether they should be separately classified. Usually the Eskimo Dog is a little shorter in the back than the Greenland, and weightier generally, but without extra height.

Size
Height at shoulder: dog 58.5-68.5cm (23-27in); bitch 51-61cm (20-24in). Weight: dog 34-47.6kg (75-105lb); bitch 27.2-40.8kg (60-90lb).

Exercise
These dogs are accustomed to pulling sleds and hauling fishing boats ashore. They would soon get bored snoozing by the fire.

Grooming
Regular brushing will keep the coat in good condition.

Feeding
Recommended would be 1½-2½ cans (376g, 13.3oz size) of a branded meaty product, with biscuit added in equal part by volume; or 5 cupfuls of a dry food, complete diet, mixed in the proportion of 1 cup of feed to ½ cup of hot or cold water.

Origin and history
These polar Spitz breeds no doubt originated in Eastern Siberia and shared a common task and ancestry with the Alaskan Malamute, Siberian Husky and Samoyed. To quote the American explorer Peary, 'there is, in fact, only one sled dog'. 111▸

Below: The rugged and good-natured Eskimo dog may not adapt well to domestic life as a house pet.

OTTERHOUND

Good points

- *Appealing*
- *Excellent swimmer*
- *Friendly*
- *Gentle with children*
- *Waterproof coat*

Take heed

- *Essentially a hound rather than a house pet, and not ideally suited to suburban living*

With otter hunting now outlawed in the United Kingdom, the Otterhound could have faced extinction, had not the last Master of the Kendal and District Otterhounds, in the Lake District, set up the Otterhound Club to ensure the survival of the breed. Without the continued interest of breeders and the show world, the Otterhound would certainly die out.

The Otterhound is an amiable, friendly animal, gentle with children and responsive to affection. However, one should not lose sight of the fact that it was a pack hound bred to kill, a background that does not ideally equip it as a household pet.

Size

Height: dogs should stand approximately 68.5cm (27in) at the shoulder; bitches approximately 61cm (24in). Weight: dogs 34-52.2kg (75-115lb); bitches 29.5-45.4kg (65-100lb).

Exercise

The Otterhound needs a lot of exercise. A unique feature of this breed is the existence of webbing between the toes. This gives the Otterhound a decided advantage in the water. Most dogs can swim, but the Otterhound excels in that ability, and is as much at home in the water as it is on land.

Grooming

A thorough brush and comb once a week should be sufficient to keep the Otterhound's coat in good condition. There is natural oil in the coat and, if bathing the animal for a show, it is advisable to do this a week beforehand to allow the coat to regain its correct texture. However, the head hair can be bathed the day before a show because this is of a finer texture.

Particular attention must be paid to the ears, as they are inclined to collect wax and can become a source of irritation to the animal. Inspect the ears regularly.

Feeding

The Otterhound is a large dog and will need up to 2½ cans of a good branded meaty diet (376g, 13.3oz size) to which biscuit should be added in equal part by volume; or 5 cupfuls of a dry food, complete diet, mixed in the proportion of 1 cup of feed to ½ cup of hot or cold water.

Origin and history

The Otterhound is an extremely old breed, and its origins are somewhat obscure. Some say it descended from the old Southern Hound and others see the Bloodhound in its ancestry. Today it is most like some of the French hounds, such as the Griffon Nivernais or Griffon Vendéen, and it is quite possible that the Otterhound springs from the same origins as these French breeds.

Otter hunting was one of the earliest field sports in the United Kingdom and King John, Henry II and Elizabeth I all kept Otterhound packs, long before foxes were thought worthy to be hunted. Many monasteries also kept Otterhounds to protect their fishponds from the nightly ravages of otters. 112▸

ITALIAN SPINONE

Good points
- *Affectionate*
- *Fine retriever of water fowl*
- *Hardy*
- *Good guard dog*
- *Easy to train*
- *Loyal companion*

Take heed
- *No drawbacks known*

The Italian Spinone is an ancient breed of gundog, much appreciated by Italian horsemen for its ability to work in marshy and wooded country. It has a soft mouth and will point and retrieve. It is good-natured and well established in its own country.

Size
Height: dog 60-65cm (23½-25½in); bitch 54.5-60cm (21½-23½in).

Exercise
Needs plenty of vigorous exercise.

Grooming
Daily brushing will be sufficient.

Feeding
Recommended would be 1½-2½ cans (376g, 13.3oz size) of a branded meaty product, with biscuit added in equal part by volume; or 5 cupfuls of a dry food, complete diet, mixed in the proportion of 1 cup of feed to ½ cup of hot or cold water.

Origin and history
The Spinone originated in the French region of Bresse but later found its way to Piedmont in Italy, its evolution being attributable to the French Griffon, French and German Pointers, the Porçelaine, Barbet and Korthals Griffon. What has emerged is a reliable gundog with a pleasing appearance, somewhere between a Pointer and a Foxhound. 112▸

Below: The friendly and rugged Italian Spinone is a popular gundog and show dog in its native country.

ROTTWEILER

Good points
- *Good temperament*
- *Intelligent*
- *Makes a good household companion/guard*
- *Reliable working dog*

Take heed
- *Responds best to kind, firm handling – not being chained or kennelled in a back yard*

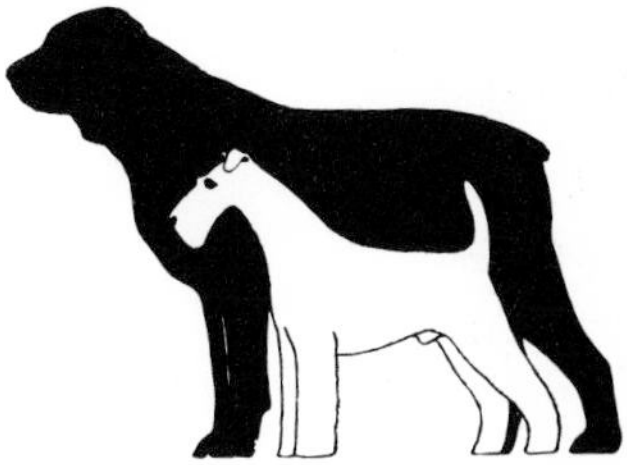

The Rottweiler is a German working dog of high intelligence and good temperament. It has been a draught dog and herder, and is still used as guard, police dog, sled dog and mountain rescue dog. In many countries it is sought after as a companion/pet and guard. It is a popular contender in the show ring and does well in obedience tests.

Size
Height at shoulder: dog 63.5-68.5cm (25-27in); bitch 58.5-63.5cm (23-25in).

Exercise
Regular walks and runs.

Grooming
Daily brushing will keep the coat in good condition.

Feeding
Recommended would be 1½-2½ cans (376g, 13.3oz size) of a branded meaty product, with biscuit added in equal part by volume; or 5 cupfuls of a dry food, complete diet, mixed in the proportion of 1 cup of feed to ½ cup of hot or cold water.

Origin and history
The Rottweiler is a butcher's dog. It comes from the West German town of Rottweil in Württemberg, where it is known as the Rottweiler Metzgerhund or Rottweil butcher's dog.

It was known in the Middle Ages as a hunter of wild boar, and later as a revered and trusted cattle dog as well as a draught dog that would draw carts for butchers and cattle dealers. Just before the first World War its abilities were recognized as a police dog and guard.

Thelma Gray of the Rozavel Kennels introduced the breed into Britain in 1936. It was developing a following until World War II, when breeding ceased, and it was not until a Captain Roy-Smith, serving with the Occupation Army in Germany, brought home a dog and bitch that a sound breeding programme was re-established, since when a few breed devotees have produced many good specimens. 177▸

Below: Excellent as a guard and police dog, the powerful Rottweiler will also make a reliable and affectionate companion for the family.

POLISH SHEEPDOG (Owczarek Podhalanski, Owczarek Nizinny)

Good points
- *Excellent guard*
- *Hardy*
- *Generally good-natured*
- *Intelligent*

Take heed
- *No drawbacks known. However, the Nizinny is generally thought to be the more docile of the two varieties*

Lowlands type

There are two varieties of Polish Sheepdog, the Lowlands Shepherd Dog (Owczarek Nizinny), which looks something like the Old English Sheepdog, and the Tatry Mountain Sheepdog (Owczarek Podhalanski), a bigger type that has something of the Retriever or Kuvasz about its appearance. They are both intelligent, good-natured, generally docile and have a keen memory.

Size
Height: Tatry Mountain Sheepdog 66cm (26in); Lowlands Shepherd Dog 40.5-51cm (16-20in).

Exercise
Plenty of exercise necessary.

Below: The Lowlands Shepherd Dog, a hardy sheepdog from Poland.

Grooming
Regular brushing; the Lowlands type will need combing with a steel comb also.

Feeding
Recommended would be 1½-2½ cans (376g, 13.3oz size) of a branded meaty product, with biscuit added in equal part by volume; or 5 cupfuls of a dry food, complete diet, mixed in the proportion of 1 cup of feed to ½ cup of hot or cold water.

Origin and history
The Tatry Mountain Sheepdog bears a strong similarity to the Hungarian Kuvasz, and both varieties are credited with having been introduced to Poland in the 4th or 5th century. They are little known outside their homeland. 180▸

OLD ENGLISH SHEEPDOG

Good points

- *Beautiful appearance*
- *Home-loving*
- *Intelligent*
- *Adaptable to different climates*
- *Excellent with children*
- *Gets on well with other animals*
- *Sound temperament*

Take heed

- *No drawbacks known*

The Old English Sheepdog, or Bobtail, is an extremely popular breed, being a devoted friend and guardian of children, with a sound, sensible temperament. It will live contentedly in a fairly small house despite its bulk.

Size

Height: dog 56cm (22in) and upwards; bitch slightly less.

Exercise

Regular walks of average length – perhaps two good walks of 20 minutes duration per day.

Grooming

Daily brushing and weekly combing with a steel comb. The hair is brushed forward to cover the eyes. I don't know how, but it *can* see! White parts are powdered for showing.

Below: The ever-popular Old English Sheepdog, a playful and devoted pet.

Health care

Check the ears for canker, and take care that dead, matted hair does not accumulate around the feet. Some Bobtails are born with that stumpy tail; otherwise it is docked to a length of 5cm (2in).

Feeding

Recommended would be 1½-2½ cans (376g, 13.3oz size) of a branded meaty product, with biscuit added in equal part by volume; or 5 cupfuls of a dry food, complete diet, mixed in the proportion of 1 cup of feed to ½ cup of hot or cold water.

Origin and history

The Old English Sheepdog is often, for obvious reasons, known as the Bobtail. How it came to England is a subject of conjecture, for the breed is said to have evolved through the crossing of the Briard with the large Russian Owtscharka, a dog related to the Hungarian sheepdogs. It was used in England as a cattle dog and guard, but nowadays is kept mainly as a much loved pet. Because of the Bobtail's reliability with children, a number have found their way into schools for handicapped youngsters. The first breed club for the Old English Sheepdog was established in Britain in 1888 and the standard has altered little in the intervening years. 180▸

BOUVIER DES FLANDRES

Good points

- *Strong and alert*
- *Easily trained*
- *Impressive guard*
- *Loyal to owner's family*
- *Trustworthy*

Take heed

- *Fierce appearance, especially with cropped ears*
- *One-person family dog*

The Bouvier des Flandres is a Belgian cattle dog, hardy, trustworthy, and – when its ears are cropped, as in its country of origin – looking the epitome of ferocity. It can be kept as a pet, but tends to be a one-person dog, though that means guarding their family as well!

Size

Weight: dog 34.9-39.9kg (77-88lb); bitch 27-34.9kg (59½-77lb). Height: dog 62-68.5cm (24½-27in); bitch 58.5-65cm (23-25½in).

Exercise

Needs plenty of exercise. Not ideally suited to town life.

Grooming

Regular brushing will keep the coat in good condition.

Feeding

Recommended would be 1½-2½ cans (376g, 13.3oz size) of a branded meaty product, with biscuit added in equal part by volume; or 5 cupfuls of a dry food, complete diet, mixed in the proportion of 1 cup of feed to ½ cup of hot or cold water.

Origin and history

The Bouvier was derived from a number of working Belgian breeds with the purpose of producing a good all-purpose dog, suitable for the rough shoot, for herding, and also as a draught dog. It was not until 1912 that a meeting was held to discuss a possible standard for the Bouvier; no agreement was reached, and devotees had to wait until after the First World War for a standard to be drawn up by the Club National Belge du Bouvier des Flandres and efforts made to improve future stock of the breed. 177▸

Below: The impressive Bouvier des Flandres makes an effective guard.

BRIARD

Good points
- *Easy to train*
- *Family pet and/or farm worker*
- *Gentle nature*
- *Good guard dog*
- *Weather-proof coat*
- *Successful show dog*
- *Loyal*

Take heed
- *No drawbacks known*

The Briard is the best-known of the four French sheepdogs – the others being the Beauceron, the Picardy and the Pyrenean Mountain Dog – although the latter won Best in Show at Crufts in 1970. Briards are good-natured, and can be kept happily either as an affectionate family pet, or for work around the farm; quite a number are finding their way into the show ring.

Size
Height: dog 58.5-68.5cm (23-27in); bitch 56-65cm (22-25½in).

Exercise
Regular, and not just a walk around the park.

Grooming
Regular brushing. The Briard takes pride in cleaning itself.

Feeding
Recommended would be 1½-2½ cans (376g, 13.3oz size) of a branded meaty product, with biscuit added in equal part by volume; or 5 cupfuls of a dry food, complete diet, mixed in the proportion of 1 cup of feed to ½ cup of hot or cold water.

Origin and history
The Briard comes from the Brie area of France, where it is also known as the Berger de Brie or Chien de Brie. It has been known since the 12th century. There is an entertaining 14th century French legend of how the Briard was given its name: in the year 1371 Sir Aubry de Montdidier was assassinated. His killer was hunted down by his dog, and it was ordained by the king that a battle should take place between the man, named Macaire, and the dog The battle took place on the Isle of Notre Dame, and the dog proved the victor. Macaire then admitted his crime and was beheaded. It is likely that from then on the Briard became known as the Chien d'Aubry, and a shield sculpted in stone was placed in the church at Montdidier, bearing a likeness of a dog's head that looks similar to the Briard of today. 177▶

Below: The Briard is an active and lively breed that can become a devoted pet and a trusted worker.

BLACK AND TAN COONHOUND

Good points
- *Fine nose*
- *Good temperament*
- *Strong and hardy*
- *Eager and alert*

Take heed
- *This breed is a working hound and needs plenty of exercise in open spaces*

The Black and Tan Coonhound is a fast, hardy, strong working hound that, like the Bloodhound, does not kill its prey. It is similar to the Bloodhound in appearance, but you can detect the Coonhound by its lack of wrinkles, characteristic of the Bloodhound.

Size
Height at the shoulder: dog 63.5-68.5cm (25-27in); bitch 58.5-63.5cm (23-25in).

Exercise
It is a working dog and needs plenty of vigorous exercise.

Grooming
Daily grooming with a hound glove. Regular ear inspection is advocated.

Feeding
Recommended would be 1½-2½ cans (376g, 13.3oz size) of a branded meaty product, with biscuit added in equal part by volume; or 5 cupfuls of a dry food, complete diet, mixed in the proportion of 1 cup of feed to ½ cup of hot or cold water.

Origin and history
The Black and Tan Coonhound is essentially an American breed, though a close relation of the Bloodhound, being identical in size and often in colour. It traces back from the Talbot Hound to the Bloodhound and the Virginia Foxhound. The Black and Tan is one of six types of Coonhound recognized in America, and is used for hunting opossum and raccoon. It is a working hound not often seen on the show bench. 179▸

Below: The Black and Tan Coonhound is fundamentally a working dog, capable of withstanding the rigours of winter, the heat of summer, and the difficult terrain over which it is required to work.

BLOODHOUND

Good points
- *Charming to look at*
- *Good with children*
- *Great tracker and trailer*
- *Ideal family pet – if you have room*

Take heed
- *Easily hurt – use only voice control*
- *Needs plenty of exercise*

The Bloodhound is a delightful animal with a nose that is second to none. It follows its quarry, but does not kill. Indeed, it is loved by children, who can accompany it on the lead, and is often kept as a family pet. Bloodhounds are popular show dogs, but individuals are still often called in by police for tracking purposes; a number have appeared in films.

Size
Height: dog 63.5-68.5cm (25-27in); bitch 58.5-63.5cm (23-25in). Weight: dog 40.8kg (90lb); bitch 36.3kg (80lb).

Exercise
Needs plenty. These dogs have to gallop. Best to join a Bloodhound club if you become an owner, and take part in organized events.

Grooming
Daily grooming with a hound glove. Regular ear inspection is advocated.

Health care
Bloodhounds are subject to torsion (stomach gases building into a bloat). A large proportion are affected and it can prove fatal if not treated within minutes. Be ready to seek immediate help.

Feeding
Recommended would be 1½-2½ cans (376g, 13.3oz size) of a branded meaty product, with biscuit added in equal part by volume; or 5 cupfuls of a dry food, complete diet, mixed in the proportion of 1 cup of feed to ½ cup of hot or cold water.

Origin and history
The Bloodhound is said to have been brought to England by William the Conqueror in 1066, and to be one of the oldest and purest of the hound breeds. 179▸

Below: These Bloodhound puppies make charming companions.

SLOVAKIAN KUVASZ (Tsuvatch)

Good points
- *Brave*
- *Intelligent*
- *Devoted*
- *Keen, alert watchdog*

Take heed
- *Needs plenty of exercise in wide open spaces*
- *Predominantly a working dog and guard*

The Slovakian Kuvasz is a lively and intelligent dog, ever watchful, and with acute hearing. Its characteristics are similar to those of the Hungarian Kuvasz.

Size
Height at shoulder is around 61cm (24in), but should not exceed 71cm (28in) for a dog, 66cm (26in) for a bitch.

Exercise
Needs plenty of vigorous exercise to stay healthy.

Grooming
Regular brushing is necessary to keep the coat in good condition.

Feeding
One to 2½ cans (376g, 13.3oz size) of a branded meaty product, with biscuit added in equal part by volume; or 5 cupfuls of a dry food, complete diet, mixed in the proportion of 1 cup of feed to ½ cup of hot or cold water.

Origin and history
The Slovakian Kuvasz is little known outside its own country. It would seem to be related to the Hungarian Kuvasz and bears resemblance also to the Owczarek Podhalanski, an ancient Polish herding breed. Indeed, Bo Bengtson and Ake Wintzell in their *Dogs of the World* suggest that the three breeds could be said to be local varieties in their respective countries of the same herding breed. The Polish and Slovakian types are sometimes known as 'Tatry' dogs, after the mountain range that stretches through both Poland and Czechoslovakia and where each has existed for a long time. 178▸

Below: The Slovakian Kuvasz is a powerfully built working dog and guard from Central Europe.

HUNGARIAN KUVASZ

Good points
- *Intelligent*
- *Excellent guard*
- *Loyal*
- *Tireless worker*
- *Gentle and patient*

Take heed
- *Tends to be a one-person dog*
- *Sensitive – should not be dealt with harshly*

The Hungarian Kuvasz may be kept as a pet and is loyal and devoted to its owner and family. It is, however, essentially a guard and will be ever watchful for intruders. It is an intelligent dog, and its name comes from a Turkish word meaning 'guardian of the peace'. It is a natural herder and has been used for big game hunting. However, its role in life is predominantly that of protector.

Size
Height at withers: dog 71-75cm (28-29½in); bitch 66-70cm (26-27½). Weight: dog 39.9-52.2kg (88-115lb); bitch 30-42.2kg (66-93lb).

Exercise
Needs plenty of exercise.

Below: The Hungarian Kuvasz is devoted to its owners but will treat strangers with suspicion.

Grooming
Regular brushing will keep the coat in good condition.

Feeding
Recommended would be 1½-2½ cans of a branded meaty product (376g, 13.3oz size), with biscuit added in equal part by volume; or 5 cupfuls of a dry food, complete diet, mixed in the proportion of 1 cup of feed to ½ cup of hot or cold water.

Origin and history
The Kuvasz has existed in Hungary for centuries, and as early as the 1490s was protecting Hungarian nobility against possible assassins. It became known as the guard dog of the privileged, only the high-born being permitted to keep one. It is a breed that has to date attained greater popularity in the United States than in Great Britain, where there are very few. 178▸

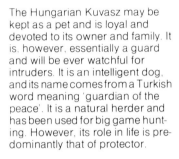

BERNESE MOUNTAIN DOG (Bernese Sennenhund)

Good points
- *Beautiful*
- *Easily trained*
- *Excellent watchdog*
- *Good with other animals and people*
- *Suitable as a pet*

Take heed
- *No drawbacks known, but it is a big dog to have around the place*

The Bernese Mountain Dog is the most internationally known of the four Swiss Mountain Dogs, the others being the Great Swiss Sennenhund (or Mountain Dog), the Appenzell Sennenhund and the Entlebuch Sennenhund. It is used as both draught dog and companion in its country of origin, but elsewhere it is gaining popularity as pet and show dog, being easy to train despite its size and strength, loyal, affectionate and docile with both other animals and humans. It is a beautiful dog, with something of the Collie in its appearance.

Size
Dog 63.5-70cm (25-27½in); bitch 58.5-66cm (23-26in).

Exercise
Needs a reasonable amount of exercise and is not ideally suited to town life or apartment living.

Below: The loyal Bernese, used as a draught dog for centuries.

Grooming
Regular brushing will keep the coat in good condition.

Feeding
Recommended would be 1½-2½ cans (376g, 13.3oz size) of a branded meaty product, with biscuit added in equal part by volume; or 5 cupfuls of a dry food, complete diet, mixed in the proportion of 1 cup of feed to ½ cup of hot or cold water.

Origin and history
The Bernese has been used as both herder and draught dog for centuries, and many a visitor to Switzerland returns with a snapshot of a Sennenhund pulling a milk cart. The types of Sennenhund are named after the regions in which they were found. They have Mastiff characteristics and are believed to have Molossian ancestry. The St Bernard, Rottweiler and Newfoundland are also related to the Sennenhunds. 178▸

ESTRELA MOUNTAIN DOG (Cão Serra da Estrela)

Good points
- *Excellent guard dog*
- *Can live in harmony with other dogs*

Take heed
- *A reserved dog with strangers*
- *Will wander if not properly enclosed*
- *Needs firm, but affectionate handling*

The Estrela Mountain Dog is a hardy animal of great power. A really excellent guard dog, it was bred to guard the flocks in the Sierra da Estrela range against wolves and marauders, and has considerable stamina. Very loyal and affectionate to its owners, but rather indifferent to others, the Estrela is intelligent and alert, but inclined to be stubborn.

The Estrela needs a special kind of home with a great deal of love, but a firm hand.

Size
Dogs: 65-76cm (25½-30in).
Bitches: 62-72·5cm (24½-28½in).

Exercise
Needs plenty of exercise.

Grooming
Regular brushing will keep the coat in good condition. The worst of the moult is quickly dealt with.

Feeding
The Estrela prefers a light diet, green tripe being a favourite. Rich, red meat is not often welcome. Biscuit is occasionally accepted. In puppyhood milk feeds are rejected at an early stage, while adults will have self imposed periods of starvation with no ill effect. The diet is sometimes a problem as Estrelas prefer a mild diet and are unlike most other breeds in their eating habits.

Origin and history
This is a dog that has existed for centuries in the Estrela mountains of Portugal. It resembles the St

Above: The Estrela Mountain Dog, a natural guard dog that needs firm, kind handling as a pet.

Bernard, but is of lighter stature with something of the Mastiff in its make-up. It was bred as a herder and guard dog.

The Estrela Mountain Dog was first introduced into the United Kingdom by Mr. Roger Pye, who sent a bitch whelp from Portugal in 1974. She produced seven pups, five dogs and two bitches, in the UK, the latter remaining while the mother returned to Portugal. Four of the pups were destined for Mrs. Marcia Dovey's Sturtmoor Kennel near Salisbury in Wiltshire. Sturtmoor has won five Top Estrela Awards. 179▶

ANATOLIAN KARABASH (Anatolian Sheepdog.

Good points
- *Affectionate*
- *Hardy and independent*
- *Intelligent*
- *Loyal*
- *Trainable*

Take heed
- *Not suited to town life*
- *Will accept others, but main loyalty remains with owner*

The Anatolian Karabash is a shepherd's guard dog of ancient lineage. It is a large, fast, vigorous outdoor working dog with a self-sufficient temperament. Such dogs are found from the Anatolian plateau of Turkey right across Afghanistan. The shepherds of Central Asia crop their dogs' ears and give them massive iron-spiked collars to help defend the flocks from predators.

The Anatolian Karabash can live outside all day, but it is much better to allow it in the house as part of the family, when it will become more amenable and a good companion.

This is a dog that will automatically identify with one person as its owner. It will accept other members of the family, and friends who have been introduced, but its main loyalty will remain with its owner.

It needs and responds to a great deal of love, and should be taken around and socialized at an early age, otherwise it may become too possessive. The Anatolian Karabash's natural inclination is to be friendly with other animals and it has a very long memory. Incidentally, when it leans heavily against you, this means that you have been totally accepted.

Size
Weight: dog 49.9-64kg (110-141lb); bitch 41-59kg (90½-130lb). Height: dog 73.5-81cm (29-32in) at the shoulder; bitch 71-78.5cm (28-31in) at the shoulder.

Exercise
As a pet the Karabash is not suited to town life, because it needs plenty of space in which to work off its energy. This it will do on its own, so normally there is no need to walk it in the conventional way. Indeed, it is said that a man would have to walk all day to give such a dog enough movement for it to be able to develop its superb body. The breed is naturally active and playful and will be happy in a large and well-fenced garden.

For such a big dog, the Anatolian Karabash moves remarkably quickly and gracefully, and speeds of 55kph (34mph) have been clocked up by the breed.

Grooming
The natural inclination of the Anatolian Karabash is to get up at intervals, especially at night, and patrol the area, bedding down in a different spot each time. This keeps its coat remarkably clean, odourless and free of parasites. However, it will benefit from regular brushing.

Feeding
The canned food requirement for a dog of this size is approximately 3 cans per day (376g, 13.3oz size), with biscuit supplement in equal part by volume, or the fresh meat equivalent, so they are by no means cheap to feed. Incidentally, all so-called soft bones may be given and are probably a necessity for the animal's proper development.

However, it is of interest that in their own country they can exist on very little, and shepherds have recounted with pride how their

Above: The Anatolian Karabash has exceptional stamina and hardiness, developed over centuries of outdoor life as a shepherd's dog.

dogs remained with the flocks for up to a week without food or water. They have two strange behavioural adaptations to help them survive, one being an alert 'hibernation' in the cruel midday Turkish sun, the other an ability to dig up gophers—a kind of prairie dog or marmot-like animal—for food.

Origin and history

Since Babylonian times, there existed in this area a breed of large, strong dogs with a heavy head. They were employed as war dogs, and for hunting big game such as lions and horses. Some spectacular examples can be seen on the very well preserved bas-reliefs in the Assyrian Room of the British Museum in London.

In their native Turkey the dogs do not herd the sheep, but patrol around them, often seeking higher ground to get a better view and a breeze. The dogs patrol the ground ahead of the flock, checking out every bush and irregularity of the terrain for potential trouble. Should they notice anything, even a moving car, they will, silently at first, split up and converge upon it at great speed. These ambush tactics are completely inborn and fascinating to watch. 179▶

TIBETAN MASTIFF

Good points
- *Handsome*
- *Strongly built*
- *Excellent guard dog*
- *Reliable temperament unless provoked*
- *Loyal to owner*

Take heed
- *Suspicious of strangers*

The Tibetan Mastiff bears a strong resemblance to the St Bernard. It is an excellent guard dog, but is good-natured unless provoked. It can be kept happily as a reliable companion/guard.

Size
Height at shoulder: dog 63.5-68.5cm (25-27in); bitch 56-61cm (22-24in).

Exercise
Needs regular vigorous exercise.

Grooming
Daily brushing will keep the coat in good, healthy condition.

Feeding
Recommended would be 1½-2½ cans (376g, 13.3oz size) of a branded meaty product, with biscuit added in equal part by volume; or 5 cupfuls of a dry food, complete diet, mixed in the proportion of 1 cup of feed to ½ cup of hot or cold water.

Origin and history
The Tibetan Mastiff is regarded as a British breed, but it originated in Central Asia, where its job was to guard flocks. Like other Mastiffs, it is likely to have descended from the Roman Molossus. 179▸

Below: The Tibetan Mastiff is a powerful guard dog from Central Asia. Basically a docile breed with strong allegiance to its owner, it will deter intruders with a show of force.

BORZOI

Good points
- *Aloof*
- *Beautiful and graceful*
- *Intelligent*
- *Faithful*
- *Striking show dog*

Take heed
- *A dignified dog, not ideal as a children's playmate*
- *Not suitable for apartments*

The Borzoi is an animal of great beauty and grace used in Russia from the 17th century for wolf hunting and coursing. Today it is often regarded more as a fashion accessory: the fur-clad silent film star accompanied by two Borzois was not a rarity!

They are dignified, good-natured animals, but somewhat aloof and not likely to enjoy playing wild games with children.

Size
Height at shoulder: dog from 73.5cm (29in) upwards; bitch from 68.5cm (27in) upwards.

Exercise
The Borzoi needs a great deal of exercise, but remember that this dog is a hunter: it is essential that it should be allowed to run only when far from livestock.

Feeding
Recommended would be 1½-2½ cans (376g, 13.3oz size) of a branded meaty product, with biscuit added in equal part by volume; or 5 cupfuls of a dry food, complete diet, mixed in the proportion of 1 cup of feed to ½ cup of hot or cold water.

Origin and history
The Borzoi was maintained for centuries by the Czars and noblemen of Imperial Russia for hunting the wolf. During the 15th and 16th centuries it was crossed with the sheepdog to provide strength, and later with various hounds to obtain more speed. However it was from the strain developed by the Grand Duke Nicolai Nicolayevitch that the present-day standard evolved. Information on present-day Borzois in the USSR is sketchy. There would appear to be more Borzois in fashionable capital cities of the world such as New York, London and Paris. 179▸

Below: Borzois combine elegance with great power and speed.

DEERHOUND (Scottish Deerhound)

Good points

- *Graceful and beautiful*
- *Hardy*
- *Happy to be with humans and to please*
- *Loving*
- *Sound temperament*

Take heed

- *No drawbacks known, if you have sufficient space*

The Deerhound is a creature of grace and beauty, mentioned frequently in the novels of Sir Walter Scott. It is strong and healthy, anxious to please and asks no more than to be its owner's devoted companion.

Size

Weight: dog 38.5-47.6kg (85-105lb); bitch 29.5-36.3kg (65-80lb). Height at shoulder: dog not less than 76cm (30in); bitch 71cm (28in).

Exercise

Needs a great deal of exercise.

Grooming

Requires very little trimming, just removal of extra shaggy hairs for show, and regular brushing. Its coat is weather-resistant, and this breed rarely feels the cold – in fact, it seems to prefer it.

Feeding

Recommended would be 1½-2½ cans (376g, 13.3oz size) of a branded meaty product, with biscuit added in equal part by volume; or 5 cupfuls of a dry food, complete diet, mixed in the proportion of 1 cup of feed to ½ cup of hot or cold water. Will need extra feed if used for coursing.

Origin and history

The Deerhound was purpose-bred to hunt with its master by day and to grace his sumptuous dining hall at night. With the advent of breech-loading rifles, the need for the hunting Deerhound ceased, as did its popularity; in Britain, it is now kept only by devotees of the breed. It is said that once you have owned a Deerhound, never again do you wish to own another breed. It is truly a gentle giant.

The breed has much of the Greyhound in its make-up, and it seems that until the 19th century the Irish Wolfhound and the Deerhound were of a similar type. Today it is easy to distinguish between the two, the Deerhound being a sleeker, lighter dog. 180▸

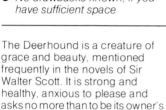

Above: Capable of great speed as a hunting dog, the Deerhound is now kept mainly as a companion, a role it fulfills superbly. As a pet the Deerhound is obedient, quiet and extremely faithful.

IRISH WOLFHOUND

Good points

- *Quiet and friendly*
- *Marvellous with children*
- *Good guard*
- *Happiest as a housedog*
- *Magnificent show dog*

Take heed

- *Gentle when stroked, fierce when provoked*
- *Needs discipline as a puppy*

The Irish Wolfhound, variously known as the Wolfdog, the Irish Greyhound and the Great Dog of Ireland, is a gentle giant, fierce only when provoked. It is intelligent, intensely loyal and slow to anger. Irish Wolfhounds do, nonetheless, have a mind of their own, so firm, gentle discipline is advocated in puppyhood.

Size

The minimum height and weight of dogs should be 78.5cm (31in) and 54.4kg (120lb); of bitches 71cm (28in) and 40.8kg (90lb). Anything below this should be heavily penalized. Great size, including height at shoulder and proportionate length of body, is the target to be aimed for, and ideally the breed should average 81-86cm (32-34in) in dogs, showing the requisite power, activity, courage and symmetry.

Exercise

Despite its size, the Irish Wolfhound does not require more exercise than smaller breeds, but it should have ample space in which to gambol. Let it have unrestricted play during puppyhood, but do not force it to take lengthy walks, rather allowing it to 'muscle up' by its own joyful activity. Irish Wolfhounds are usually taught both to walk and to move at the trot while being led; as they are so powerful, obedience is essential.

Grooming

Brush regularly, and remove long, straggly hairs from ears, neck and underside with finger and thumb. This is a natural-looking breed, which is not difficult to groom.

Feeding

At least 2½ cans (376g, 13.3oz size) of a branded meaty product, with biscuit added in equal part by volume; or 5 cupfuls of a dry food, complete diet, mixed in the proportion of 1 cup of feed to ½ cup of hot or cold water.

Origin and history

The Irish Wolfhound is the national dog of Ireland, and its original role was to kill wolves. It is spoken of in many legends, but almost certainly came from Greece with the invading Celts, circa 279 BC. The best-known story of an Irish Wolfhound concerns the dog Gelert, given as a gift to Llewellyn, Prince of Wales, by King John of England around 1210. Prince Llewellyn went hunting, leaving the faithful Gelert in charge of his baby son. On his return he could see only Gelert, with blood on its mouth, and, thinking it had killed the child, he drew his sword and slew the dog. It was only then that he saw, nearby, the body of a wolf, and heard the happy chuckle of his child. Gelert had killed the wolf and saved the child. Full of remorse, Prince Llewellyn ordered a statue to be erected in memory of Gelert, and the dog's name has lived on through the centuries.

The first breed standard for the Irish Wolfhound was set down in 1885, after Captain George Graham, a Scot in the British Army, had spent 23 years restoring the breed from near extinction. 180▶

LEONBERGER

Good points
- *Derived from sound breeds*
- *Handsome*
- *Lively temperament*
- *Intelligent*
- *Good watchdog*

Take heed
- *Little known outside Germany, Holland, France and Belgium*
- *Needs plenty of space*

The Leonberger is a strong, sound dog, used for protecting livestock and as a draught dog in Western Germany and certain other European countries. It was derived from animals of sound temperament, and is beginning to create interest internationally. A breed member was exhibited at Crufts soon after World War II, but it is doubtful if any specimens were bred in England.

Size
Height: dog 76cm (30in); bitch 70cm (27½in).

Exercise
Would need adequate space and exercise to thrive.

Grooming
Normal daily brushing needed.

Feeding
Recommended would be 1½-2½ cans (376g, 13.3oz size) of a branded meaty product, with biscuit added in equal part by volume; or 5 cupfuls of a dry food, complete diet, mixed in the proportion of 1 cup of feed to ½ cup of hot or cold water.

Origin and history
The Leonberger is a German dog derived through crossing the Landseer-type Newfoundland with the Pyrenean Mountain Dog, the result being a most attractive breed of yellow to reddish brown colour that is gradually becoming known outside Germany and the bordering countries. 181▸

Below: The strong and elegant Leonberger, an attractive watchdog.

PYRENEAN MOUNTAIN DOG (Great Pyrenees)

Good points
- *Can be kept indoors or outdoors*
- *Easy to train*
- *Family protector*

Take heed
- *A working dog, happiest with a job to do*
- *Does not like strangers taking liberties*
- *Needs plenty of space*

The Pyrenean Mountain Dog is a natural shepherd dog bred to guard flocks in the Pyrenees. Nonetheless it has become a popular household pet with those who have the space and income to keep such a large dog. Mr and Mrs Prince's Bergerie Knur won Best in Show at Crufts in 1970.

They are hardy and good-natured, and become devoted to the entire family. They are not keen on approaches from strangers, however, and accidents have occurred when show visitors have been tempted to give a pat.

Size
Height at shoulder: dog at least 71cm (28in); bitch at least 66cm (26in). Weight: dog at least 49.9kg (110lb); bitch at least 40.8kg (90lb).

Exercise
Normal requirements. Strangely, for such a big fellow, the Pyrenean will adapt to town or country, and be content with walks of average length. Its gait is unhurried, giving the impression of a powerful animal moving steadily and smoothly.

Grooming
Regular brushing will keep the coat in good condition.

Feeding
Recommended: at least 2½ cans (376g, 13.3oz size) of a branded meaty product, with biscuit added in equal part by volume; or 5 cupfuls of a dry food, complete diet, mixed in the proportion of 1 cup of feed to ½ cup of hot or cold water.

Above: The Pyrenean Mountain Dog, one of the largest and strongest of present-day breeds. Given plenty of space, it will make a trustworthy and easy-going companion.

Origin and history
The Pyrenean was a royal favourite in the French court before the revolution. It has never regained the same popularity, though it is widely known and frequently exhibited. It comes from the area from which it takes its name and was once used to guard sheep, and also fortresses, wearing a spiked collar like that of the Mastiff. The breed became known when shepherds found a ready market for their pups with tourists. 181▸

MAREMMA SHEEPDOG (Pastore Maremmano Abruzzese)

Good points
- *Great stamina*
- *Beautiful*
- *Intelligent*
- *Natural guarding instinct*
- *Weather-proof coat*

Take heed
- *Will treat its master as an equal – this breed is not renowned for obedience*

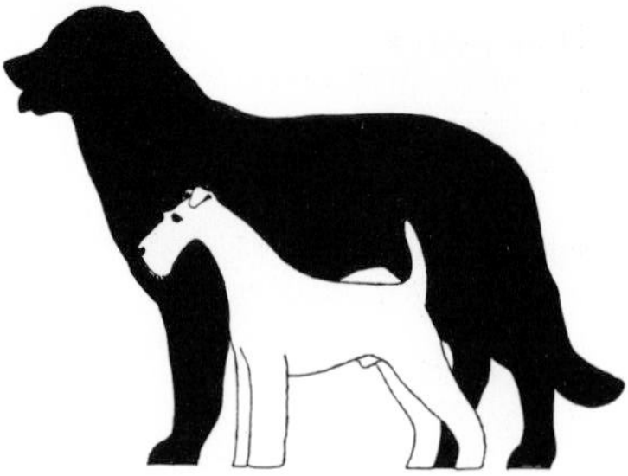

The Maremma is a dog that cannot tolerate discipline and, although it becomes fond of its master, it would consider it a weakness to show it. The dog will guard the entrance to its master's home, but will not lie across his feet. It will not forget kindness, or forgive injury, and will protect the family. The task of this breed was never to work sheep as would a Collie or German Shepherd Dog, but to defend the flocks from wolves, bears and thieves.

Size
Some latitude permitted with a minimum of 65cm (25½in) for a dog, 60cm (23½in) for a bitch.

Exercise
Exercise is a necessity for the breed's well-being in its formative years, but excessive exercise is not a vital need when the animal is mature. Rather than covering a long distance, their daily walks should be made as varied and interesting as possible, and – despite the fact that they are not particularly obedient – it is important that they should have some off-the-lead freedom. Walking on a hard surface will help to keep the dog's nails in condition. Rain will not have an adverse effect on the Maremma's coat. All it needs after a soaking is a good rub down. The dog will clean itself and soon be gleaming white again!

Grooming
Grooming should be carried out regularly, preferably with a wire dog brush and the occasional use of a good cleansing powder. A bath should be given once a year – more often if absolutely necessary – but this is a scrupulously clean breed that attends to its toilet fastidiously. During grooming the ears should be checked carefully for infection.

Feeding
The diet of the Maremma must contain adequate calcium, which can be given in either tablet or powder form. It is very necessary because of the extraordinary growth rate of Maremma puppies. Two meals daily are recommended for the breed, with perhaps some 'goodnight' biscuits. Recommended would be 1½-2½ cans of a branded canned product (376g, 13.3oz size), with biscuit added in equal parts by volume; or 5 cupfuls of a dry food, complete diet, mixed in the proportion of 1 cup of feed to ½ cup of hot or cold water.

Origin and history
It is believed that the Maremma sheepdog may have evolved from the ancient white working dog of the Magyars, and they have been bred exceedingly true to type on the Maremma plains and hills by Tuscan farmers.

The first known record of what is believed to be the Maremma was made 2000 years ago when Columbella (about AD 65) mentioned a white dog, and Marcus Varro (116-27 BC) gives a standard for a sheepdog that would seem to describe the Maremma of today. 181▸

KOMONDOR

Good points
- *Will live indoors or in a kennel*
- *Loyal*
- *Excellent guard*
- *Seldom sheds*
- *Good with other animals (in the family)*

Take heed
- *Will not tolerate teasing*
- *Wary of strangers*

The Komondor (pronounced Koh-mohn-dohr – the plural is Komondorok) is a large white dog of imposing bearing, very strong and agile for its size. Nobody can mistake a grown dog for any other breed. It is covered with a full coat falling in tassels or cords and looks like an old-fashioned string mop.

This is a loyal dog whose purpose in life is to guard the property and charges in its care. It does not attack without provocation but trespassers will not be tolerated.

Size
Weight: dog about 49.9-61.2kg (110-135lbs); bitch about 36.3-49.9kg (80-110lb). Height: dog average 80cm (31½in), minimum 66cm (26in); bitch average 70cm (27½in), minimum 60cm (23½in).

Exercise
Puppies are large and active and require a lot of exercise for good development. A grown dog is maintained in good condition on a moderate amount of exercise. In a city this will have to be given on a lead.

Grooming
The Komondor has a thick, heavy, double coat; the shorter undercoat is woolly and soft, the outer coat longer, coarse and wavy. The combination of the two types of hair forms naturally into tassel-like cords, the cords being a type of controlled matting. It is never brushed or combed. It forms naturally, with the owner aiding by controlling the size of the cords in areas where matting is too large.

Bath the Komondor when it gets dirty, wetting the coat thoroughly and using a canine shampoo; rinse thoroughly, and wring with towels. A grown dog will take a long time to dry. Cords do not come out when you wash the dog; indeed, they will tighten up with age and washing. The dog requires standard care for eyes, pads and nails.

Feeding
Recommended: at least 2½ cans of a branded canned product (376g, 13.3oz size), with biscuit added in equal parts by volume; or 5 cupfuls of a dry food, complete diet, mixed in the proportion of 1 cup of feed to ½ cup of hot or cold water.

Origin and history
The Komondor was bred for centuries to guard flocks and property from thieves and predators on the Hungarian plains. It has worked with and without other dogs, first herding the semi-wild Hungarian sheep, later protecting whatever herds and property required a large and commanding dog as guard. Bred into the dog is an instinct to guard and to take responsibility for making decisions. The Komondor naturally protects whatever is entrusted to it – if not sheep, then goats, cattle, and chickens on a farm or ranch, or cats, dogs and children if it is a family companion. 181▸

BULLMASTIFF

Good points

- *Affectionate*
- *Trustworthy*
- *First-class guard*
- *Good with children*

Take heed

- *Remember its ferocious past; if you have one, make sure it is trained and temperamentally sound*

The Bullmastiff is an extremely strong breed, obtained through crossing the Mastiff with the Bulldog. At one time it had an almost unequalled reputation for ferocity, but today's specimens tend to be lovable and trustworthy, despite their power and size.

Size

Height at shoulder: dog 63.5-68.5cm (25-27in); bitch 61-66cm (24-26in). Weight: dog 49.9-59kg (110-130lb); bitch 40.8-49.9kg (90-110lb).

Exercise

Needs regular exercise. A child or lightweight adult would not be able to hold on to the lead.

Grooming

Regular brushing will keep the coat in good condition.

Feeding

Recommended: at least 2½ cans (376g, 13.3oz size) of a branded meaty product, with biscuit added in equal part by volume; or 5 cupfuls of a dry food, complete diet, mixed in the proportion of 1 cup of feed to ½ cup of hot or cold water.

Origin and history

The Bullmastiff is said to have been evolved 200 or 300 years ago by crossing the Mastiff with the Bulldog, as a guard dog against poachers, the bulk of the dog weighing down intruders without actually harming them. It was not until later that they attained their reputation for ferocity, despite novelist Charlotte Brontë's loving references to her Bullmastiff Tartar. Nowadays the breed has become a big softie whose appearance alone would deter. However, such large dogs need skilful handling. 182▸

Below: The Bullmastiff looks fierce but will make a lovable pet with sensible handling and training.

NEAPOLITAN MASTIFF

Good points
- *Immensely strong*
- *Excellent guard*
- *Friendly*
- *Courageous*

Take heed
- *Make sure the specimen you buy is physically sound*
- *Not really the most suitable breed for apartment living!*

The Neapolitan Mastiff is a large, imposing dog, usually depicted wearing a spiked collar. It is an excellent guard, but is reputed to have a docile and friendly temperament, being unlikely to attack except on command.

Size
Height: dog 65-72.5cm (25½-28½in), bitch 60-68.5cm (23½-27in). Weight: 49.9-68kg (110-150lb).

Exercise
Like most dogs of its size, it is happiest when given a job to do and with a reasonable area in which to exercise.

Grooming
Regular brushing will keep the coat in good condition.

Feeding
Recommended: at least 2½ cans (376g, 13.3oz size) of a branded meaty product, with biscuit added in equal part by volume; or 5 cupfuls of a dry food, complete diet, mixed as 1 cup of feed to ½ cup of water.

Origin and history
One scientific classification of the Neapolitan Mastiff puts it in the Molossoid group. It is a guard and defence dog, a police dog and a tracker, of Italian origin, more specifically Neapolitan. Whether Italy's Mastiff ever did battle in the arenas of Rome is debatable, but geographical evidence gives credence to this theory. 182▸

Below: The forbidding Neapolitan Mastiff, rarely seen outside Italy.

MASTIFF

Good points
- *Brave*
- *Good-natured*
- *Excellent guard*
- *Intelligent*
- *Loyal*
- *Quietly dignified*

Take heed
- *Likes to have a job to do*

The Mastiff is a large, powerful dog that makes a formidable guard and loyal companion, becoming devoted to its owners. It is suspicious of strangers, and happiest when given a job to do.

Size
Height at shoulder: dog 76cm (30in), bitch 70cm (27½in).

Exercise
Regular normal exercise, but preferably with a purpose.

Grooming
Daily brushing will keep the coat in good condition.

Feeding
Recommended: at least 2½ cans (376g, 13.3oz size) of a branded meaty product, with biscuit added in equal part by volume; or 5 cupfuls of a dry food, complete diet, mixed in the proportion of 1 cup of feed to ½ cup of hot or cold water.

Health care
Their size can contribute to limb joint problems. Check with your veterinarian if you suspect trouble.

Origin and history
The Mastiff is an ancient breed that was treasured by the Babylonians, fought in the arenas of Rome, and has lived in Britain since the time of Julius Caesar. In the Middle Ages the Mastiff was used as a guard dog and also for hunting. St Bernard blood has been introduced, in an effort to restore the Mastiff to something of the size of its early splendour. Numbers today are fairly low. 182▸

Below: One of the world's well-established breeds, the Mastiff commands respect by virtue of its sheer size and noble bearing.

GIANT SCHNAUZER

Good points
- *Easy to train*
- *Excellent with children*
- *Fearless*
- *Fine guard*
- *Good-natured*
- *Playful*

Take heed
- *Slow to mature*
- *Wary of strangers*

The Giant Schnauzer is the largest of the three Schnauzer varieties, (the other being Miniature and Standard), with which it shares the qualities of good humour, intelligence and devotion. It has been used for security and as a messenger in the armed services; it works well in obedience competitions, and is a good ratter—ratting was, after all, the Schnauzer's original job. However, this giant variety is little seen in America or Great Britain, where the Miniature variety is popular, but the Standard Schnauzer less so.

Size
Height: dog 65-70cm (25½-27½in); bitch 60-65cm (23½-25½in).

Exercise
Needs plenty of vigorous exercise.

Grooming
This is a breed that requires a certain amount of care if it is to do its owner justice. Daily grooming with a wire brush or glove is necessary, and those quizzical whiskers have to be combed. The coat has to be stripped with a serrated stripping comb, or the dead hair plucked out with finger and thumb. Ask the breeder for a grooming chart, or at least a demonstration, before tackling the job yourself—especially if your heart is set on the show ring.

Feeding
Recommended: at least 2½ cans (376g, 13.3oz size) of a branded meaty product, with biscuit added in equal part by volume; or 5 cupfuls of a dry food, complete diet, mixed in the proportion of 1 cup of feed to ½ cup of hot or cold water.

Above: The Giant Schnauzer, a lively, good humoured companion.

Origin and history
Descended from German sheepdogs and cattle dogs, this, the largest Schnauzer, was evolved through interbreeding with the smaller Schnauzer varieties. It was first shown in Munich in October 1909 under the name 'Russian bear Schnauzer', the breed being classified as a working dog in Germany in 1925. 182▸

GREAT DANE

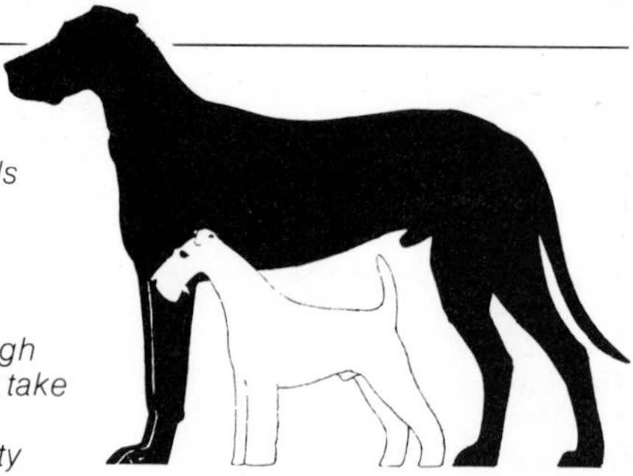

Good points
- *Devoted*
- *Gets on with other animals*
- *Good-natured*
- *Easy to train*

Take heed
- *Not the dog to have a rough and tumble with – it might take it seriously!*
- *Not renowned for longevity*

The Great Dane is a wonderful companion, devoted to the family, slow to anger and ready to accept other pets. Despite its size it does not object to apartment life, provided it has plenty of walks. It is easily trained. Regrettably this is a breed that is not renowned for its longevity.

Size
Minimum height: dog 76cm (30in); bitch 71cm (28in). Weight: dog 54.4kg (120lb); bitch 45.4kg (100lb).

Exercise
Regular exercise on hard ground would be recommended.

Grooming
Daily grooming with a body brush. *NB* The Great Dane needs warm sleeping quarters.

Feeding
Recommended would be up to 4 cans (376g, 13.3oz size) of a branded meaty product, with biscuit added in equal part by volume; or 5 cupfuls of a dry food, complete diet, mixed in the proportion of 1 cup of feed to ½ cup of hot or cold water.

Origin and history
The Great Dane has existed in Britain for many centuries and is thought to be a descendant of the Molossus hounds of Roman times. In the Middle Ages they were used to chase wild boar, to bait bulls and as body guards.

Interest in the breed was roused in Germany in the 1800s by Bismarck, who had a penchant for the Mastiff, and by crossing the Mastiff of southern Germany and the Great Dane of the north produced a Dane similar to the type known today. It was first exhibited at Hamburg in 1863, being shown under the separate varieties of Ulmer Dogge and Dänisch Dogge. In 1876, it was decided that they should be shown under the single heading of Deutsche Dogge, and they were acclaimed as the national dog of Germany. This breed is sometimes referred to as the Apollo of the dog world. 182▸

Above: The Great Dane is a truly magnificent breed in temperament, size, stamina and devotion.

ST BERNARD

Good points
- *Friendly*
- *Loyal*
- *Adores children*
- *Easy to train*
- *Supremely intelligent*

Take heed
- *Hindquarters prone to weakness*
- *Needs plenty of space*
- *Not renowned for longevity*

The St Bernard is a gentleman; powerful, but gentle. It adores children and is loyal and affectionate, coupled with which it is supremely intelligent and proves very easy to train.

Size
The taller the better, provided that symmetry is maintained; thoroughly well proportioned, and of great substance.

Exercise
Do not give the young St Bernard too much exercise. Short, regular walks are advocated, rather than long, tiring ones.

Grooming
Daily brushing will be sufficient.

Feeding
Frecommended would be up to 4 cans (376g, 13.3oz size) of a branded meaty product, with biscuit added in equal part by volume; or 5 cupfuls of a dry food, complete diet, mixed in the proportion of 1 cup of feed to ½ cup of hot or cold water.

Origin and history
The St Bernard is a descendant of the Roman Molossian dogs. It is named after the St Bernard Hospice in the Swiss Alps, to which it was introduced between 1660 and 1670, where it became famed for rescuing climbers in the Alps. One dog, Barry, is credited with saving 40 lives between 1800 and 1810. The first St Bernard to come to Britain arrived in 1865. The breed had a boost in popularity in the 1950s, when a St Bernard played a prominent role in the British film *Genevieve*, and it is also associated by almost everyone with advertisements for a well-known brandy. 183▶

Below: The St Bernard is a powerful but benevolent giant of a breed.

NEWFOUNDLAND

Good points

- *Excellent guard, but fierce only when provoked*
- *Fine swimmer*
- *Marvellous with other animals and children*
- *Intelligent*
- *Affectionate*

Take heed

- *No drawbacks known*

The Newfoundland is a gentle protector of children and family that gets on well with other animals and makes a thoroughly reliable companion and guard; it is slow to attack unless provoked.

Size

Average height at shoulders: dog 71cm (28in); bitch 66cm (26in). Weight: dog 63.5-68kg (140-150lb); bitch 49.9-54.4kg (110-120lb).

Exercise

Regular exercise on hard ground.

Grooming

Daily brushing with a hard brush.

Feeding

Recommended would be up to 4 cans (376g, 13.3oz size) of a branded meaty product, with biscuit added in equal part by volume; or 5 cupfuls of a dry food, complete diet, mixed in the proportion of 1 cup of feed to ½ cup of hot or cold water.

Origin and history

The Newfoundland is the traditional life-saving dog, an animal with the over-powering instinct to carry anything in the water safely ashore. It originates from the north-east of Canada, into whose protective harbours fishing boats of other nations have habitually come to avoid bad weather. It is believed that ships' dogs mated with the local working dogs, whose ancestors probably included Red Indian dogs and Basque sheepdogs, to produce the Newfoundland. Particularly famous is the Landseer variety, with black and white markings; it is so named because of its portrayal by the British painter Sir Edward Landseer (1802-73). 183▸

Below: The Landseer Newfoundland, a celebrated variety.

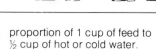

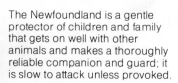

Index

Page numbers in Roman type refer to text entries; *italic* numbers refer to photographs; **bold** numbers to colour artwork illustrations.

M

N

O

P

R

S

Parts of a Dog

1 Ear
2 Skull
3 Eye
4 Stop
5 Foreface. The foreface, nose and jaws make up the muzzle
6 Nose
7 Jaws. The fleshy parts of the lips and jaws make up the jowls
8 Lips. Pendulous upper lips are called flews
9 Cheek
10 Neck
11 Shoulder
12 Upper arm
13 Elbow
14 Forearm
15 Wrist
16 Stopper pad

This annotated drawing shows the main anatomical parts of a dog and the accepted terms used to describe them.

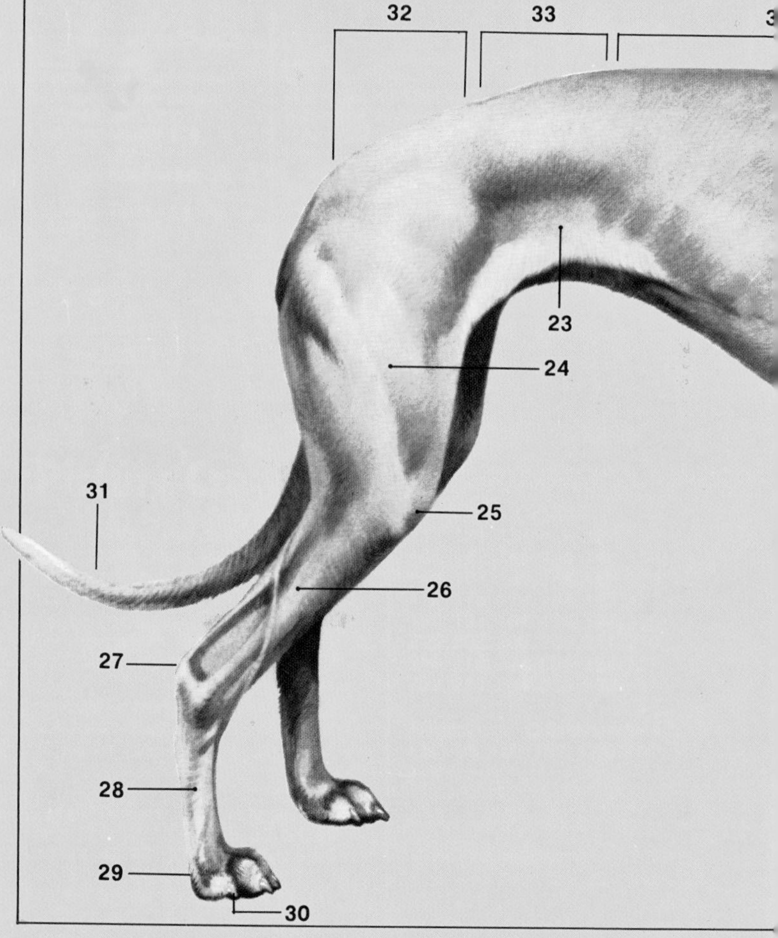